ALSO BY E. L. DOCTOROW

Welcome to Hard Times
Big as Life
The Book of Daniel
Ragtime
Drinks before Dinner (play)
Loon Lake
Lives of the Poets

WORLD'S
FAIR

E. L. DOCTOROW

WORLD'S FAIR

RANDOM HOUSE NEW YORK

Library of Congress Cataloging in Publication Data

Doctorow, E. L., 1931–

World's fair.

I. Title.
PS3554.03W6 1985   813'.54   85-10728
ISBN 0-394-52528-0
ISBN 0-394-54909-0 (lim. ed.)

Manufactured in the United States of America
Typography and binding design by Jo Anne Metsch

For R. P. D.

A raree-show is here,
With children gathered round . . .

Wordsworth
The Prelude

WORLD'S FAIR

ROSE

I was born on Clinton Street in the Lower East Side. I was the next to youngest of six children, two boys, four girls. The two boys, Harry and Willy, were the oldest. My father was a musician, a violinist. He always made a good living. He and my mother had met in Russia and they married there, and then emigrated. My mother came from a family of musicians as well; that is how, in the course of things, she and my father had met. Some of her cousins were very well known in Russia; one, a cellist, had even played for the Czar. My mother was a very beautiful woman, petite, with long golden hair and the palest blue eyes. My father used to say to us, "You think, you girls, you're beautiful? You should have seen your mother when she and her sisters walked down the street in our village. Every head turned, they were so slim, their bearing so elegant." I suppose he did not want us to get conceited.

I was four when we moved up to the Bronx, a big apartment near Claremont Park. I was a good student, I went to P.S. 147 on Washington Avenue; when I was graduated from there I went to Morris High School. I completed all my courses and graduated, and reenrolled to take the program of commercial courses there and got enough credits to graduate all over again if I chose. I knew now how to type, how to keep books, I knew shorthand. I was very ambitious. I had paid for my own

3

piano lessons by playing for silent movies. I watched the screen and improvised. My brother Harry or my father used to sit right behind me to see that nobody bothered me; movie houses were still primitive and they attracted a bad element. After my courses, I found a job as private secretary to a well-known businessman and philanthropist named Sigmund Unterberg. He had made his money in the shirt business and now spent a good deal of his time doing work for Jewish organizations, social welfare, that kind of thing. There were no government bureaucracies in social work, no programs as there are now, everything charitable came from individuals and the private agencies they created. I was a good secretary, Mr. Unterberg would dictate a letter to me and I could take it right on the typewriter, without an error, and so when he was finished I was finished and the letter was ready for him to sign. He thought I was wonderful. His wife was a lovely woman and used to invite me to tea with them, to socialize with them. I suppose I was by now nineteen or twenty. They introduced me to one or two young men, but I never liked them.

I by now was interested in your father. We had known each other since high school. He was extremely handsome, dashing, he was a good athlete; in fact, that's how I met him, on the tennis courts, there were clay courts on Morris Avenue and 170th Street and we were each playing there. You played tennis in long skirts in those days. I was a good tennis player, I loved sports, and that's how we met. He walked me home.

My mother did not like Dave. She thought he was too wild. If I went out with another boy he would ruin the date. He would hang around outside our house even if we hadn't arranged to do anything together and when he saw another boy coming to pick me up he'd do terrible things, he'd pick a fight, or stop us and talk when I was with this other boy. He would warn the other boys to treat me with respect or he would come after them. Naturally, he frightened a few of them away, it was very annoying, I was furious, but somehow I would not break off with him as my mother advised. In the winter we went ice-skating, in the spring he would surprise me with flowers, he was very romantic and over the course of these years I was falling in love with him.

Things were different then, you didn't meet someone and go out and go to bed with them one two three. People courted. Girls were innocent.

ONE

Startled awake by the ammoniated mists, I am roused in one instant from glutinous sleep to grieving awareness; I have done it again. My soaked thighs sting. I cry, I call Mama, knowing I must endure her harsh reaction, get through *that,* to be rescued. My crib is on the east wall of their room. Their bed is on the south wall. "Mama!" From her bed she hushes me. "Mama!" She groans, rises, advances on me in her white nightgown. Her strong hands go to work. She strips me, strips the sheets, dumps my pajamas and the sheets, and the rubber sheet under them, in a pile on the floor. Her pendulous breasts shift about in the nightgown. I hear her whispered admonitions. In seconds I am washed, powdered, clean-clothed, and brought to secret smiles in the dark. I ride, the young prince, in her arms to their bed, and am welcomed between them, in the blessed dry warmth between them. My father gives me a companionable pat and falls back to sleep with his hand on my shoulder. Soon they are both asleep. I smell their godlike odors, male, female. A moment later, as the faintest intimation of daylight appears as an outline of the window shade, I am wide awake, blissful, guarding my sleeping parents, the terrible night past me, the dear day about to dawn.

These are my earliest memories. I liked when morning came to climb down from their bed and watch my parents. My father

6

slept on his right arm, his legs straight, his hand coming over
the pillow and bending at the wrist against the headboard. My
mother lay curled with the curve of her broad back touching his.
Together under the covers they made a pleasing shape. The
headboard knocked against the wall as they stirred. It was ba-
roque in style, olive green, with a frieze of small pink flowers and
dark green leaves along its fluted edges. On the opposite wall
were the dresser and mirror of the same olive green and fluted
edges. Sprays of the pink flowers were set above the oval brass
drawer pulls. In my play I liked to lift each handle and let it fall
back to hear the clink. I understood the illusion of the flowers,
looking at them, believing them and then feeling the raised paint
strokes with my fingertips. I had less fondness for the bedroom
curtains of sheer white over the window shades and for the
heavy draperies framing the curtains. I feared suffocation. I
shied away from closets, the dark terrified me mostly because I
wasn't sure it was breathable.

I was an asthmatic child, allergic to everything, I was attacked
continually in the lungs, coughing, wheezing, needing to be
steamed over inhalators. I was the mournful prodigy of medicine, I knew the mustard plaster, the nose drop, the Argyrol
throat swab. I was plugged regularly with thermometers and
soap water enemas. My mother believed pain was curative. If it
didn't hurt it was ineffective. I shouted and screamed and went
down fighting. I argued for the cherry-red mercurochrome for
my scraped knees and I got the detested iodine. How I howled.
"Oh stop the nonsense," my mother said, applicating me with
strokes of searing pain. "Stop it this instant. You make a fuss
over nothing."

I had difficulty with the proportions of things and made reasonable spaces for myself in what otherwise was an unfairly giganti-
cized home. I liked to sit in the shelter of the piano in the parlor.

It was a Sohmer upright of black mahogany, and the cantile-
vered keyboard made a low-lying roof for me. I enjoyed the
patterns of rugs. I was a familiar of oak flooring and the skirts
of upholstered chairs.

I went readily to my bath in part because the tub was of
reasonable dimensions. I could touch its sides. I sank walnut-
shell boats in the tub. I swamped them in tidal waves and then
I quieted the water.

I was also aware that for some reason my mother's relentless
efficiency was suspended when I was in my bath. Other than
calling in to me from time to time to make sure I hadn't
drowned, she left me in privacy. The pads of my fingers would
wrinkle before I rose from the bathwater to unplug the drain.

Of the wooden kitchen table and chairs I made a fortress.
Here I had surveillance of the whole vast kitchen floor. I knew
people by their legs and feet. My mother's sturdy ankles and
large shapely calves moved about on the pinions of a pair of
ladies' heeled shoes. From sink to icebox to table they went
accompanied by the administrative sounds of silverware clattering, drawers sliding open and shut. My mother took confident
solid steps that made the glass doors of the cabinets tremble.

My little grandmother inched her feet forward without lifting
them from the floor, just as she drank her tea in tiny sips. She
wore high-laced shoes of black whose tops were hidden beneath
her long limp skirts, also black. Of all the family Grandma was
the easiest to spy on because she was always in her thoughts. I
was wary of her, though I knew she loved me. She prayed sometimes in the kitchen with her prayer book lying open upon the
table and her old-fashioned shoes flat on the floor.

My older brother Donald could not be spied upon. Unlike
adults he was quick and alert. Targeting him for even a few
seconds before he knew I was there was a great triumph. I
lingered one day in the hallway outside the open door of his
room. When I peeked around the corner his back was to me, he
was working on a model airplane. "I know you're there, Mr.
Bubblenose," he said without a moment's hesitation.

I valued my brother as a confident all-around source of knowledge and wisdom. His mind was a compendium of the rules and regulations of every game known to mankind. His brow furrowed with attentiveness to the proper way of doing things. He lived hard and by the book. He was an authority not only on model building but on kite flying, scooter racing, and the care of pets. He did everything well. I felt for him the gravest love and respect.

I might have been daunted by his example, and the view I had through him of everything I had to learn, except that he had the generous instincts of a teacher. One day I was with our dog, Pinky, in front of our house on Eastburn Avenue, when Donald came home from school and put his books down on the front stoop.

He plucked a large dark leaf from the privet hedge under the parlor window. He placed the leaf between his palms and cupped his hands to his mouth and blew into the gap formed by his adjacent thumbs. This produced a marvelous bleat.

I jumped up and down. When Donald made the sound again, Pinky began to yowl, as she did also when a harmonica was played in her presence. "I want to try," I said. Under his patient instruction I chose a leaf like his, I placed it carefully on my palms, and I blew. Nothing happened. He arranged and rearranged my little hands, he changed leaves, he corrected my form. Still nothing happened.

"You have to work at it," Donald said. "You can't expect to get it right away. Here, I'll show you something easier."

The same leaf he had used for a reed he now split in half simply by pressing the heels of his palms together and flattening his hands.

My brother was very fine. He wore the tweed knickers and

ribbed socks and shoes with low sides of a young man. A shock
of straight brown hair fell over one eye. His knitted sweater was
dashingly tied by the sleeves around his waist and his red school
tie was loosened at the knot. Long after he had taken our maniac
dog into the house, I conscientiously applied myself to the tasks
he had set me. Even if I couldn't get the hang of them right away,
I knew at least what had to be learned.

Donald was like my mother in applying himself resolutely to the
demands and challenges of life. My father was a different sort.
I thought he got to where he was by magic.

He would let me watch him shave because I rarely saw him
except in the mornings. He came home from work long after my
bedtime. With a partner, he owned a music store in the Hippodrome, a famous theater building on Sixth Avenue and Forty-
third Street in Manhattan.

"Good morning, Sunny Jim," he said. He had noticed early
in my life that each morning I woke smiling, an act of such ex-
traordinary innocence that he had ever since commented
upon it. When I was a baby he lifted me into his arms and we
played a game: he puffed up his cheeks like a hippopota-
mus and I punched the air out, first one side of his face, then
the other. No sooner was the job done than his eyes went wide
and his cheeks refilled and I had gigglingly to do it all over
again.

The bathroom was lined in squares of white tile and all the
fixtures were white porcelain. An opaque crinkled window
seemed to glow with its own light. My father stood in the diffuse
sunlight of the white bathroom after he had partially dressed—
shoes, trousers, ribbed undershirt, suspenders looping off his
flanks—and brought his shaving soap to a lather in its mug.
Then he applied the lather to his face with an artful slopping of
his shaving brush.

He did this while humming the overture to Wagner's *The Flying Dutchman*.

I loved the scratchy sound the brush made on his skin. I loved the soap as it turned from a froth to a substantive lather under his rubbing. Next, he held taut from its hook on the wall a long leather strop about three inches wide, and upon this he wielded his straight razor back and forth with a twist of the wrist. I failed to understand how something as soft as leather could hone something as hard as a steel razor. He explained the principle to me, but I knew it was just another example of his magic powers.

My father did sleight-of-hand things. He could appear to remove the top joint of his thumb, for example, and then put it back. Behind the screen of one hand, you'd see the thumb of the other come apart and then the space between the two halves. Like all good tricks, it was horrifying. He'd lift the thumb off and then put it back with a little twist, and hold it out for my inspection and wiggle it to assure me that it was as good as new.

He was full of surprises. He punned. He made jokes.

As he shaved, here and there tiny springs of blood quietly leaked through the white foam and turned pink. He did not seem to notice but simply went on shaving and humming.

After he had rinsed his face and patted it with witch hazel, he parted his shiny black hair in the middle and combed each side back. He was always well barbered. His handsome pink face shone. He smoothed his dark moustache with the tips of his fingers. He had a thin straight nose. He had vivid sparkling brown eyes that sent out signals of a mischievous intelligence.

Assiduously he applied the lather remaining in his shaving mug to my cheeks and chin. In the medicine cabinet was one of my wooden tongue depressors; every time I required a visit from our family physician, Dr. Gross, I was given a new one as a present. My father handed me a depressor so that I could shave.

"Dave," called my mother as she rapped on the door. "You know what time it is? What do you *do* in there!"

He grimaced, ducking his head between his shoulders, as if we were, both of us, naughty boys.

My father always made promises as he went off to work.

"I'll be home early tonight," he told my mother.

"I have no money," she said.

"Here's a couple of dollars to tide you over. I'll have cash this evening. I'll call you. Maybe I can pick up some things for dinner."

I pulled on his sleeve and begged him to bring me a surprise.

"Well, I'll just see what I can do," he said, smiling.

"You promise?"

Donald was already at school. When my father left I'd have nothing to look forward to, so I watched him to the last second. He was portly, though trim enough in one of his suits with the vest buttoned tight. He checked the knot of his tie in the mirror in the front hall. When he set his fedora on his head at the stylish angle he affected, I ran into the parlor so as to be able to see him as he came out the front door. Down the steps he skipped, and turning to wave, and smiling at me as I stood in the parlor window, he strode off down the street in that brisk jaunty gait of his. I watched him turn the corner and from one moment to the next he was out of sight.

I understood the reach of his life. I understood him as living by nature as a sojourner. He went forth and returned. He covered ground. His urges and instincts even on his one day off pointed away from home.

He rarely kept his word to return in time for dinner or to bring me something. My mother could not abide his broken promises. She was forever calling him to account. I saw that this did no good. By way of compensation he brought me things when I least expected them. A surprise surprised. It was a kind of teaching.

TWO

My mother ran our home and our lives with a kind of tactless administration that often left a child with bruised feelings, though an indelible understanding of right and wrong. As an infant I was bathed with brisk, competent hands and as a boy fed, clothed and taken through unpleasant events with strong admonitions to behave myself. I was not to express dissent. I was to stop the nonsense.

She was a vigorous buxom woman in her late thirties. A strong will beamed in her clear blue eyes. There was no mistaking her meaning—she was forthright and direct. She construed the world in vivid judgments. She felt strongly that even little boys bore responsibility for their actions. For example, they could be lazy, selfish, up to no good. Or they could be decent, kind, truthful, honest. However they were, so would their fate be decided.

All about in the air were the childhood diseases—whooping cough, scarlet fever, and, most dreaded of all, infantile paralysis. She believed children were at risk to the extent that their parents lacked common sense. "I saw that Mrs. Goodman at the Daitch Dairy," she said coming in from her shopping one day. "Poor woman, I don't envy her. Her daughter wears a brace on her leg and will for the rest of her life. She cried telling me this. But she let the child swim in public pools on the hottest days of the summer, so what else could she expect?"

Her stories dazzled me. Their purpose was instruction. Their theme was vigilance.

In the mornings, with my father and brother Donald out of the house, my mother threw open the windows, she plumped up pillows and quilts and laid them across the windowsills in the sun. She washed dishes and put clothes to soak in the laundry tub. She swept and ran the Electrolux vacuum cleaner. Everything she did was a declarative act. Her mastery of our realm was worth my study.

My mother wanted to move up in the world. She measured what we had and who we were against the fortunes and pretensions of our neighbors. That my brother and I were properly clothed; that my father was self-employed; that we paid the rent on time, the telephone bill, the electric light bill: these were the elements of a composition she wanted the world to understand as the quality of our family.

When she was ready to do her marketing, she changed into a belted dress and shiny black shoes and put on a straw hat whose brim she turned up on one side. A little ribbon ran around the crown. She applied red lipstick and went off with her pocketbook tucked under her arm.

At the end of an afternoon she sometimes rested on the sofa for a few minutes and read the newspaper. In contrast to my father, who held the paper open at arm's length at the breakfast table, my mother, reclining, held the paper at the spine with one hand and slapped the pages left and right with the back of the other.

"I don't trust that doctor," she said of the physician attending the Dionne quintuplets. "He likes the limelight too much."

In the evenings, after dinner, with everything quieted down, she sat in the living room and read a novel from the rental library while she waited for my father to come home. I sometimes watched her when she didn't know it. After a while she would close the book in her lap, her legs would be tucked under her, and she would stare at the floor. She worried a lot about my little grandmother, who was sickly and had spells. But I think she worried mostly about my father.

My father was not a reliable associate, I was to gather. Too many things he said would come to pass did not. He was always late, somehow he would suppose he could get somewhere or accomplish something in less time than it actually took him. He created suspense. He was full of errant enthusiasms and was easily diverted by them. He had, besides, various schemes for making money that he did not readily confide to my mother. She seemed most of the time to be aroused to a state of worry regarding his activities.

When he was late my father was evasive, which seemed to justify her anger. He had a weakness for cards, I heard my mother tell her best friend, Mae. He liked to gamble and could not afford to.

I understood that my father seemed to elude my mother's ideas for him. He did not comport himself appropriately, given the hard times we were living in. I knew he was unreliable, but he was fun to be with. He was a child's ideal companion, full of surprises and happy animal energy. He enjoyed food and drink. He liked to try new things. He brought home coconuts, papayas, mangoes, and urged them on our reluctant conservative selves. On Sundays he liked to discover new places, take us on endless bus or trolley rides to some new park or beach he knew about. He always counseled daring, in whatever situation, the courage to test the unknown, an instruction that was thematically in opposition to my mother's.

The conflict between my parents was probably the major chronic circumstance of my life. They were never at peace. They were a marriage of two irreducibly opposed natures. Their differences created a kind of magnetic field for me in which I swung this way or that according to the direction of the current. My brother seemed to be more like my mother in his love of rules and a disposition for the proper doing of things. I, a quieter, more passive, daydreaming sort of child, understood my father with some sympathy, I feel now—some recognition of a free soul tethered, by a generous improvidence not terribly or shrewdly mindful of itself, to the imperial soul of an attractive woman.

15

My mother's one indulgence was to play the piano, which she did with authority, as she did everything. She had paid for her own lessons as a girl by working as an accompanist for silent movies. She was very good. What I liked, when she sat down to play, was that her rigorous thought was suspended. Her expression softened and her blue eyes shone. She sat with her back very straight, like a queen, her arms outstretched, and she filled the house with beautiful music that I thought of as waterfalls or rainbows. She could sight-read any score placed before her. When Donald brought home a new lesson from the Bronx House Music School, he would ask her to play it through just to hear how it was supposed to sound.

Donald was up to "Für Elise," by Beethoven. He had already mastered Schumann's "The Wild Horseman."

I expected someday to take piano lessons too. In the meantime I toyed with the keys, experimented with sounds, with the moods and feelings I could produce in myself by arranging my fingers on several keys at once and hammering away.

Under the glass counter near the cash register in my father's store downtown were shelves of toy instruments for children. I had one of every kind. I tooted a penny whistle, I blew a Hohner Brothers Marine Band harmonica, I got sounds from an ocarina, known also as a sweet potato because of its shape.

The easiest thing to play was a kazoo, not an instrument at all, but an oval tin tube with a piece of waxed paper screwed taut in a hatch halfway down its length. The paper vibrated as you hummed into the kazoo, and *"Voilà,"* as my father said, you were a musician.

I liked to march down the hall all the way from my room at the back of the house to the front door while playing the kazoo with one hand and waving a flag with the other.

THREE

We lived at 1650 Eastburn Avenue. We occupied the ground floor, and our landlords, the Segals, the second or top floor. To distinguish our way of living from that of the families who tenanted the apartment houses prevalent in the Bronx, we called ours a "private house." It was of red brick and had a flat roof. A stoop of eight white granite steps led down from the glass-pane doors to the street. To one side of the stoop, under the windows of our front parlor, was a little square of earth contained on three sides by a privet hedge. Here I built roads and dwellings—a whole city, in fact—for a society of small brown ants, whose reluctance to inhabit it never discouraged me.

I remember the light on Eastburn Avenue. It was a warm and brilliant bath that bleached the brick houses of red and of yellow ocher, the ruled sidewalks, the curbstones of blue Belgian block, into a peaceful and forbearing composition.

I imagined houses as superior beings who talked silently to each other.

At noon the sun shone from the top of my favorite toy, a Railway Express truck like the ones that occasionally made deliveries in the neighborhood. My truck was dark green, with solid matching green wheels and tires of hard rubber, and red fron-

tier-style Railway Express lettering on the sides. The two rear
doors unbolted and swung open exactly in the manner of the
real ones. The steering wheel, which actually worked, was
mounted at the correct angle, an undeviatingly horizontal on an
absolutely vertical shaft. The sound of the motor, an electric
whine, I supplied myself. I liked to push my truck over the cracks
in the sidewalk and the obstacles of pebbles and sticks.

The sun baked the sidewalk so that it felt good on the knees
and the palms of one's hands.

Across the street was a six-story apartment house, and two
more private houses like ours, with droopy, heavy-leaved trees
in front; up at the corner of Mt. Eden Avenue, the south end of
the block, was the tile-roofed red brick mansion of Mrs. Silver,
the widow of Judge Silver, a state Supreme Court Justice. My
mother had told me that. This mansion was on a raised lawn
behind a retaining wall of round stones cemented together. I
never saw Mrs. Silver up close, but my mother assured me she
was a fine woman who did not think she was better than anyone
else.

I could see past the corner of Mt. Eden Avenue to the plane
trees of the Oval, a small park with benches circling the garden
beds of tulips, where the mothers and children gathered in the
afternoons. A string of such ovals bisected the width of Mt. Eden
Avenue all the way up the hill west, to the Grand Concourse.

On the far side of the Oval was the beginning of Claremont
Park, or the big park, as we called it; from my vantage point it
was a great swatch of forest where the land went green.

If I turned in the other direction, I saw the north end of the
block, 173rd Street. Here there was no greenery, but another
apartment house whose entrance was around the corner, and,
across the street, the enormous schoolyard with its chain link
fence of P.S. 70. This was Donald's school and I would go there
too.

Everything we needed was close by. Beyond P.S. 70 was
174th, where all the stores were. I had been born in a small
lying-in hospital at the corners of Mt. Eden and Morris avenues,
just a block west. The Mt. Eden Center, the temple where my

old grandma went on Friday nights to pray, was also on Morris Avenue.

Most of these buildings and parks and houses were not more than ten or fifteen years old. It was a new neighborhood. I think the light was so clear and broad because of all the open space that allowed the sun to come down evenly. There were no big buildings or narrow alleys to make sharp angles and deep shadows and block out the blue of the sky, as was the case downtown in Manhattan, at my father's store.

In the street I preferred my own company to whatever miserable wretch of a child wanted to pit his ideas and requirements for me against my own. Alone, I could be happy. I assumed everyone's will was stronger than mine. This attitude may have come of my situation as a severely younger brother.

Because I was eight years younger than Donald I was something of a novelty among his friends—like a puppy or a kitten. I grew up being instructed, led about and mauled by older children. There were great numbers of them. As an infant I had held on to the sides of my carriage in terror as one or another of these louts pushed me along the street as fast as he could. They would have contests, a sort of Eastburn Avenue Olympics in occupied baby-carriage racing. Their tender ministrations poked ice cream pops into my face, or, in winter, pulled my hat down over my eyes so that I would not suffer from the cold. They were not cruel, merely dangerously boisterous. Their names were Seymour, Bernie, Harold, Stanley, Harvey, Irwin, and so on. In my mind they are like a chorus of noisemakers. Not faces or voices I recall, but horns, bladders, ratchets, and wheezing party favors that someone blows into your face.

In my own consciousness I was not a child. When I was alone, not subject to the demands of the world, I had the opportunity to be the aware sentient being I knew myself to be.

But I did have a companion of sorts, the family dog, Pinky. My father had brought her home without warning. We had named her for the color of the inside of her pointed ears. She was a long-haired dog, a sort of terrier, white, with a thin snout and dark bright eyes. She was smart, she seemed to understand words. She had a good trick, which was to drink water from the fountain in the Oval: she stood on her hind legs and held the pedestal basin with her front paws.

But when my mother put Pinky out with me, she tied her leash to a root branch of the privet. This was because the dog was totally untrained and ran away whenever she had the opportunity. And she was fleet. My mother was not fond of her. My father was. Donald, of course, loved her. I loved her but could not control her. If I held her leash, she pulled me all over the place until I fell. She got away from me almost every time. I didn't like that.

As I played in front of the house Pinky sat and watched me or barked at passing cars and lunged against her restraint. This particular morning we both heard a roar from the north end of the block. The dog barked furiously. Around the corner came the Sanitation Department water wagon. An enormous cylindrical tank was mounted on the flatbed of a Mack truck. The entire equipage was painted khaki, suggesting perhaps its origins during the World War. As it turned into our street two fanlike jets of water shot out of the nozzles suspended under the tank. Oh what a sight! An iridescent rainbow moved like a phantom light through the air, disintegrating as millions of liquid drops of sun and forming an instant torrent in the gutters at the curbstones. The water wagon rolled by with a fearsome roar and hiss. I ran along the sidewalk to feel the driest edges of the great spray. Behind me Pinky was barking and rearing against her collar. Then, from one moment to the next, the nozzles shut off, the truck went into another gear and turned the corner at Mt. Eden Avenue, and was gone from sight. But the air was cool and fresh. The street was black and shining. In the raging course of water flowing swiftly along the curb I tossed a Good Humor ice cream stick. Other children had appeared and dropped in their sticks and twigs. We followed our boats back down the block as they turned and twisted in the current, followed them down the gentle incline of Eastburn Avenue to their doom, a waterfall pouring into the sewer grate at the corner of 173rd Street.

I could count on seeing the water wagon in warm weather every couple of weeks. Less frequent appearances were made by the coal trucks. They came in early autumn, usually, while the temperature was high.

These trucks were of great interest to me. They were so heavy, so massive, especially when loaded with their mountains of coal, that only a clanking chain drive could turn their wheels. They were like rolling houses. One day a delivery was made to 1650. The coal truck backed up to the curb, parking almost at right angles to the sidewalk. It was the lawless arrogance of the mighty. The driver jumped out, bare to the waist, heavily muscled, like the truck. He was whiter in the chest than in the arms and he had a red bandanna around his neck. I recognized him as brother to the men who held the jackhammers and swung the picks and axes in the street-repair gangs. He disdained even to hear the barking dog. He threw a lever and the truck bed rose, tilting back on its hydraulic lifts so slowly, and with such grinding protest, as to transform itself in my mind into a screeching rearing dinosaur. When and only when the loaded bed stood at a dangerously slanted angle, almost at the vertical, did he bring it to a stop and throw open the sluice gate at the back: the great smoking avalanche of black stone poured itself onto the sidewalk.

Now, I had anticipated the event by untying Pinky and moving back with her to see things from a distance. There was a garage next to our house with a double set of folding doors. It belonged to the adjoining private house whose entrance was around the corner on Mt. Eden Avenue. It was set farther back than our front steps and so made a kind of playing area. I had looped Pinky's leash to the broken handle of one of the doors. The great tumbling slide so terrified her that she snapped her leash and ran off.

I did not realize this. I was too intent on watching the driver, who now climbed into the truck, straddling the side of the bed with a flaunted animal daring, and with a long-handled broom pushed the lingering chunks of coal out the chute. When this was done, he leaped nimbly to the ground, brought the truck bed back to the horizontal with a resounding clang, and drove away, sprinkling a thin trail of coal in the street behind him.

I contemplated the pyramid of slag in front of my house, in wonder for the weight of it, with some increased sense of the hierarchy of being, how the mass of it had been manipulated to do human bidding. I felt its substance keenly. I felt through my feet the earth as gravity.

I waited for the coming up from the alley with his shovel and wheelbarrow of Smith, our black janitor, who inhabited the basement.

He appeared. He didn't seem to notice me, which I counted as my good fortune.

Smith was a huge man, bigger and more muscular than the coal-truck operator. His slow gliding walk and slow speech, as resonantly basso as the voice at the bottom of a cavern, was to me consistent with the size of him. He wore overalls in winter or summer. He smelled of coal dust and ashes and whiskey. His hair was grey. His skin was black with a rich purple tone, he had raised scars on his face, his eyes were bloodshot, and he was now, as always, regally, imperially angry.

Piece by piece, he was going to move the coal to the coal bin.

He shoveled not from the top, where I would have, but from the bottom. When he filled the barrow, he stuck the shovel like a spear into the coal pile, lifted the handles and, his arm muscles tensing, rolled the wheelbarrow down the alley to the cellar. When he came back out again, he did not look at me, but I was the only one he could have been talking to when he said, "That dog done gone."

At this same moment I realized I had not for some time heard Pinky barking. Of course I ran into the house and got my mother. We went looking. We went from one end of the block to the other. Pinky was nowhere to be seen. The calamity of her loss panicked my small heart. As we half ran, half walked, my mother questioned me: had I noticed which way she'd run? how could I not have seen her break away? and so on. The judgment was explicit. My mother was sorely put out with me. At the same time she expressed the hope that Pinky might finally have run away forever. "With luck she'll never come back," my mother said.

This was her way—to express concern from opposite sides of the crisis.

I was ready to cry. Then I saw her. She was crossing Mt. Eden Avenue from the Oval to the big park. Her leash trailed behind her. "Pinky!" We ran across the street. "Pinky!" I shouted.

She ignored us. At this moment a car bore down on her. She had never understood cars. Now she froze in the middle of the street. She flattened herself head to tail, pressing her snout between her front paws, and the car passed over her.

"Oh my God," my mother said. We ran across the Oval and into the street. The car, a Nash or Hudson, I wasn't sure which, did not stop. The driver hadn't even seen her. Pinky was where she had hunkered down, she had not moved. She looked up at us with her dark eyes shining in terror. A big chunk of hair was gone from her back. She whimpered. "Oh Pinky," my mother said and got down on her knees and hugged the dog she despised. Pinky stood up trembling. Other than her skinning she was no worse for wear. She trotted home obediently behind us, I holding the remainder of the leash with both hands.

Cars were built high off the ground and so the dog survived. We were all to praise her for her instructive reaction before the oncoming car; we did not tell each other how stupid she was for having gotten in front of it in the first place. My mother put Vaseline on Pinky's scrape, and within an hour it was as if nothing had happened.

And I went back to watching Smith. He was working slowly and steadily in that way of skilled laborers. After the last barrowload was put away he came back out and hosed the sidewalk. The big penumbra of black dust dissolved. Then, everything clean and fresh again, Smith slowly went back to his basement.

I sat alone in the silence on the front stoop. My dog was safe. I sat there on the steps and looked into the peaceful shining street. In the passage of this sun-filled afternoon, it was as if the monumental event of the coal truck had never occurred, and that weightless light, and the iridescence of sprayed water, were, after all, the reigning forces of the universe.

Some black-and-white eight-millimeter film records a moment when I was commissioned by my brother to hold the spring-wound Universal movie camera that our father had brought home to us. The camera was not much larger than a pack of cigarettes, though much heavier. My job was to press the button and photograph Donald and his friends grouped around Pinky in the sun in front of the double folding garage doors alongside our house. First you see a sedate composition of boys standing and kneeling like a team around its mascot. Pinky barks and strains at her leash, which Donald has trouble holding. The group is waving, smiling, but then Pinky jumps, knocks over one of the kneeling boys, and soon the whole company are falling over themselves, laughing and shouting and mugging for the camera while the dog gets loose among them. They bang into each other grabbing for her. As you watch this scene the film seems to waver, the subjects careen out of frame and back, and Donald, disengaging himself from the extras, advances toward me with a frown. He shakes his head, waves his hands, and indicates with his characteristic expression of intense concern that I am doing something wrong. His scowl looms into the shot —I was determined to keep the button pressed as long as I could.

ROSE

By the time the war started, World War One, I had through Mr. Unterberg gotten interested in social welfare work. He had said to me watching the way I dealt with people who came into the office, that I had greater abilities than secretarial. I was very sensitive to poor people, and sometimes going to the settlement house on some errand of Mr. Unterberg's I would see these people in need and talk to them and try to help them. So he got me a job working for the Jewish Welfare Board, dealing with immigrants and their problems. The Board had set up a model tenement apartment up on 101st Street and First Avenue —up near the vinegar works. I taught the immigrant women and men how to live in the modern world. How to keep clean, store food, make beds, all that sort of thing. It was astonishing how little people knew, how uneducated and green they were. It was touching, you could not help being moved to see the struggles they had to understand, to learn, their desire to make good in America. I, having been born here, had no idea of my own parents' struggle, they too had come as young people not knowing the language, the ways of the new world, but at least they had skills, my father had a profession, he had work the day he landed, he was always very proud of telling us that. My father always knew how to make a living, and he worked till the day he died. He was extremely responsible, for him the family was everything, he not only got himself work but other musicians too, he became a sort of booking agent for musicians in addition to working himself. I learned ambition from him.

At any rate, working for the Jewish Welfare Board, when the war started I was naturally involved with that. Teams of us used to travel to the armories to serve coffee and doughnuts and talk to the soldiers and maybe dance with them at their functions. It was all chaperoned, all proper. Your father by then was in the Navy, he was training to be an ensign at the Webbs Naval Institute on the Harlem River, and as usual, he was devilish; he would each night climb over the fence and sneak out to see me without official leave. He did things like that. He would come to wherever I was working—we did this work in the evening—and there he would be in his blue sailor suit, one sailor among hundreds of soldiers and it could be quite a problem for him, the rivalry between soldiers and sailors being what it was, and he was totally outnumbered and still he'd take me away from these other boys with whom I'd been talking or dancing. He was lucky not to be killed.

Then in 1918 we had the terrible flu epidemic, and my two older sisters, my dear sisters, one twenty-three, the other twenty-four, they each contracted the flu and within months of each other they both died. To this day I don't like to think about it. I saw my poor mother turn old before my eyes. It was never an easy life, she was the hardest-working person I had ever seen, and how they had struggled the both of them to make a good life, and bring us up properly and see to it that we had some prospects for our own lives, some promise. It was not easy raising six children on the wages of a free-lance musician, however responsible he was; and in those days, of course, there was nothing that made running a home easy; you washed clothes with a washboard, you scrubbed them by hand in the sink. I used to do that myself, and you shopped every day because there was no refrigeration, and you cooked from scratch, there were no conveniences in cooking any more than in anything else. She had never had help. And these two beautiful young women got sick and died. She lost her two oldest daughters! I've blocked it all out, I don't remember the funerals. I try not to picture those girls. I don't remember any of it, only that that time in my mind is blank, a grey space, an emptiness.

When I was twenty-three I eloped with your father. We went to Rockaway Beach and we got married. What had happened is that my brother Harry, who was always very protective, went to Dave and he said, "You and Rose have been going out for eight years. She's twenty-three and she wants to get married. She would like to marry you, but if you won't she doesn't want to see you anymore. You either marry her or stay away." Well, you remember your father. He had a most unusual mind. He didn't think the way other people thought, he was unconventional, his ideas were different. Even then. I knew he wanted to marry me. But he didn't like to be told what to do, he never liked that. So the answer was to marry in this scandalous way, to elope, and get married by a justice of the peace rather than formally in a synagogue with a bridal veil and a celebration with the families' blessing. He disliked religion, your father. He was very modern, interested in the new ideas—just as he loved new gadgets he loved new ideas. He believed in progress. He'd learned some of this from his father, Isaac, a wonderful man, very scholarly, but not pious. For Isaac religion meant superstition and poverty and ignorance as it had in the old country. He was a socialist, your grandfather Isaac, he believed the problems on earth in life— food, shelter, education—should be solved on earth. The promises of Heaven didn't interest him. So your father had a background in these sorts of ideas. We went out to this remote beach community and married and set up house there. Both families were outraged and hurt. We lived a block from the ocean away from everyone else. I loved it there, it was very beautiful. Every day Dave took the train into the city. He worked for a man named Markel, who was in the phonograph business. After World War One, phonographs—Victrolas we called them—became popular. Markel liked Dave and taught him the business. That is how he got into it, through that man. For a while before we were married, I worked for Markel too, keeping the books, running the office. Dave had gotten me that job.

At any rate, though it was sometimes lonely in Rockaway, that was more than compensated for by the ocean and the sky and the privacy. We didn't have our families on our backs. You don't know what that meant. To have come from a large family living together, to have grown up in apartments and city streets. Now we were alone and we had privacy and we had space. It was a wonderful time in our lives. When we went out we went down to the Village, Greenwich Village. It was very much the thing then. Your father had a gift for making friends, meeting people, and he naturally gravitated to people of intelligence, people with fine minds and radical ideas. Well, in the Village that's the way things were, lots of young people thinking new thoughts and living differently from everyone around them. We had artists for friends, and writers. We read the latest books, listened to poets reading their poems in living rooms, in garrets in the Village. We knew Maxwell Bodenheim, who was then a very well known Village poet, we even met Edna Millay, who was already well known outside the Village. We ate in restaurants where actors and playwrights ate; I remember one, you walked down a few steps from the street, Three Steps Down, that was the name of it, and there we found ourselves sitting at a table next to Helen Hayes. How young and beautiful she was.

George Tobias, the actor, was a friend of ours. He was a young man then. He later went to Hollywood. And Phil Welch, a reporter for the *New York Times*. Phil admired your father very much. We had wonderful friends. Only now do I see that our lives could have gone in an entirely different direction.

FOUR

Winters, with their short and darkening days, were difficult. When it stormed, snow got down my collar, inside my galoshes and under my sleeves. Despite my mother's bundling me in several layers of clothes, all sealed in by my snowsuit, I was wet and freezing in a discouragingly short time considering everything I had had to go through to get out the door. I moved lurchingly, stiffly, breasting the snow like some tiny golem.

But the season had its revelations. I stood one afternoon at my front steps with a gale blowing and immense drifts of snow filling the block, banking against the parked cars, and making dunes of the stone stoops of the private houses. It was awesome, furious, but afterward, the sky clearing, the stars appearing in the dusk, I breathed the sharpest coldest air as some draft of incredibly clear and delicious water. In a moment my senses were alert and settled me in a stillness of perception as quiet as the snow. No cars moved, no people were in sight, and then, silently, the streetlamps came on like the assurance of survival of the buried.

Another day, a Saturday, with the sun shining and two feet of fresh snow on the ground, I discovered Donald and his friends in the backyard. Inspired perhaps by the legendary Admiral Byrd, they had undertaken to build an igloo. I did not usually venture into the backyard. It meant first of all going down the alley past Smith's door. And it was an enclosed space with stone retaining walls on three sides. It was a place to be trapped. At the rear our house and the one across the alley were three stories high and included car garages at basement level. Not that anyone had a car. Over a wood fence on the retaining wall at the back of the yard loomed a tenement with clotheslines strung from all the windows to an enormous creosoted pole planted just behind the wall.

But with Donald in the backyard, I ran right down. Talking, chattering, arguing, working away with their jackets thrown off, shirttails hanging, woolen watch caps askew, the friends were cutting blocks of snow with one of Smith's coal shovels and laying out a circular foundation. Their faces were red and their breaths were spouts of steam. As they slowly built the igloo up on an ever-decreasing circumference, I watched with a sense of the anti-material oppositeness of the thing; bit by bit, it was eliminating itself as an idea from the light of the sun. I felt that what was being built was not a shelter but some structured withdrawal from the beneficence of the lighted day, and my excitement was for invited darkness, the reckless enclosure, as if by perverse and self-destructive will, of a secret possibility of life that would be better untampered with. I jumped up and down in a kind of ecstasy of my own being, inducing deliberately from my frame a series of spasms of shivers of concentrated awareness. Little by little the light was being blacked out, and when the final block of wet snow was installed at the apex of the hemisphere, my brother, who had been working as the inside man, disappeared entirely.

I was very impressed. It was a marvel of an igloo for anyone to have built, let alone five or six arguing, pushing, shouting boys. Donald dug his way carefully out the side and then they all built a crawl-through entrance, a kind of hemicylindrical foyer. Then a hose was brought out to play water over the igloo so that it would freeze up hard. Then they punched an air hole in the top with a length of broomstick and the thing was done.

By the next day the igloo had become the talk of the neighborhood. Not only children but adults came down the alley from the street to have a look at it: Dr. Perlman, our family dentist and friend, who lived in the apartment house across the street; Mrs. Silver's chauffeur, who lived over the garage of the late Justice's mansion on the corner; Lieutenant Galardi of the Sanitation Department, who lived on 173rd Street; and several other mothers and fathers I didn't know by name.

My mother had donated a square of old carpet and a candle and the five builders had settled in, only sometimes deigning to respond to the importunings of the children outside who wanted a turn. Actually, they soon grew bored of occupying the thing, learning fast enough that the real excitement had been the building of it; but it was almost as good lording it over their friends and those who were younger, designating this or that one to take a turn, and instructing him as to the rules of deportment once he was admitted. For a while they had considered charging admission, but settled instead for barter offered in bribe—one child paying with a small American flag on a stick, which they embedded in the top like Peary at the North Pole, another a candy bar, another a half-eaten peanut butter and jelly sandwich, and so on. As younger brother of one of the founding architects, I had a special relationship to the igloo, being one of the first guests permitted entrance and, thereafter, more or less free to enter and exit at my own judgment at such moments as the crowd inside was not too great. It was a source of considerable amazement to me how, in this hemisphere of snow, my house, my yard and the Bronx, New York, disappeared in space and time. I was further engrossed by the paradox of the warmth of a structure made of solid ice. You sweated in there, it was so hot. You took off your hat and snowsuit jacket or you were, almost immediately, glisteningly hot as on the hottest day of summer.

The igloo lasted physically long after the builders and everyone else grew bored with it. Inside a week it was almost totally forgotten. It began to shrink, but maintained its geometry even as it grew smaller and greyer and less interesting. I had discovered this about ice cream cones too—that they maintained their original proportions even as they were consumed. Long after I had lost any interest in sitting inside the igloo I nevertheless took pleasure from its integrity of form, almost as if my brother and his friends had used the magic of an ethereal idea as something to hand—like the most skillful magician.

Eventually I joined some other children working at the igloo and kicking it down into a pile of solid snow. It seemed as important to do that as it had been to go inside and sit down when the thing was in its fresh, crystal glory and all the world was reduced to the cold and silent space of an Arctic night, and the faces of your fellow humans looked at you, red and expectant, with the light of the candle flame filling the centers of their widened eyes.

FIVE

As my birthday, January 6, approached each winter I anticipated it with the conviction that the number six was sacramental, my number, the enumeration of my special being. It was like my name, which was mine alone. The holiday season and the New Year seemed to me just a lighting of the way, an advance fanfare for the culminating event, like all the motorcycle policemen in their slouch caps and riding boots, and with their captains in the sidecars, roaring down the street ahead of the President.

My mother inadvertently confirmed my feeling by considering my birthday, as she did every ritual, in its historical context.

"Can you imagine not wanting this golden little boy?" she said to her friend Mae as they sat in the kitchen having tea. We were waiting for the first of my party guests.

In my white shirt and tie and my short pants held up by attached suspenders, I stood by my mother's side leaning my elbows on the table and indolently eating a cookie. She combed her fingers through my blond hair and I shook my head as a horse shakes his mane.

"Give him to me if you don't want him," Mae said, who was an unmarried woman. She winked at me. Unlike my round-armed mother, Mae was skinny. She wore thick eyeglasses that made her eyes small. And she smoked cigarettes, which my

mother did not do. With her elbow crooked, Mae held the cigarette between her index and middle fingers and she pointed it
at the ceiling.

"Oh, we like him now all right, I suppose," my mother said.
She pulled me up on her lap. "Now that he's here, we'll keep
him."

More than once my mother had told me that I was a mistake.
What this meant I both knew and did not know, in that way
children have for getting just enough of the sense of something not to want to pursue it in detail. The idea that I was
not expected or striven for did not injure me, however. I felt
assured of my mother's love, as troublesome as I may have
found it.

"He's always been difficult," she said proudly. "Full of surprises, from the day he was born. A breech birth no less."

"An acrobat," Mae said.

"I'll say. Except the acrobat didn't walk till eighteen months.
And you remember the trouble I had weaning him?"

"Maybe now that he's a big four-year-old fella he'll take it easy
on you," Mae said, smiling at me through the smoke.

At that moment the doorbell rang, and in anticipation of my
first guest I wriggled out of my mother's arms, slid my arched
spine over her knees, and landed on the floor under the table,
and crouched there. "Aren't you going to answer the door?" my
mother asked. But I had no intention of doing that; I only
wanted to hide.

The day was momentous, but parties were mixed blessings.
You got presents, all right—pick-up sticks, or crayons, or flat
boxes of modeling clay in many colored strips—but they were
the lesser presents of party admissions. And we all had to sit at
the table with ridiculous pointed paper hats, and paper plates
and noisemakers and popping balloons and pretend to a joyful
delirium. In fact, a birthday party was a satire on children directed by their mothers, who hovered about, distributing Dixie
Cups and glasses of milk while cooing in appreciation for the
aesthetics of the event, the way each child was dressed for it and
so on; and who set us upon one another in games of the most

acute competition, so that we either cried in humiliation or punched each other to inflict pain.

And it was all done up in the impermanent materials of crepe paper, thin rubber and tin, everything painted in the gaudy colors of lies.

And the climax of the chaos, blowing out the candles on the cake, presented likely possibility of public failure and a loss of luck in the event the thing was not done well. In fact, I had a secret dread of not being able to blow out the candles before they burned down to the icing. That meant death. Candles burning down to the end, as in my grandmother's tumblers of candles, which could not be tampered with once lit, memorialized someone's death. And the Friday-night Sabbath candles that she lit with her hands covering her eyes, and a shawl over her head, suggested to me her irremediable grief, a pantomime of the loss of sight that comes to the dead under the earth.

So I blew for my life, to have some tallow left for the following year. My small chest heaved and I was glad for my mother's head beside mine, adding to the gust, even though it would mean I had not done the job the way one was supposed to, with aplomb.

Grandma lived in the room next to mine. She was a desiccated, asthmatic little woman who wore high-laced shoes and all manner of long old-fashioned dresses, and shawls, usually black. She lived a very private life, which made me wary of her. She stayed in her room for hours on end, and often came out in such a thoughtful, brooding state as not to notice what was going on around her.

She was very slender and tiny with delicate features. But her face was all wrinkled and her complexion was sallow. She wore her long wavy grey hair neatly braided and coiled when she was feeling well, and uncombed and flying when she was unwell. Like my mother, she had the palest blue eyes. But they looked at me, these eyes, either with great smiling love and animation, or with no recognition in them at all. I never knew on any given day whether Grandma would know and love me, or stare at me as if she had never seen me before.

Had I known precisely what her trouble was, it might have helped to remove some of the terror of her in my mind. My mother only told me what a sad hard life she had had. She had lost two children many years ago. And the year before I was born, her husband, who would have been my grandfather, had died. In this view Grandma's behavior was appropriate. But then why did she insist that my mother taste everything she put before her on the table? Grandma would not eat anything if my mother did not taste it first. She believed my mother, her own daughter, was trying to poison her. She sat with her hands in her lap and stared at her food. So now, whether Grandma was feeling that way or not, my mother tasted everything conspicuously before she served it. And she did that with everyone, even me. She sipped from my glass of milk and set it down before me, a practice I came to regard as normal.

Sometimes, when everything was all right, Grandma helped my mother with the cooking. In fact, she was a good cook, and knew things my mother didn't know. "Oh Mama," my mother said, "why don't you make your wonderful cabbage soup." I could tell my mother loved Grandma—she lost her self-assurance when Grandma was not well. She worried about the old woman terribly. She could not get her to go to a doctor. My father was kind to Grandma, but was not around her enough to worry about her. Donald, I suspected, was as shy of her as I was, though he tried not to show it. He sometimes gave Grandma his arm so that she could descend the front steps more easily when, the weather being mild, she was persuaded to get some air. Grandma negotiated steps the baby way, bringing both feet together on each level.

She spoke mostly in the other language, the one I didn't understand. When she felt all right she blessed me and kissed me on the forehead and produced pennies from her change purse and pressed them into my hand. "For a good boy," she said. "So he should buy something." She pulled me to her, and with my face lodged in her skeletal shoulder she muttered an instruction to God as to the good health He must always assure me. Since these love words were in the other language, as her curses were on her bad days, they made me similarly uneasy.

I knew the name of the other language: Jewish. It was for old people.

Grandma's room I regarded as a dark den of primitive rites and practices. On Friday evenings whoever was home gathered at her door while she lit her Sabbath candles. She had two wobbly old brass candlesticks that she kept well polished. She had brought them many years ago from the old country, which I later found out was Russia. She covered her head with a shawl, and with my mother standing beside her to keep the house from burning down, Grandma lit the white candles and waved her hands over the flames and then covered her eyes with her wrinkled hands and prayed. The sight of my own grandma performing what was, after all, only a ritual blessing seemed to me something else—her enacted submission to the errant and malign forces of life. That an adult secretly gave way to this sentiment I found truly frightening. It confirmed my suspicion that what grown-ups told me in my life of instruction was not the whole truth.

Grandma kept her room clean and tidy. She had a very impressive cedar hope chest covered with a lace shawl, and on her dresser a silver hairbrush, and comb. There was a plain slat-back rocking chair under a standing lamp so she could read her prayer book, or Siddur. And on an end table beside the chair was a flat tin box packed with a medicinal leaf that was shredded like tobacco. This was the centerpiece of her most consistent and mysterious ritual. She removed the lid from this blue tin box and turned it on its back and used it to burn a pinch of the leaf. She applied a match and blew on the leaf as my brother blew on punk, to get it started. It made tiny sputtering pops and hisses as it burned. She turned her chair toward it and sat inhaling the thin wisps of smoke—it was a treatment for her asthma. I knew it helped her breathing, and that it was scientific, having been purchased from Rosoff's Drugstore on 174th Street. But the smell was pungent, as if from the underworld. I didn't know, nor did any of my family seem to know, that this medicinal leaf my Grandma burned was marijuana. Even had they known, it would have held no significance, since it was readily and legally available without prescription. But to this day the smoke of grass produces in me memories of the choking harsh bitter rage of an exile from the shtetl, a backfired life full of fume and sparks, like a Fourth of July held in an open grave and projecting on the night a skull's leer and a clap of crossed bones.

One of my favorite ways to spend Grandma's pennies came along Eastburn Avenue in the afternoons: Joe the Sweet Potato Man. He pushed a small unmarked cabinet on wheels. Inside the cabinet was a kind of oven of homemade design, the fuel being charcoal. Joe raised the hinged top lid and reached down practically to his armpit to withdraw one of his roasted sweet potatoes. He was an impassive man who wrapped himself in sweaters and coats, obviously scavenged, and a watch cap over which was a peaked khaki hat of rough wool. He wore old Army shoes, cracked and splitting. Over all his clothing he had tied a shoulder-to-ankle waiter's apron not recently washed. This costume suggested great authority to me. With his large hands, dirt uniformly running under his nails, Joe slapped the potato on the cart, pulled an enormous knife from its wooden sheath and sliced the potato in half lengthwise. He then stuck the tip of the knife into a can and withdrew a slab of butter, which he inserted in a slit made almost simultaneously in the meat of the potato, and, after sheathing the knife, wrapped the purchase like a cornucopia in a torn half sheet of the *Bronx Home News* so that you could hold the potato and eat it without burning your fingers.

For this golden, sweet, steaming hot feast I gave up two pennies. Another, and I could have the potato whole.

Joe went along his impassive way as, with dusk descending on the cold blue-grey sky over the Bronx, I sat on my stoop and ate his remarkable cuisine. It was not only something to eat but something to warm my hands against, as if I had plucked a tiny hearth from an elf's house.

Sometimes when my mother was going shopping I went along so that I could spend my money at the candy store on the corner of Eastburn and 174th Street. Many different things were to be had for a penny, candies of various kinds, Fleer's Double Bubble gum, or some shoe leather, which was what we called a pounded sheet of dried apricot, or Indian nuts that fell from the chute of a glass canister after you deposited the coin and twisted the key, or, what I usually went for, a shot-glassful of sunflower seeds poured into my hands by the proprietor.

I put the seeds in my jacket pocket and followed my mother from store to store as I cracked the shells one at a time between my front teeth and withdrew each seed with the tip of my tongue. I did this without missing a thing that was going on around me. In fact, the steady and relentless crunching of Polly seeds brought my gaze to sharp focus. One next to another, stores were built at street level in the sides of apartment houses. The street was astir with cars, trucks and horse-drawn wagons. It interested me that horses could, without any reduction in speed, raise their tails and leave a trail of golden dung.

The old Italian who repaired shoes managed to conduct his business without speaking English. His shop was a dark little basement store throbbing with the running motors and looped and slapping belts of leather trimmers and buffing wheels. Each wheel was stained with shoe polish of a different color. My mother held out a pair of my father's shoes. "Heels and tips," she said, and the old man, barely looking up from a shoe he clutched to his chest while he carved its sole to size, nodded and grunted something in Italian. My mother asked him the cost and when the shoes would be ready. She addressed him in English and he replied in Italian, and the negotiation was completed to everyone's satisfaction. As we left he grabbed a handful of nails and put them in his mouth: he was about to attach the sole.

A few doors down was the Atlantic and Pacific Tea Company, where a man in an apron stood behind his wooden counter and ground up coffee to order and collected the items you asked for from the shelves behind him. If what you wanted —a box of junket, for example, or Cream of Wheat—was too high for him to reach, he grabbed it with a long pinching stick whose ends he could contract by squeezing the handle. The box flew through the air and he caught it. Then, with the purchases stacked in front of him, he wrote the cost of each on a brown paper bag with a small pencil he took from behind his ear and totaled the row of sums smartly, and then used the same bag to pack everything. I liked this store because of the coffee smell and the sawdust on the floor. I liked sawdust as long as it was dry.

In Irving's Fish Store, the sawdust was often wet. Irving's had a kind of swimming-pool atmosphere about it. The walls were bare of shelves. Everything was white. Two holding tanks of live fish were along the wall where the customer came in. Water ran in them continuously. Irving's apron tended to be wet and red with fish blood. He was a big jovial man. "Hello, Missus!" he said to my mother as we walked in. He was scaling a big brown fish. Fish scales flew through the air, some sticking to his glasses like snow. "How are you, sonny boy?" he said to me. "I want some salmon, Irving," my mother said, "but only if it's not expensive." Irving came around from behind his counter, took a short-handled net from the wall and ran it around the dark tank, where I could see the shadows of several fish slithering in panic. They looked elusive to me, but in a second or two Irving had raised one twisting and curling in the net and dripping water on the floor. "I saved this beauty for you," he said to my mother. He slapped the salmon down on the counter and held it pressed against the wood block with one hand while with the other he banged it on the head with a heavy wooden mallet. The fish went still. I admired Irving's fast hands. My mother turned away, but I watched as he sliced off the salmon's head with one of his large

41

knives, eviscerated it, washed it under the faucet, and sliced it up in steaks. I recognized the salmon now.

Our last stop was Rosoff's Drugstore, on the corner of Morris Avenue. Large glass jars of red and blue liquid stood on display in the window; what they were meant to suggest I had no idea, but I liked the way the sunlight went through them and lit the colors. Also on display was a brass mortar and pestle, whose function I understood because my grandmother had one just like it to use in the kitchen to pound nuts and seeds. There were also various mysterious items made of red rubber. Inside the store I breathed an atmosphere of sweet soaps and bitter medicines, rolled bandages and anodynes, sodas, salts and pungent tinctures. Along the walls were glass cabinets that went all the way up to the patterned tin ceiling. Mr. Rosoff reached the upper levels by means of a railed ladder, which he rolled along the wall. He climbed the ladder for the implement of porcelain or the bottle, box, packet or tin the customer called for. He was a tiny sweet-tempered man with a round face and a soft voice. He politely inquired about the health of everyone in the family, particularly my grandmother. He shook his head in sympathy as my mother told him. He wore a starched white short-sleeved tunic buttoned to the neck, like a doctor's, and could offer such medical services as taking out things that had gotten into your eye—rolling your eyelid back and dabbing off the offending mote with a bit of cotton. He had done that for me.

My mother made a purchase, a box that Mr. Rosoff placed precisely in the middle of a sheet of dark green wrapping paper, which he had torn from a big roll on his counter. His pudgy hands flew about the box like bird wings and in a matter of seconds the green wrapping had been folded over, tucked in at the corners, triangulated at the ends, and tied around with white string from a spool hanging from the ceiling above his head. To break the string he looped it around each hand and gave a smart tug.

When we left I asked my mother what was in the box. She didn't want to tell me. "It doesn't concern you," she said. But

I persisted. I had no more Polly seeds and no more pennies. "What did you buy," I said. "Tell me." She strode along. "Tell me," I whined.

"Oh stop it, they're sanitary napkins. Are you satisfied?"

I was not satisfied because I didn't know what sanitary napkins were, but I knew from her tone that I had used up my allotment of questions and so pursued the matter no further.

SIX

It was early spring when my uncle Billy came to live with us. He was an older brother of my mother's, a gentle ineffectual man down on his luck. Claremont Park was beginning to turn green. Uncle Billy moved into Donald's room, and Donald came down the hall to stay in my room, which was actually a bit larger. I was thrilled by this arrangement but Donald was deeply affronted. "It's only for a little while," my mother told him. "Till Billy gets back on his feet. He has nowhere else."

Donald lay on his bed and threw a hardball toward the ceiling and caught the ball in his first baseman's glove, one-handed. He did this over and over. Sometimes the ball hit the ceiling. A polka-dot pattern of black marks began to appear there. Sometimes the ball missed his glove and thudded on the floor and under the bed. I retrieved it for him.

Uncle Billy was a divorced man, something quite rare at this time, and he had the further distinction of having been a successful bandleader in the nineteen twenties. He was not insensitive to the disruption caused by his joining the household. Before he had finished unpacking his suitcase, he came into our room with a rolled cloth under his arm. His vest was unbuttoned. "You boys ever see this?" He gave the cloth a flap and spread it on the floor. It was a rectangular banner of purple velvet with gold lettering, all in capitals, and a border of gold.

44

On the floor it was like a room rug. Before I could work it out Donald said, " 'BILLY WYNNE AND HIS ORCHESTRA.' "

"That's right," Uncle Billy said. "You hung that over the bandstand everywhere you played—'Billy Wynne and His Orchestra.' That was me in the good old days."

Donald and I were awed. We hadn't known he was that famous. He leaned against the doorjamb with his hands in his pockets and began to tell us about the hotels he had played, the nightclubs. "We were booked for two weeks in the Ambassador," he said. "And we stayed for thirteen." He had a reedy voice, up in his head. I was too shy now to look at him directly. But he had the hurt blue eyes of that side of the family, though smaller and closer together than my mother's or grandma's. He had a double chin and had thinning hair combed carefully sideways to hide his scalp. His nose was red and bulbous. When he laughed he had teeth missing.

I felt the velvet with my fingertips. "You boys keep it," he said.

"Don't you want it?" Donald said.

"Naah, take it. It's a nice souvenir of the good old days."

We thanked him. He turned to go. "You know the first orchestra ever to broadcast over the radio?"

"Billy Wynne?" Donald said.

"That's right. WRPK Pittsburgh, 1922."

How Uncle Billy had lost his orchestra was never made clear to me, but it seemed to have had to do with a crooked business manager as well as his own ineptitude. He'd had numbers of jobs in the years since. He fit into the house easily enough—in a matter of a week or two it felt as if he had always lived with us. He was a decent, kind man. My mother appreciated his help in dealing with Grandma. Uncle Billy talked to the old woman and pacified her. She was glad to see him, but she also shook her head and cried, seeing how poor he'd become. "Mama," he said, "don't you worry about a thing. I've got a coupla aces up my sleeve."

In fact he was now working for my father in the Hippodrome music store downtown on Sixth Avenue. They went off to the subway together every day. My father's theory was that Billy would bring customers into the store. Some of them might even remember his name. The salary wasn't much, but he could earn commissions on the big items. Uncle Billy was grateful. He was not an educated man and regarded the books in my parents' house with great respect. I saw him once pick up a book and squeeze it and riffle its pages and put it down and smile and shake his head. When my father talked to him about politics, or history, he felt honored. "Dave," he'd say. "You should've been a professor."

"Thanks, Willy," my father said. I noticed both my father and my mother used the names Billy and Willy interchangeably as if there were no difference. Later I found out my mother's family's name was Levine. So Billy Wynne was Willy Levine. After I worked that out I always called him Uncle Willy.

Uncle Willy sometimes did tricks for us, and I remember one trick in particular that was my favorite and that he did very well. He'd stand in the doorway to my room and make it appear that a hand belonging to someone else just hidden from view was grabbing him by the throat and trying to drag him away. He would choke and gasp and his eyes would bulge and he'd try to tear at the clawlike hand; his head would disappear and reappear again in the struggle, and sometimes it was so realistic that I'd scream and rush to the door and beg him to stop, jumping up and swinging on the arm of the malign killer hand, which, of course, was his own. It didn't matter that I knew how the trick was done, it was terrifying just the same.

With the lengthening of the days I stayed out longer. Warm breezes blew into the evening. The new leaves of the privet were pale green. People opened their windows and came out of doors, women with their baby carriages, children at games. I studied the more difficult or daring games against the time when I would be old enough to play them: hit and span, which took you into the gutter and was waged with one's best marbles; the infernally difficult paddle ball, in which a small red ball connected to a paddle by a long single strand of rubber was hit so that it would fly off and return to the face of the paddle to be hit again. (Rhythm was everything.) And the variations of baseball, including stoop ball, punch ball and stickball; and also the ball games utilizing the sides of buildings or the cracks in sidewalks, such as slug or hit the stick.

Of course the ice cream vendors appeared—going very slowly and jingling their bells till a child came running. The Bungalow Bar truck was roofed like a fairy-tale house. A Good Humor pop, at a dime, was twice as expensive, but if your stick had the words GOOD HUMOR burned into it you'd get a free one. Competing with these motorized corporations was the swarthy steadfast Joe. The Sweet Potato Man was now dressed for the spring in a strawhat with the top punched out and his pushcart retooled to sell ices. Impassive as ever, Joe gave you for your two cents a scoop or ball of shaved ice over which he pumped the vile syrup of your choice—cherry, lemon or lime. The concoction was served in a small pleated paper cup that was so porous it soon took on the color of the syrup.

The mothers themselves came out for Harry's vegetable wagon, the fruits and vegetables displayed in their wooden crates in tiers, steeply raked, and the prices of things scrawled on paper bags still folded flat and stuck over slats in the front of the crates. A spring scale hung from three chains. Harry was a thickset, red-faced man with a gravel voice and an incantatory salesmanship. He packed up the purchases of one customer while calling up to the windows the catalogue of what he had for sale, how good it was, and how fairly priced, in a kind of double mode of communication, the soft voice for the already sold customer, the loud voice to broadcast for the customer still to come. I liked Harry's horse too, an ancient flea-ridden creature with sores on his back who chewed the oats from his feed bag in a way to capture my interest, slowly but tirelessly, with the glassy eyes of a superior contemplation.

47

Less frequent visitors were the knife and scissor sharpeners who worked on the trucks with their noisy footpedal grinding wheels that sent sparks off the steel, sparks being to me the most suggestively volatile phenomena, so quickly self-consuming as almost not to exist; and peddlers wearing derbies who bought used clothes and carried them in enormous packs on their backs; and junk dealers who pushed two-wheeled carts piled high with newspapers and rags and flattened tin cans and broken chairs and beds and boxes of dishes; and men ringing doorbells to sell cartons of fresh eggs, or magazine subscriptions, or red paper poppies from the American Legion; and bearded men in black hats and black winter coats who came begging at the door with coin boxes and letters of credentials from yeshivas. "My God," said my mother one day, closing the door after still another transient had rung the bell, "is there no end to this? When my father brought us to the Bronx when I was a little girl, he didn't know the whole Lower East Side would follow."

These itinerant peddlers, beggars and entrepreneurs were often unwholesome-looking or shabby or dirty and had dull blackened eyes from which all light had departed, but I don't ever remember feeling threatened by any of them.

One day a Department of Public Works crew appeared to repair a pothole. Their truck carried tar pots and towed a two-wheeled cart that was a kind of stove for heating their asphalt. The stove made a roaring sound as it fired. The crew raised and dropped long-handled flat-irons to flatten the smoking asphalt fill. One of the workers wore a pin-striped suit and vest, and a grey fedora. He was dressed just like my father. But his suit was creased and dirty, and because he was warm his tie was loosened. His hat was pushed back. I was alarmed. I had hoped he was the boss, but the boss was sitting in the truck and reading the newspaper.

When the job was done, this man in the suit swung his long-handled tar iron over his shoulder, just like the others, and followed the truck up the street as it slowly went looking for the next pothole.

Late each spring a Parks Department traveling farm exhibit encamped in the big park, Claremont. With great excitement of her own my mother took me to see it one day. We crossed Mt. Eden Avenue and the Oval, and the other direction of Mt. Eden Avenue, and then we were at the foot of the park's retaining wall of rounded stones. We raced up the flight of stone stairs. It was a huge wonderful park, with playgrounds and fields and tree-shaded paths. It was cool compared with the street. In a wooded meadow were the tents and trucks of the traveling farm. There was no gate, no entrance. Suddenly we were among the sheep and their lambs, cows and calves, horses with their foals, all of whom seemed to lend themselves in gentle patience to the touches of city children. Only an occasional bleat or whinny suggested they would rather be somewhere else. But the geese and ducks squawking about in clipped-wing panic would not let us get near them, which seemed to me a logical reaction, a mark of their intelligence, in fact. I was invited to hold a rabbit, which I did. Animals were warm. I touched a foal's back too lightly and the hide twitched, as if I were a fly. A wooden pen, about the size of a sandbox, held a rippling of peeping chicks, as if a bright yellow flag of the sun was waving over the ground. Hay was played out to the animals in their pens; I smelled the hay, and the manure, and it was not entirely unpleasant, it was a forceful array of smells that alerted you, somehow, to an insistence on more life than you knew. Smiling suntanned young women in light green dresses lectured from the back steps of trailers. We were guided with our mothers' blessings amid the animals in their fecundity, and invited to enjoy the reality of them, which I fervently did.

But the truest and most daring expeditions of spring were mounted by my father, whose restlessness drew us ever out-ward. Usually on Sundays he preferred to visit his mother and father, my grandma and grandpa, who lived north of Kingsbridge Road on the Grand Concourse. But in this season he was too much with the fullness of himself and his good feeling to do the ordinary thing. And so one Sunday we went to the tennis courts on Morris Avenue and 167th Street—a good walk—and he played tennis first with my mother, hitting the white ball back and forth over the net, and later with Donald, whom he instructed in the forehand and backhand strokes. "That's the way," he said. "Good. Good one." I was too small to hold the wood racket with one hand. When my turn came, I hit with it as if I held a baseball bat. I didn't want to do it long because I was afraid of hitting the ball into another court and disturbing someone. "Don't worry about that," my father said. I thought he looked splendid in his white ducks and shirt and tennis shoes, his dark eyes flashing as he lunged this way and that to stroke the ball. It seemed effortless as he did it, he was always where the ball was. "You've got to bend your knees," he said. "You've got to anticipate. Keep your side toward the net. Bring the racket back, and when you swing, follow through." I was having too good a time to listen carefully. My mother played well; although she didn't move quite as fast as my dad, she hit the ball smartly and it flew right back to him. She was not awkward as you would expect a girl to be. She wore a white dress and a sunshade tied around her hair, and white ankle socks with her shoes.

There were many courts. I counted twelve. Around the entire compound was a fence of chicken wire. The courts were red clay and made the bottom of my socks red. The white lines were whitewashed on with lime and had to be redone by the court attendant because they were rubbed out by the players' shoes.

My father was always rousing us up to do things. It was his idea to persuade his friend Dr. Perlman, the family dentist who lived in the apartment house across the street, and who owned a car, that the two families should have a picnic in the country. And so we did. I did not relish the drive sitting on my mother's lap in the back of Dr. Perlman's black Plymouth. I didn't know if it was true of all Plymouths, but it certainly was of Dr. Perlman's, that it seemed designed to lurch and jerk and drift and lurch again but never to travel at a steady rate. Somewhere on the Saw Mill River Parkway north of the Bronx, my green color was noted, and I was dumped over the back of the front seat to sit up there with my father and Donald, the little front swivel window pushed out wide to give me the breeze.

But then we were out in the country, as far out as I had ever been in my life. The country was an endless pathless park. We were in a broad meadow of millions of buttercups. We ran races in the sun, Donald and I and the Perlmans' boy, Jay, who was a bit younger than I but taller and stronger, which did not endear him to me. My father called the races with a newspaper rolled up as a megaphone and my beret on the top of his head. His vest was open, his jacket lay on the ground. My mother and Mrs. Perlman, a woman with a limp, and Mae Barsky, sat on blankets in the shade of a tree and set out the sandwiches and fruit and lemonade. Donald took home movies with our Universal camera. My father throws a ball at the camera. My father bats. My father stands facing Dr. Perlman, a big horse-faced man with rimless glasses, and he waves his arms in a hocus-pocus circle and points his two index fingers and Dr. Perlman disppears. Someone has produced ice cream and I am eating a Melorol happily, smears of it all over my mouth. I smile and wave at the camera.

This was a place called Kensico, an Indian name. The field we played in was at the foot of a high sheer bluff covered with bushes and trees and vines. The tracks of the New York Central ran along the top of the bluff. Trains came along, but they were so high above the meadow and the trees they seemed no bigger than toy electric trains. Whenever we heard the whistle of the locomotive, we stopped what we were doing and stood still in the grass before we saw it. And then it appeared, the tiny train, and we waved and the engineer, who was too small to be seen, blew his whistle in greeting.

But the spring had its maniac leer, some dissolving smile of menace that I couldn't quite catch sight of. The whole earth was pushing up, everything was turning out and open. My arms and legs hurt, and my mother told me I had growing pains. I thought I would rather not feel myself growing. I felt my heart banging and understood life as something that lived itself in you, an irresistible animating power that was mindless enough to go out of control, like the spring in a windup toy that without warning would run amok and bust itself to pieces.

A genial man from the neighborhood whose name was Ziggy walked past my house every day. His head was the size of a watermelon; the little features, including the tiny smiling mouth, were way up front. Ziggy walked with mincing steps, shuffling, his knees bent, his too-heavy head bobbing this way and that so that it appeared it might topple him over at any moment. Ziggy laughed and clapped his hands like a baby when he saw something that pleased him. My mother told me she'd heard he was a mathematical genius.

Even among children, people of my own ilk, there were some who didn't act right or were tremblingly uncoordinated or had half-grown limbs or clubfeet. I knew a pair of twin boys my age —they came to my first few birthday parties; one was normally nasty and verbal, the other a saint of retardedness. They were identical twins and when little had sat side by side in one of those double strollers of brown wicker.

From the tenement behind my backyard all sorts of urgent and enraged cries rose on the spring night. My room was in the rear of our house, just over the garage. The clotheslines were strung from tenement windows to the creosoted pole like the cables of a bridge. I saw things I wasn't looking for, people in the lighted windows in their underwear, women pulling themselves out of their corsets. Prowling about, sometimes at dusk, or on cold mornings of rain when everyone still slept, strange youths not from the neighborhood came vaulting over the fences into our yard. They climbed the retaining wall and disappeared. These were boys who hated boundaries and straight lines, who traveled as a matter of principle off the streets, as if they needed to trespass and show their scorn of property. They wore felt hats with the brims cut away and the crown folded back along the edge and trimmed in a triangle pattern. They wore undershirts for shirts and high-top sneakers without socks. They carried cigarettes behind their ears. Slingshots stuck out of their back pockets. They were the same boys who rode the backs of the trolley cars by standing on the slimmest of fenders and holding on to the window frames with their fingertips. They wrestled sewer covers off their seats and climbed down in the muck to find things. They were the ones, I knew, who chalked the strange marks on our garage doors.

I had noticed these chalk marks one day while in the yard. Donald and his friends were building a Ping-Pong table. It was to be a marvel of a table, hinged in the middle and painted regulation green with ruled edges. It was to rest on sawhorses. Donald and his friends were quietly and cooperatively building their table for a contentious Ping-Pong tournament full of shouting. I caused them to look up from their work by pointing out the sign on the garage doors. I wanted to know what it was.

I hadn't expected their complete attention. They stopped what they were doing and stood and looked at the chalk scrawl. Donald stepped up and raised his arm, and used the sleeves of his sweater as an eraser. The other boys were equally solemn. They took the whole thing seriously. "It's bad," Donald told me. "Whenever you see one of these, make sure to erase it. Use your shoe sole, spit on it, rub it with dirt, do anything. It's a swastika."

My mother added to this intelligence later the same day. "The next time you see one of those boys you tell me," she advised. "If you see someone who obviously is not from this neighborhood and doesn't belong here, don't stand around, but come inside and tell me. Or tell Donald. These boys think they're smart. They'd like to be Nazis. They're disgraceful. They carry knives. They confront Jewish children and say they killed Christ. They rob. You come inside if you see them."

And so my horizons were expanding. As I understood it, beyond Eastburn Avenue, on the far side of Claremont Park and down the hills, were the East Bronx neighborhoods, pockets of Irish and Italian poverty, that were the source of these depredations. These Irish and Italian neighborhoods were far below us, in valleys that rang with trolley-car bells and shook with the passing of elevated trains, where people lived in ramshackle houses with tar-paper siding amid factories and warehouses.

I had the good fortune to be living in this neighborhood, but its borders were not inviolate. That my house was of red brick, which I knew was essential from the tale of the three little pigs, evoked in me feelings of deepest gratitude. However, in bed at night, after the light was out, I heard outside in the dark sometimes the kicking over of ash cans, or a police siren, and then closer to my ear but somehow less audible, the breath of someone watching me. And in my sleep figures would loom in threatening gesture and just as suddenly recede into colored swirling points, as if I myself had been spread-eagled on a wheel spinning so fast that the colors melted together and became a target.

ROSE

Only now do I see that our lives could have gone in an entirely different direction. We were young and energetic. But little by little the two families were accepting us. The shock was wearing off. This began when Donald was born. Another generation! Donald was born at St. Joseph's Hospital in Rockaway Beach. A Catholic hospital. The nurses there were lovely to me, the nuns. It was a wonderful hospital and they took everyone in, it didn't matter to them. The only thing was the nurses wore habits and in the front lobby on the wall was an enormous gold cross, and in each room was a crucifix that was quite specific, with a painted Jesus on the cross. Well, you can imagine, when it was time for the birth my whole family traveled all the way from the Bronx, and for them the occasion was to be celebrated in the traditional way, with cake and wine and a little whiskey, so there were, in addition to my mother and father and sister Bessie and my brothers Harry and Billy, my aunts and uncles and cousins. Here they came dragging all the way from the Bronx, which was quite a trip then, nobody had cars, nobody could afford them, you took buses and the elevated train and then the real train, it took hours. And they had bags and shopping bags and gifts. And when they walked into St. Joseph's and saw that big cross on the wall, they were stunned. One of my uncles, an extremely religious man, a ridiculous pompous man, took one look and turned around and walked out and went right home—Aunt Minnie's husband, Uncle Tony, he was English, he wore homburgs, he had a very high regard for himself. Then Minnie followed him, of course, she always let him lead her around, and one or two of the others, but my mother, a blessed dear woman, she and my father stayed, they were no less religious than Uncle Tony. The crosses on the walls were a profound offense to them, but they didn't let it faze them, they knew what was important, and what was important was that they had a new grandson and that their daughter wanted them there.

The circumcision was done by a regular doctor in an operating room, that was the way we wanted it, we didn't want a mohel; and the Sisters had set aside a room where we could all gather and have our cake and wine. They were what they were, and we were what we were, and it all worked out fine. Even the Mother Superior came in and had a sip of whiskey. I had gotten along very well with all the Sisters and I liked her very much and I was honored that she came.

Your father was very funny. He was in the city working when Donald was ready to be born. Donald was not expected for another week or two. I went to the hospital alone, and by the time they called Dave I had given birth. He came rushing out and the first thing he said to me was "Why didn't you wait!" Can you imagine? He was so excited, so solicitous. Donald was a tiny baby and had jaundice the first few weeks of his life and we were very worried about him, Dave was worried. When we brought him home, all wrapped up, a tiny little face peering out of his blankets, you should have seen how proud his father was, how excited!

But that was the beginning of the return to the families. With the baby we were respectable in their eyes. Or it seemed that way. My mother-in-law in particular kept urging Dave to bring us back to the Bronx. "You're so far away," she said, "we're all here, it's not right both families so close to each other in the Bronx and you and Rose and the baby so far away." Then too it was a matter of having help, of being able to call on someone; Dave had a good job, but we couldn't immediately afford nurses or live-in maids, I needed my mother. I needed her to tell me how to do things, I didn't want to make mistakes. It was so much work, washing and boiling diapers, sewing clothes, our old family doctor Dr. Gross was in the Bronx, and so on. These were all considerations. But I think I would have stuck it out in Rockaway if Dave had wanted that. He seemed to give in, maybe he was scared by the responsibility, maybe he felt it would be easier commuting to Manhattan from the Bronx than from Rockaway; he could leave later and be home earlier; but who knows what he thought, in many ways he was very mysterious, very secretive, your father; and in those days husbands didn't help out particularly, the division of labor was very clear-cut and everyone abided by it, so who knows what he felt. But somehow the decision was made. We found an apartment on Weeks Avenue and Mt. Eden Avenue next to Claremont Park, it was right back in our old neighborhood. So back we went, and my heart sank, I had loved it so in Rockaway. I loved the salt air, I loved the sea and the sky. Everything was so bright and fresh. It wasn't till we were ensconced in our new apartment that I realized how sorry I was.

SEVEN

You learned the world through its dark signs and also from its evil devices, such as slingshots, punchboards and scumbags. I found a slingshot one day that was beautifully made. Someone had taken great pains with it. The Y-shaped frame was a shaved piece of tree branch with close to symmetrical arms. The sling was a heavy band of rubber in the absolute center of which was strung a pouch of soft leather. The key stress points were tightly and evenly wound with kite string. I immediately placed a small round stone in the pouch and let fly. It didn't go very far. I tried again, this time pulling back on the rubber as hard as I could with my right hand and holding my left arm stiff, my hand clenching the frame handle. The stone went like a bullet, pinged a car door, leaving a dent, and then bounced off the carriage of a child sitting in the sun next to my house.

The mother was furious. She went up the steps of my house and rang the doorbell. But even before my mother came to the door I had dumped the slingshot in the ash can. It was powerful magic, it had some animating force of its own, well beyond the strength in my child's arms. No wonder it was, with the spring-blade knife, the weapon of choice of the swastika youths.

One day I was sitting with Pinky on the steps and an older boy stopped and offered me a chance on a punchboard, a cardboard packet with a grid of little holes fitted with white paper plugs.

At the top was a cartoon of a girl in harem pants dancing with her arms over her head. For a nickel I might win a dime, fifty cents, or even five dollars. The nickel in my pocket was for ice cream, but I turned it over to him. Punchboards were made in Japan, a country specifically known to all children as the source of cheap toys and novelties that broke very quickly. With the punch key, a miniature version of the kind of key used to open a sardine tin, I pushed out my chance, a tightly folded accordion-pleated piece of paper a half-inch long. I unfolded it with the seller looking over my shoulder. I felt his hot breath on my ear. The chance was blank. I experienced the loss of my nickel.

Later Donald questioned me. "Was the punchboard full?"

"Yes, I was the first."

"If the punchboard is honest," Donald said, "and you have only the kid's word on that, then when you buy your chance affects the odds. Do you know what odds are?"

"No."

"Well, look, if the board is half punched and the kid tells you the prize money is still unclaimed, then you have a better chance of winning. Do you get it? Your odds are better."

I strove to understand.

"Well, you'd better forget it anyway," Donald said. "It's gambling. Gambling is illegal. You can get caught. Mayor La Guardia took the slot machines out of the candy stores and now he's after the punchboards. It's in all the papers. So you might as well forget the whole thing, if you know what's good for you."

I was prepared to do that. A couple of years later I would overhear some boys in school describing an older girl as a punchboard. I was unable to make the metaphorical leap, though understanding something bad was being said.

But the scumbag, ah the scumbag, here was an item so loathsome, so evil, that the very word itself was too terrible to pronounce. There was a seemingly endless depth of dark meaning attached to this word, with intimations of filth, and degradation, touching on such dark secrets as the young prince of life that I was would live in eternal heavenly sunlight not to know. In order to learn what a scumbag specifically and precisely was, beyond the foul malevolence of the sound of the word, you had to acquire knowledge of sick and menacing excitements to a degree that would inflict permanent damage to your soul. Yet of course I did learn, finally, one summer at the great raucous beach of crashing waves and sand-caked bodies known as Rockaway.

The beach was something my mother and father could agree on. Why they favored Far Rockaway at the sea edge of Brooklyn I did not quite understand. It was an enormous journey getting there. Perhaps my memory is faulty, perhaps we never made a day trip to Far Rockaway but rented a bungalow there for a week, in the summer, in the years when my father was doing comparatively well. But I remember, after a subway ride downtown, standing in the cavernous waiting room of Penn Station. We had with us bundles and blankets, newspapers and picnic baskets. High above was the vaulted roof of steel and translucent glass. The steel ribs that buttressed the roof were curved as delicately as scrollwork. Holding everything up were slender black-steel open columns taller than the columns that supported the elevated tracks on Jerome Avenue. The sun came through the roof on planes of dust, giving everything a pale greenish color and hushing the vast babble of all the people waiting for their trains, and the redcaps with their baggage dollies, and the echoing public address system announcements.

Yet even after the train trip to the seaside there was a long walk in the sun through blocks of one-story bungalows and across streets half filled with sand.

Rockaway might be overrun with sunbathers, the boardwalks jammed, not a place to lie down, but with my father leading the way we encamped miraculously enough in a space that hadn't been seen as possible by anyone except us. And there we were on a ridge of wet sand, facing the Atlantic Ocean.

My mother grew happy, the characteristic expression of concern lifted from her face, which now shone with a blissful contemplation as she tugged on her rubber swim cap and waded into the surf. It was as if she was alone, and not another human being around her. My father, who was more accustomed to relaxing and enjoying himself, reclined on the blanket and read his newspapers, interrupting himself every now and then to lie back on one elbow and point his face into the sun.

The trouble was, I had difficulty with the idea of changing into or out of a bathing suit in public. My father swam way out past the breakers, and when he came back he thought nothing of letting his black wool tank suit dry right on him in the sun. Donald too wore his belted bathing trunks through many swims. But my mother insisted that when I was wet, if I wasn't going into the water again, I had to change out of my suit into a pair of dry shorts.

I didn't understand the logic of this—that it was all right to be wet in the water but not on land. My father tried to arbitrate. "Why be uncomfortable," he said. "You put this blanket around you and slip off your suit underneath, and put your pants on. Nothing to it, one two three."

I was not persuaded. I saw other children changing this way and I knew their shame when they saw me watching. My mother thought I was being ridiculous. Yet I had never seen her change her clothes in public, nor my father, nor anyone but another child. I had heard it said of a little girl I knew how silly she was to refuse to wear a simple pair of cotton briefs for a bathing suit. "You have nothing up there to hide," her mother told her, pointing at her chest. "Nobody cares." What could she have possibly revealed to the world but that she lacked what she was supposed to have? We were not equipped as adults; we were small and without hair. That was the reason for modesty. Yet our dreams and desires were great shadows on the sun, enormous looming fearful attacks of unnamed chaos of the heart. To be undressed was to seem to be a child, a degrading state.

So I was taken to the public bathhouse behind the boardwalks —I suppose our bungalow was too many blocks away—and in the hot still air of a box of dark wood, a rented key for ten cents on an elastic loop attached to my wrist, I hurriedly changed. The air was motionless, woodsmoked. I had latched the door but someone could get down on his knees and peek underneath because the door did not reach the ground. People were changing in the other cubicles. I heard voices from all directions. I peeked through the cracks to make sure no one on either side was watching me: I was looking at monumental square inches of naked flesh. I heard the snap of elastic. I heard distant giggling. I heard a slap. I heard an urgent female demand to be let alone.

And then I found, stuck to my big toe, a flattened tube of whitish rubber. Instinctively repelled, I flicked it off with a shake of my foot.

The beach at Rockaway in 1936: Monoplanes with enormous wings slowly pulled banners of the alphabet through the sky. Washed in on the surf were dead jellyfish and the shells of horseshoe crabs, upside down, like shallow bowls. In the cold dark sand under the boardwalk I came upon a veritable garden of those flattened rubber things. They were stiff, not pleasant to touch, they lay pasted together and they smelled bad. Everything from the sea smelled bad—bulbous oily pods of green weed, jellyfish, half-eaten shellfish and those white rubber things under the boardwalk. I picked one up. "Don't touch it!" my brother said. "Don't you know what that is, you dope?"

Oh what a roaring sun-blasted life on the beach! Tiny piping holes bubbling in the sand. Birds with legs like toothpicks scurrying in front of the wavelap. Gulls hovering in windplanes off the sandbank. Donald and I ran to the shaded precinct of the boardwalk arcades. Sea winds blew through the open game rooms. We stood in our bare feet and bowled wooden balls down chutes, we spun the wheel to make the miniature steam shovel in the glass case clutch the prize. We wanted the real penknife, the silver cigarette lighter. We got only the gumballs.

Sand is in my crotch. I am turning red, the sun is inflating me. I eat sandwiches on the blanket, I drink cherry Kool-Aid, which is like liquid Jell-O. All speech is shouted, the surf crashes, I fear only two things, the water crashing up at my feet and the desert hordes of human beings among whom I may get lost. Crying children are walked by fully dressed policemen among the families on their blankets. Life is raw here; more policemen in their dark shirts and trousers and garrison caps, and with their heavy belts and guns, stand on the boardwalk overlooking the masses of bare bodies. Behind them big clown faces smile down from the false front of the amusement park. They are not fooled. Bad things are happening everywhere. Lifeguards bring in an exhausted child. An ambulance backs up to the steps of the boardwalk leading to the beach. I dig banks of sand around me. I create structures to support me, I bury my own leg to the knee. I am in the salt and the sun and the sea of voices. It all crashes over me, but I am not drowned.

It seems to me now that in this elemental place, these packed public beaches in the brightest rawest light of day, I learned the enlightening fear of the planet. Everywhere I looked men stood on their hands or climbed to other men's shoulders. Women of flesh slept ground into the sand. Beyond any name's recognition, under the shouting and teeming life of the world's public on their tribal Sunday of half-nude ceremony, was some quiet revelation in me of unutterable life. I was inspired in this state of clarity to whisper the word *scumbag*. It was as if all the sound had stopped, the voices, the reedy cry of gulls, the sirens and the thunderous surf, for that one word to be articulated to illumination. I felt through my fingers the sand pour of bones, like some futile archaeologist of a ground-up mineral past. I recognized the heat in the sand as some invisible power of distant light. And from the glittering blue water I took its endless motion and unimaginably frigid depth. All of this astonishingly was; and I on my knees in my bodying perception, worldlessly primeval, at home, fearful, joyous.

EIGHT

It must have been that summer or not long after that my little grandma's mental condition worsened. She took to running away. I was outside the house one afternoon when the front door opened and down the steps she came. She cursed and shook her fist at me. Her hair was uncombed. I backed away, but when she reached the bottom of the stoop she wandered off in the opposite direction, giving me the distinct impression that she had cursed me only because I was in her line of sight. She turned the corner at 173rd Street and was gone.

I ran and got my mother, who was at the laundry sink scrubbing clothes. She hadn't even known Grandma had left. Wiping her hands on her apron, my mother ran after her. She found the old woman and brought her back, but that was only the first of several episodes in which Grandma, crying and calling curses down on our house, wrapped a shawl around her shoulders and ran off.

In her curses she suggested that it would be a good thing if cholera were to kill us all. My mother numbly translated for me when I asked her what was being said. Another eventuality Grandma hoped for was that a company of Cossacks on their horses would ride us down. My mother cautioned me not to take these remarks at face value. "Grandma loves us," she said. "Poor Grandma doesn't know what she's saying. She's remembering her life as a little girl in her village in Russia, when these things happened. Cholera killed people when they drank water that was contaminated. The Cossacks were horse soldiers of the Czar, who mounted pogroms against Jewish settlements. She never forgot, poor thing."

I understood and did not take Grandma's madness personally. In fact, I tried to be friendlier to her when she was sane, to show her I loved her. I took to bringing her her tea in the morning when she got up. She liked that. My mother might look in on her to see that she was all right and then in the kitchen pour her tea for her in a glass, and put the glass in a saucer, with two cubes of sugar next to it, and in my two hands I would carry the glass of tea down the hall.

But now we all had this additional worry of Grandma disappearing at any hour of the day or night. We worried that she would be hit by a car, because she wandered in the street so intently involved with her inner rage that she paid no attention to cars. When Grandma fled, if Uncle Willy was home, he would go get her. He was the best at it. He sighed, and put on his shoes, and went out and followed after her with mild consoling words of the gentlest reproach. "Oh Mama," he said, "come back, it's getting chilly and you'll catch cold. Come, Mama, no you don't mean that, don't say that, you know how sorry you feel afterwards when you talk that way. Come home, *Mamaleh,*" he said and held his hand out with the palm up, like a man extending an invitation to dance; and many blocks from Eastburn Avenue with her rage vented, and her curses cursed, she turned and allowed herself to be escorted home.

Naturally, the neighbors knew of our trouble. Children in the street got out of Grandma's way, but were so fascinated they followed her at a safe distance. My mother's mortification was intense. With Uncle Willy out in the middle of the street trying to lead Grandma back inside, my mother waited in the shadows beside the parlor window where she couldn't be seen. She cried and shook her head and bit her lip. "What did I do to deserve this?" she muttered, not unlike Grandma. "God in heaven, what have we done to deserve this!"

And one night Grandma disappeared entirely and no one could find her. My father finally called the police. Hours went by. Nobody went to bed, not even me. Then a green-and-white police car pulled up to the curb in front of our house. Two policemen got out and opened the rear door, and gently assisted Grandma out of the car and up the front steps as if they were her footmen. She was quite docile. They told my father they had found her on a street bridge overlooking the New York Central tracks all the way over on Park Avenue.

There was some message to me in all of this that did not address itself to my rational being as a good boy. But all I knew consciously was that I was making mistakes of recklessness and getting into trouble. I was wild. I tore up my knees from running too fast and falling. My knees or my elbows recorded these events with scabs. I was rarely clear of them. One afternoon in my room I heard my brother coming home from school; I ran the length of the house down the hall to the front door. Donald was ringing the bell, I saw his shadow on the curtain; the door was glass-paned from its top to its bottom. Running, my hand outstretched for the doorknob, reaching, reaching, what could account for my excitement? Did I have something to tell him? Did I have some story about Pinky? Or was it only that I knew Donald coming home from school commenced the day's action? My hand missed the knob and went through the glass door. I felt the slash of an inanimate evil. Without so much as the caesura of a drawn breath I was first shouting in joy, then screaming in shock. Pain tore through my hand, and the mess of my own red substance was on the curtain. My mother running from the back of the house, my brother calling her, the door opening, glass falling to the floor, I stood looking at my palm, blood pouring down my arm. Ripples of terror went through the community of my home, as each person had in turn to learn and respond to

the awful event. I was being tourniqueted, washed, soothed, but
at the same time an investigative procedure had been initiated,
my mother searching from my brother's answers to her questions the possibility of his having been responsible for this
event, while he defended himself righteously, loudly and
adeptly, and my grandmother was with her hand on her cheek
coming along down the hall and shaking her head and saying
"*Gottenyu, Gottenyu,*" thus suggesting the cosmic forces once
again assailing us all. Pinky was furiously barking, and Uncle
Willy, awakened from a nap on his day off, was simply trying to
get the news of how this had happened, since nobody had taken
the time to stop and tell him. Eventually, from the center of all
of this, sobbing fitfully as I stood, hand extended for the operation over the bathroom sink, and winced as my mother removed
shards of glass with a tweezer, I nevertheless found an inner
certitude and calm, perhaps in advance of my willingness to stop
crying or feeling sorry for myself. Everyone stood around me
and watched. Thus the element of performance added itself to
my behavior and I realized the advantage to my small being—
the smallest lowest ranking voice in the family, in constant attendance to any one of this pantheon of powerful creatures I
lived with, each with a different strength and call upon my loy-
alty, each entitled to tell me what to do and how to do it—I could
not fail to realize the power residing in me at this moment. I was
an instrument of fearful prophecy. More than that, I knew I had
found the weakness of their adult strength and resolution—that
misfortune could reach them through me. Even my grandma
was diverted to total attention.

It is a heartening knowledge that comes sooner or later to all
children that they can achieve parity. I had seen time and again
in the streets a child hurting himself and then being spanked by
his mother for hurting himself—pain added upon pain, which
seemed cruel or stupid until it became clear that the mother
intuited the malign exercise of the child's act. She was being
hurt and so she responded in kind. My mother did not ever hit
me for hurting myself, not having the sufficient distance from
me or cynicism to do so; there was too fine an appreciation in

her for the eternal hazards given to consciousness, poor woman, here she was in the Depression, with her sick mother, her improvident brother, her two children, a yapping dog, and maintaining an entire family while in economic dependency to her unpredictable husband. To her my injury might save me from worse if it could be seen to be a lesson.

"All right," she said, "stop that whimpering. It's not so bad. Maybe you'll know now not to run through the house like a maniac."

In some emblematic measure of this sentiment my mother decided to tailor a wool suit for me. I endured many fittings before the thing was done. Early one afternoon of an autumn Sunday I emerged from our house all decked out in a camel-colored tunic and matched leggings and on my head a color-coordinated beret of dark brown. I could feel the grip of the elastic band on my forehead. The buttons on my tunic went all the way up to the neck, the top one tightly fastening the military-style collar. I felt contained. At the ankles of the leggings was a row of snaps, simulating spats. The leggings came down over the tops of my new tightly laced shoes of brown leather.

I rode up and down the sidewalks for a while on my tricycle. My father joined me a few minutes later and we had a catch in front of the setback garage doors next to our stoop. I lurched after the ball when I dropped it. I couldn't move that well. Also I didn't want to forget myself and fall and tear the new suit or get it dirty. As soon as my mother came out, we would head past P.S. 70, across 174th Street, and up the Eastburn Avenue hill to the Concourse, where we would take the bus to visit my father's parents, my grandma and grandpa, who lived north of Kingsbridge Road. Donald was old enough not to have to go. It was a beautiful cold sunny day and I had to squint to see the ball coming at me. My father wore an overcoat open over his dark double-breasted suit and tie. His hat was set at the usually jaunty angle. We were waiting for my mother and then would be on our way.

At this moment an itinerant photographer came around the corner and walked toward us with a box camera on a tripod over his shoulder, and with a small pony trailing behind him. My father's face lit up. "You've got a customer!" he called, waving at the man, and from one moment to the next my day turned bad, as if the sky had suddenly filled with dark clouds.

I didn't want my picture taken. I didn't want to get on the pony. It was a shaggy dull-eyed thing and I could see the breath coming out of its nostrils. I knew immediately it was a badly used animal with a cynical spirit. But this was the kind of fortuitous event that made my father happy. Life declared itself in him. "It's just the thing, just the thing!" he said. I disagreed. We exchanged views. The unctuous photographer felt privileged to join the argument on my father's side, saying the pony loved to have children sit on his back. I knew his game. Finally my father could contain himself no longer. He lifted me under the arms and set me on the pony's back, my legs split wide over the saddle. I felt the pony stomp and stir about. The saddle seemed to me loose and creaking. The pony whinnied and took a step or two. My father was holding one hand on my back and holding the reins with the other while the man busily set up his camera. I felt the shuddering animal life of the pony between my legs, I had never sat on a horse before and I would not stick my feet in the stirrups. "Get me down!" I shouted, and I put up such a fight, squirming and sliding and threatening to fall by my vehement twistings and kickings, that the pony started to clip-clop about, turning in circles on the sidewalk. The photographer now tried to soothe him, patting his neck and gripping his mane, and my father, holding me under the arms and not lifting me off, said, "You're all right! Don't you see you're all right? This little pony is more frightened of you than you are of him. Stop shouting so, stop screaming, you're all right, nothing to be afraid of, come on, you can do it, give it a try."

There I was, buttoned down and collared in the tight, almost suffocating fit of my mother's vision, and my father was urging me to heights of daring and adventure.

I thought in my desperation of a compromise. I would permit my picture to be taken, but on my tricycle, not on the pony.

I still have that picture. My little hands clutch the handlebars. My feet rest on the block pedals of the oversized front wheel. I am in my matching jacket and leggings of stiff wool. The beret is only slightly askew. I am allowing my adorable self to be commemorated in his new outfit. I am a good-looking open-faced towheaded child and I am smiling as I have been instructed; but it is a tentative wary little smile, my deportment in life, ready to placate, appease, if that will work, but my foot on the pedal, ready to fly me away, if it doesn't.

It wasn't as if I weren't eager to learn their ways and take the instruction I was given and assume my place in life. But each of my deities spoke from a different strength and to different aspirations. All around me was the example of passionate survival, but I could never be sure, as I held in me the conflicting arguments of how it was done, what was the margin for error, the tolerance for wrong moves.

NINE

Extending from my mother and father were two family wings, unequal in strength, making our flight erratic. My grandma and grandpa on my father's side were not people of means, living in a three-room apartment a few miles to the north of us. But they were whole, complete, they took pride in themselves and their children—my father being one of three, the others my aunts Frances and Molly—and they had clear views on most things. We rode up there on the red-and-black Concourse bus, which had a long engine hood and doubled rear wheels and spare tires chained to the back and torturously shifted gears. I enjoyed the ride, but once it was over, I had the visit to get through. Not that I didn't love my grandma and grandpa; they were warm little old people who beamed at me and pressed food upon me, and kisses. But there was danger there.

My grandma liked to put out a lace tablecloth on the big dark table in their dining-living room. She served tea in her good china with its pale green and white sliced-apple motif, and also Uneeda crackers and homemade plum jam with cloves in it and a big cut-glass bowl of fruit, and a smaller bowl of pistachio nuts. Most often too we brought cake from a bakery. And everyone sat around the table and talked. My grandfather had a wonderful way of paring an apple, with his own pocketknife, so that the peel came off in one continuous strip. Sometimes, one or the other of my aunts was there but without my cousins, who, like my brother, were old enough to get out of such visits. So there was nothing to do. I stared through the double windows into the courtyard. My grandparents lived in the back of a house, off the street, and I found myself looking at opaque lace curtains or drawn shades. I sat under the big table radio in the corner of the room next to my grandfather's favorite chair and tried to find something interesting to listen to—not too easy in the middle of a Sunday afternoon when the New York Philharmonic seemed to be the brightest choice. Or I wound up the big console Victrola in their bedroom and put pennies or nutshells on the spinning turntable and watched them fly off. Sometimes I leafed through a picture book I had brought along, sometimes I browsed through my grandfather's bookcase in the foyer beside the front door. He owned many books, some of them in Russian. They were stuffed in, every which way. Each shelf had its own glass door that lifted up from the bottom and slid back under the shelf above. But there were so many books the doors wouldn't slide. From my grandfather I first heard the names Tolstoy and Chekhov. He owned sets too—uniform editions, such as *The World's Great Orations* and the *Harper's Picture Encyclopedia of the Civil War*. I liked to look at the steel engravings of the Army of the North doing battle with the Army of the South. Each scene was protected by the thinnest sheet of paper.

Another diversion was the dumbwaiter in the kitchen. My grandmother let me open the little door in the wall and poke my head into the black air shaft. Odors of ash and garbage rose on the cold black air. A thick rope bisected the column of darkness. I could pull on this rope and bring into view the wooden box on which the tenants delivered their garbage to the superintendent.

My grandmother hobbled busily about, she was a bent woman with glasses and thin yellow-white hair, which she kept parted in the middle, braided, and tightly coiled in a bun. Her eyes watered and her hands were palsied, but her afflictions didn't seem to daunt her. She bustled around to great effect and never sat still. She was in charge. My grandfather by contrast was a very slow-moving, slow-talking, gentle, slight man, with thick grey hair cut close; he was partial to a tan cardigan sweater, which he wore always over a white shirt and tie, brown pants and house slippers. He smoked odd oval-shaped cigarettes, Regents, which came out of a grey-and-maroon box. He liked me to press my palm against his and measure our hands; this was the way he kept track of my growth, he said. My growth was a matter of enormous pleasure to him. Invariably he was encouraged to find my hand had increased in size since our previous measurement. He patted me on the back of my neck. He was a retired printer. He had emigrated from Russia as a young man from the Minsk district—this had been the old country too of my grandmother. Apparently they had known each other as children, but only after they had come separately to America did they renew their acquaintance, conduct a courtship and marry. It was a matter only of momentary fascination to me to imagine my dear old grandfather Isaac as an erect black-haired young man, even younger than my father; to imagine him, for instance, lifting my father in his arms as my father sometimes did me. My father called him Papa. I did not dwell on these paradoxes. I think I did not entirely believe in them. Besides, my grandfather spoke so philosophically from such thoughtful distances of wisdom that no fanciful illusion could be maintained for very long about his being anything else but a grandfather. He told me that three times, in three separate presidential elections, he had cast his ballot for someone named William Jennings Bryan. Yet he was a socialist and came of a generation of enlightened Jewish youth who understood, as Bryan did not, that religion was a means of holding people in ignorance and superstition and therefore submissive to impoverishment and want. I did not really understand what he told me; but as he repeated these ideas and phrases over time, I was comfortable with their sentiments and was finally able to identify him as a critic of prevalent beliefs. He was in opposition—that I understood. In his bookcase were authors whose names were familiar to me before I knew who they were or what they stood for: Ralph Ingersoll, Henrik Ibsen, George Bernard Shaw, Herbert Spencer. Although my grandmother was pious, and kept a kosher home, my grandfather was an atheist. He treasured a book by Thomas Paine called *The Age of Reason,* and used its arguments, and some of his own, to tease my grandmother and point out to her the absurdities and contradictions in her literal readings of the Old Testament. " 'My own mind is my own church,' " he said, quoting Paine. Yet, as she proudly told us even in her irritation with him, he had read the entire Bible many times and knew it better, God help him, the atheist, than she did.

So this was a substantive household, an establishment in history next to which my mother's poor dependent half-mad Mama in her widow's weeds was no match. Nor my hapless, self-effacing formerly famous uncle Willy. You had to go see my father's mother and father. They had a home. They were progenitors not only of my father but his two sisters—the elder, my aunt Frances, and the younger, my aunt Molly. And each of these ladies in her way had much to contribute to my sense of this family's complexity. My aunt Frances was married to a successful lawyer and lived in Pelham Manor, in Westchester County, a Christian community over the city line. Aunt Frances not only owned a car but knew how to drive it, which was quite unusual for a woman. When she drove she wore white gloves. She was very gracious and soft-spoken and naturally dignified, like my grandfather; her two sons were at Harvard. My father's younger sister, Molly, by contrast had her mother's earthy practical ways. Molly was in addition a comedienne, an irreverent, brassy, unkempt woman, as blowsy as her sister was well groomed. Molly smoked cigarettes, whose ashes invariably dropped on the bosom of her dress. She squinted in the cigarette smoke. She read a newspaper my father thought a terrible rag—the *Daily Mirror*—because its coverage of horse racing was the best in the city and because it featured a columnist, Walter Winchell, whom she adored. She played the horses, as did her husband, Phil, a cabdriver. They had one daughter, my older cousin Irma. When the whole family was gathered in my grandparents' small apartment on a Sunday afternoon, the two old people spoke English with strong inflections of Yiddish, Frances spoke in the cultivated tones of an upper-class Westchester matron, and Molly in a heavy Bronx accent. Somewhere in the middle of this mélange of styles and meld of social intention stood my father. His older sister had done well, and his younger had rebelliously married beneath her. His was the fate not yet decided. When it came to my father the stakes were high. He was the one son. Would Frances turn out to be the family exception or would Molly? It was not only his own destiny that was at issue but the final judgment still to be made of all of them.

How did I know this? On those darkening Sunday afternoons I only half heard the conversation. It would start quietly enough, filled with pleasantries, and then, almost imperceptibly, go bad. On this day my grandmother Gussie picked up my new hand-tailored camel tunic to examine my mother's sewing. "Very nice," she said, her eyebrows rising, her mouth turning down at the corners. "And lined too, no less. My daughter-in-law stops at nothing."

Behind this remark was my grandmother's penury. She took the position that my mother was impractical and careless with my father's money. My mother knew this was untrue. It was a terrible slander and it hurt her deeply. It hurt her that my grandmother Gussie felt privileged to give her opinions as to the way my mother dressed her children, how she ran her house, and whether or not she took proper care of her husband. Though Grandma's tone was sweet, her style was sly and indirect. She could bring my mother to tears, as she had now done. My tempestuous mother started to yell and my father told her to lower her voice. I looked for the pictures in books. I wound the Victrola and let the turntable spin. My grandparents maintained two goldfish in a bowl; I stared at the goldfish, studying their ways.

The visit was clearly over. My mother would not say good-bye. She put on my coat and buttoned it, and she took my hand and walked out of the door. My grandfather came after us in his slippers. "Rose," he said in the hallway. "Forgive Gussie. That's the way she is, she means no harm, she has the greatest respect for you."

"Oh Papa," my mother said. "That is not respect. That is not even civility. You are a compassionate, kind man, perhaps too kind." She hugged Grandpa, and we went down the stairs to the lobby and waited for my father. She could not sympathize with whatever anxiety of universal judgment, or perhaps God's, led my grandma on. The old woman made her regularly understand that she was not good enough to be married into this family, that she was not good enough for my father, that she was not what he needed.

I lived in the weather of my mother's spirit, and at these times, after these visits, the sky grew black. My father came down the stairs and he was whistling, as he did when something bad had happened and he was trying to be cheerful about it. We stood in the dusk at the bus stop. "Why do you let her talk to me that way?" my mother said. "Don't you care how I feel? Nothing I ever do is good enough, nothing is ever right enough. If I wash one of her dishes she will wash it after me. And you like that behavior. You like that viciousness. Never once have you defended me from dear sweet Gussie."

But the argument between my mother and father didn't really begin until they got home. Here the sight of the pathetic remnants of her own ancestry magnified the injustice she felt: Did anyone on my father's side ever inquire about her mama's health? My father's whole and thriving family treated her like dirt and her poor mother like a social pariah. Did they ever invite Mama on a Sunday? Did they ever invite Billy? I went into my room and closed the door, but it was no good, it was too interesting. It was as if my father had caught my grandma's point of view, just as my mother insisted.

But then he offered a criticism of my mother that I knew, in part, to be accurate. "You always think the worst," he said. "You're suspicious and distrustful." She told him to go to hell. He called her a fishwife. Mythic realms were indeed the territories of these disputes. Ascriptions of good and evil flew back and forth like furies, like phantoms, to take shape as sweet truths or malign imputations. Truth hovered above everything waiting to alight, and as I grew older I saw that it never did anywhere, for any length of time. I felt guilty that I preferred the company of my grandma and grandpa up on the Concourse to my sick little grandmother in the room next door. I sometimes saw my grandma Gussie as truly mischievous, jealous and up to no good. But I could not believe anything bad about any one of these people for very long, because they all seemed to love me so much.

TEN

In fact, love was what it was all about. However painful it might be, as sure as heat or freezing cold or storms were in the nature of weather, the daily tempest of my life among these elemental powers—the screams, demands, disagreements—was the nature of love. But they had their sly ways: I secretly grieved for the dark mysterious things my parents did in the privacy of their relationship. I didn't know quite what these things were, but I knew they were shameful, requiring darkness. They were never referred to or acknowledged in the light of day. This aspect of my parents' life lay like a shadow in my mind. My mother and father, rulers of the universe, were taken by something over which they had no control. How problematical that was, how unsettling. Like my little grandma with her spells, they were afflicted in the manner of some kind of possession, and then afterwards they seemed to be normal again. I could not talk about this to anyone, certainly not my brother. If he didn't know about it he was lucky. The devastating truth was that there were times when my parents were not my parents; and I was not on their minds. It was not a subject to dwell upon. I resented the early hour of my bedtime, in part because it was earlier than anyone else's bedtime, in part because it brought on that vast period of darkness when those things happened about which I had insufficient knowledge; I could only make do, like a detective with the barest of clues, inaudible words, an indefinable sound of panic, a dim light, going on and off, all of it enfolded and obscured in my sleep-drugged state.

But I was coming to rely on my brother in some way that my parents' vehemently intense life together did not allow me to rely on them. Donald was steadfast. He lived his earnest life as one human being, not as half of two. He was still within reach. He taught me card games, easy ones like War and Go Fish, and a hard one, Casino. We played on the floor, where I was comfortable. He held my hand as we walked to the candy store. He was at home when my parents went out at night. The sight of Donald doing his homework suggested to me the clear and purposeful intention of life and its march to a visionary future. He would soon be graduating from P.S. 70 and going on to high school. He was now thirteen or so. Painstakingly, with his characteristic frown of concentration, he constructed airplane models of balsa wood, as light as feathers, and hung them on sewing thread from the ceiling of our room—snub-nosed racing planes, and a Ford Trimotor. The skins on the wings and fuselage were thin colored papers stretched taut by dampening. He was also building a solid wooden Strom-Becker model of the China Clipper. He read *Popular Mechanics* and pulp detective-story magazines, and in a magazine called *Radio Craft,* which my father had brought him, he found instructions for the building of a crystal radio set at a cost of sixty-five cents. He was saving his money.

Of course we had our problems. When his friends were around he tended not to want me to be with them, but I understood that, even as I complained and pestered him. It was a matter of principle with me to pester Donald and his friends. Of course they were not without resources in dealing with this. They knew my weaknesses, that, for instance, if anyone around me cried, I cried too. It was true, I caught crying as if it were a communicable disease, I couldn't help it, I was a walking dust mop of emotions. Donald pretended to cry to get rid of me. In fact, he had refined the art of it by only threatening to cry, holding his arm up to his eyes and issuing one preliminary sob and peeking out from under his arm to find me biting my lip, my eyes filling, ready to bawl for no reason, not even knowing what the matter was, the pain, but only that whatever it was, it was overwhelming and impossible to endure. I was burdened with this terrible affliction, just as my friend Herbert from Weeks Avenue had crossed eyes, or a little boy who played in my park had inward-turning feet. There was nothing to do but hope to grow out of it, this awful teariness. First it would hit me in the throat. Then it affected my ability to see, I had to close my eyes. It was a form of shyness or sorrow for the world's hard life. Sometimes my brother and his friends Bernie and Seymour and Irwin would, all together, pretend to cry; and I would be made so tearful by this mass assault that even knowing they were teasing me and even after having them emerge from their pretense laughing and jolly, I would find myself uncontrollably sobbing, as if a substantive wrong had taken place, like a bashed thumb or a cut, or the loss of something precious. And then, of course, it took forever to wind down, a trail of heartbreaking hiccuppy sobs issuing from me for several minutes as I went about my business.

Weakness and insufficiency seemed always to be my lot. I suffered from dust and pollen, colds, coughs, flus. At times of seasonal change I more or less lived in bed. All of this led, without my understanding it, to a crisis in my relationship with my brother. My parents concluded one day that Pinky, our dog, would have to be gotten rid of because I was allergic to her.

I t was her hair that was the problem, not her character. She shed her white hair on the rugs and on the furniture. Donald would not believe this was a reason for losing his dog forever. "You don't like her," he said to our mother. "That's what this is all about. You never have liked her."

"That's a false charge," my father said, coming to my mother's defense. "On occasion she has saved Pinky's life." He

had us there. One day the dog had come up from the basement and my mother had noticed, as none of us did who were
Pinky's champions, that she was dragging herself about with
uncommon listlessness. My mother saw a speck of something
green on the tip of Pinky's nose. "Oh my God," she said, "this
stupid dog has eaten rat poison." Quickly she whipped up a
couple of raw eggs in a bowl and put the dog and the bowl in
the grass yard, a tiny patch on the south side of the house
under the windows of Donald's room. Pinky slurped up the
eggs and vomited, as my mother had expected she would, and
thus her life was saved.

But the argument continued for several days. During this time
we had reason to reflect on our history with this dog. She had
been run over several times, and was no worse for wear. The
green-poison story had become famous, although, as my mother
told it to our neighbors, she did not want to admit that anything
resembling a rodent could have needed the serious attention of
a poison in our basement, and so she had represented that
Smith had left open a can of some sort of janitorial substance
of industrial strength and this was what the stupid dog had
gotten into. Pinky had also enlightened our lives one day by
giving birth to three or four puppies on Donald's bed, an event
I peeked in at from the doorway and could accommodate with
brief glimpses. Little squirming pups were coming out of her
backside. She attended to everything with her tongue. Her ears
were flat and her demeanor uncharacteristically solemn, and as
each moving creature emerged she licked it and licked it and, in
the same manner, herself and the bedspread, like the most responsible and decorous of dogs. Something my brother called
the afterbirth she consumed in its entirety. I had not quite
worked out the concept of procreation. It was not a matter in
which anyone in my family thought I needed instruction. I was
amazed that my mother was not angry at the mess Pinky was
making. In my mind materials from the inside of the body were
abhorrent to one degree or another; I included puppies. Yet a
big shallow box was found and made into a nursery with shredded newspaper, and the dog Pinky, now given the astounding

title of Mother, retired there to nurse; and eventually the puppies were placed.

All of this was in the nature of a lifelong commitment, my brother argued. Pinky to us and we to her. How could we kick out our dog at this point in all our lives together? Was nothing sacred? Other less drastic measures might be taken. Perhaps he could vacuum the entire house every day. Yes, he would be prepared to do that! Maybe Pinky could spend more time out of doors. He could train her not to run away. She might be kept in the cellar. And so on.

Donald was skilled in disputation, he was a good student and was able to call up all manner of appeals from the fields of science, ethics, and psychology, but none of them seemed to work. "It's not fair," he said in what I thought was his most trenchant remark, "it's not fair that an entire family should lose its dog just because one baby pipsqueak gets a runny nose." Nevertheless he seemed to believe that there was still time, still room for negotiation, and perhaps my parents did somehow give that impression. Even as he rehearsed me to make a passionate protest of my own, which I was earnestly prepared to do between sneezes and eye-watering coughs, Donald was talking to his friends to try to get one of them to keep Pinky. His idea was that with the dog gone, were I to show continuing signs of allergic hysteria, then it would be proven not to be Pinky's fault and she could be brought back home. In any event, he went off to school one morning, and while he was gone my parents struck: With the help of our family friend, the dentist Abe Perlman, who lived across the street, my father took time off from work so as to transport Pinky to a place he insisted was the closest thing to an ideal existence for a dog, a place called the Bide-A-Wee home. Here Pinky would be cared for and have other dogs for friends. After a day or so she would not even miss us. I was very nervous about this and insisted on hugging the dog even though that might bring on an asthmatic attack. I asked for full particulars about the Bide-A-Wee home, I wanted to accept its credentials at face value because I didn't want to be a sniveling wheezing sissy all my life. I did not miss the heavy meaningful glance between my father and Dr. Perlman, nor the barely concealed smirk on that man's face as he assured me the dog would be loved even more where she was going than in our house, but I decided to believe everything would be all right. I did not think that was possible, but still stood, irresolute and uneasily pacified, on the sidewalk as they drove away in Dr. Perlman's Plymouth with Pinky sticking her head out of the window because Dr. Perlman's driving made her carsick, just as it did me.

When Donald got home from school and found no Pinky, and heard my report to him, he became enraged. His green eyes grew large. "You believed that baloney about the Bide-A-Wee home? They took her to the ASPCA! They put her to sleep! You let them trick you! Pinky is dead and it's your fault!" He threw down his books, grabbed his fielder's mitt and began to pound the pocket. He paced up and down. "I hate you!" he said. "I hate Mom and I hate Dad and I hate Dr. Perlman, but most of all, I hate you, because you caused the problem in the first place. You're a little shit. Get out of here! Go on. Get out," he said. He pushed me into the hallway and slammed the door.

I went outside. The more I thought about the situation, the worse I felt. A panic of grief rose in me. Implicit in what my brother said was the truth, I knew, that adults could be loved but never trusted; only Donald could be trusted. He had always told me the truth, he was passionately attached to reality and could always be relied upon to tell me exactly how things were. He showed me how to do things, and when I did them the way he said they should be done—you hold the bat this way, you catch the ball so—they worked out just as he predicted. Donald was never wrong. I had failed him, I had betrayed him, I had let them take our dog off to be killed. Our Pinky dead! I was to blame. I sat on the front stoop. I was stunned and sick. I knew the most terrible of states, irremediable damnation. I had done something fainthearted and it could not be made right, it was a disastrous act, irreversible. Some terrible chord of self-knowledge rang in me. Pinky, now invested with my moral soul, had fled and for the last time. She would never come back, running in that fleet abandoned fur-flattened way of hers, across streets, through yards, through tunnels, over bridges, under cars, but farther and farther from me, far past any range of my calling, heedless of my despair.

I was not as advanced a being as my brother. In my anguish it never occurred to me to be angry at my parents. I could perceive their characters, but I could not go on to make moral judgments of them. All my wit was spent in avoiding their critical judgments of me.

Yet now, here, I surely must have resented the clear evidence of the adult's crass disregard for the feelings of children. It was so devious of them to have gotten rid of Pinky in this way. Evading confrontation with his thirteen-year-old son and conning his five-year-old, my father had spirited away the family dog. Was it difficult for him? I knew he liked Pinky. When he walked her he took her off the leash and knew how to talk to her to keep her with him. Perhaps he regretted the decision to get rid of her. The urgency to do it would have come from my mother. But he was charming, my father. He did not raise his voice, he cajoled. He did not give commands, he appealed to reason. He rarely used physical force, unlike my mother who would swing away at the drop of a hat. I recognized the evasive style of the kidnapping as his.

My father loved tricks, gentle practical jokes, "now you see it, now you don't" kinds of things. He loved word games, riddles. I first heard Zeno's paradox from him, the runner halving the

distance to the finish line, and halving it again, getting closer
and closer but never reaching it. He loved puns and limericks.

> A queer old bird is the pelican
> His mouth holds more than his belly can
> He can hold in his beak
> Enough food for a week
> And you wonder how the hell he can.

He could not resist buying a volume of light verse if he happened to see one in a bookstore. He liked Sir Arthur T. Quiller-
Couch:

> The lion is the beast to fight,
> He leaps along the plain.
> And if you run with all your might
> He runs with all his mane.

He relished the lore of the trickster in song or story. He had
great appreciation for the legendary entrepreneur P.T. Barnum.
He told me how Barnum had had a problem keeping people
moving through his exotic animal exhibits so that more paying
customers could be admitted. Barnum's solution was to put up
a sign at the exit that said THIS WAY TO THE EGRESS. And the
people poured through thinking an egress was another rare
animal.

My father in his early forties was vigorous, ambitious, and
struggling to make a go of things. He lived zestfully the code of
the insider. He sold radios, Victrolas, sheet music. The stock of
records in his store was vast, thousands of shellac records in
brown paper sleeves and great heavy albums of operas and
symphonies, European recordings as well as American, classical,
jazz, swing. He even carried the records of obscure black folk-
singers from the South. He really knew his business, and some
of the artists on labels he carried came into his store to buy the
records from him. He was always very proud of knowing and
dealing with famous musicians. "Stokowski came into the store

today," he would tell us when he got home. Or, "Rubinstein's secretary called and gave me an order worth fifty dollars." I understood the value of the inside position. On those exciting Saturdays when I went downtown with Donald to my father's store, I saw how the people came in, I saw how he controlled what they bought by his advice and counsel, I was proud of him. He wore a blue pin-striped suit and vest and a red tie. His skin was pink and his brown eyes bright and alert. I didn't like his partner, though, Lester, a tall, unctuously hearty man with blond hair combed in a pompadour. He was in charge of the radio section. Lester had discovered that a certain percentage of customers could be counted on to bring radios in for repair that had nothing wrong with them. The residential hotels in the neighborhood were equipped with direct current. Usually the plug had been inserted in the power outlet the wrong way; by simply reversing the prongs of the plug, Lester could get the radio to work. Instead, he told the customer that the repairs would take several days; he would dust the innards, polish the cabinet, and write up a bill, having fixed a radio that was in perfect working order. "Oh, by the way," he would say as the customer was leaving with his radio, "just reverse the plug if nothing happens when you turn it on. It works fine now." My father had a kind of aesthetic appreciation for his partner's larceny. He said he held Lester down to reasonable amounts so that no one customer was stung for very much. But he told us of this practice expecting us to appreciate its humor. It was in the nature of being in the know, on the inside.

He took great pleasure from a book he brought home, an anthology of mistakes made by schoolboys on their exams and in their compositions. The mistakes were called "boners" and he read them to us. The chief animals of Australia are the kangaroo, larkspur, boomerang, and peccadillo. Medieval cathedrals are supported by flying buttocks. Shakespeare lived at Windsor with his merry wives. The two most important rivers of Scotland are the Firth and the Forth. In Pittsburgh they manufacture iron and steal. Four animals belonging to the cat family are the father cat, the mother cat, and two kittens. Acrimony, sometimes called holy, is another name for marriage. . . . Some of these made everyone laugh, some of them just my father laughed at. It was under his guidance that I would send away for my first Little Blue Books at five cents each, from the E. Haldeman Julius Company in Girard, Kansas: *Ventriloquism Self-Taught* and *Tales of Hypnotism and Revenge.* He was teaching me the available recourses in a universe run by humorless women. He himself had a mother he loved and must contend with, just as I did. My grandmother Gussie up on the Concourse had strong opinions and liked to control things. My grandfather Isaac was a bookish, peace-loving man with an intellect, like my father. So there was some cosmic scheme behind my father's puns and limericks and love of language games, a representation of the moral universe grounded in the archetypal male and female relation. Where had it come from? It was a peasant vision, a thing of funny papers and dialect jokes. It cut across all borders. It had come from the old country. In the street I heard from children its darker vulgar representations: A wife is something you screw on the bed and it does all the housework.

ROSE

Things went along smoothly for a while. My mother was an enormous help and comfort. Every day at lunch I'd wrap up my baby and put him in his carriage and go to my mother's house for lunch. I loved my parents. My brother, my older brother, Harry, was staying with them temporarily while looking for a job. So it was like old times for me, my family right around the corner. My mother was a dear sweet woman, so quiet, a very religious woman. She was one of the original members of the synagogue and the Sisterhood, she was there when they laid the first brick. I was close to her and I was happy taking care of my tiny child and making a nice home for my husband. He was making good money then. He worked for a man named Markel in the record business. That is how he got into it. Markel was some sort of jobber or distributor of phonographs and phonograph parts. This was a very good business in the 1920's— before radios, before anything else. People bought those old phonographs with big horns and they bought records to play on them and to dance to, and it was the first home entertainment besides playing your own music. Windup Victrolas first, then electric ones. It was a revelation to people accustomed to hearing music only at the concert hall. So that was the business. I didn't like Markel, he had shady ways, I had worked for him myself for a while as secretary and bookkeeper. Dave had gotten me the job. But then I saw what Markel was like and I left. He used to order things from the manufacturers, Victor, Edison, all of them, and then he wouldn't pay his bills. The office was a loft in the East Twenties. He had a whole floor with his office and the stockroom, and there was a fire escape at the window behind his desk. People in those days sent the sheriff around when they couldn't collect money due them. When he heard the sheriff coming up the stairs, this terrible man Markel would run down the fire escape. Your father was out selling all over the city. And so I was left to deal with the problem. I didn't like that. That's when I quit and found work with Sigmund Unterberg, and then through him with the Jewish Welfare Board. Now I think Markel was a bad influence on your father. True, he taught him a good business. But what else did he teach him? It was at this time, I think, that your father got interested in gambling, in card playing, and I think that was Markel's doing. Dave had a zest for adventure, he always dreamed of a big killing. It made him vulnerable. As fine as he was, as refined and cultured—and he loved good music, he loved opera—he indulged in bad things. And I never knew what was happening, he never told me anything, he gave me an allowance and that was that.

At any rate Dave's younger sister, Molly, had her baby prematurely after she and her husband, Phil, the cabdriver, had separated. So there was Molly with this sickly little baby and what was her mother Gussie's response? She wouldn't have anything to do with her. And her fancy older sister, Frances, up in Westchester had washed her hands of her. The thing about Molly was that she was the rebel in the family, the black sheep. She never finished high school, she went with riffraff, and she married someone beneath her. Phil was a decent fellow but not too smart. He spoke badly. But that wasn't the problem. The problem was that Molly after marrying him had taken up with another man. Bob, I think his name was. So it was a terrible mess. Molly begged to come and stay with us. She had no place to go. I went to the hospital to see her and she wept so. I liked Molly. She was the only one in that family besides Papa, besides Grandpa, that I felt comfortable with. She did not put on airs, she did not give me the feeling that I was not as good as she was. So I said to her come stay with us. And Dave agreed.

Now, we only had a three-room apartment at that time on Weeks Avenue. So it was quite a sacrifice. It was a light, large, airy apartment, but there was only one bedroom. So Molly slept in the bed with me and Dave slept on the couch. I had not expected her to stay long. I thought she would make some arrangement, put her life together, and after a week or two she would be gone. But that was not to be. She stayed for months. I had a girl in to help me clean and wash Donald's diapers. Donald was maybe a year old then. But the girl would not wash Molly's baby's diapers. So I had to do that myself, for this little infant girl, Irma. And where was Molly? She was out running around. This Bob kept coming to the house and taking her out on dates. Her husband, Phil, would come at night and start raising hell and shouting. The neighbors complained. It was the scandal of the whole house. I was going out of my mind. Your father had come to like having Molly in the house. He said to his mother one day, "Mama, I was thinking of increasing Rose's allowance." He asked his mother about everything. And there I was, taking care of Molly and her child, paying for everything out of the ordinary family budget, and the old lady said—I heard her right in the next room, we had gone there for a visit—"No, it's enough, she has enough, it's quite sufficient." Can you imagine? That terrible woman? I am taking care of her own daughter, she and her other daughter have done nothing, and she says that? Dave belonged to them. He never consulted me, he told me nothing. His mother was his consultant.

As you can imagine, I was very unhappy. My life was not good. I was not sleeping with my husband, it was very upsetting. There was no privacy. I tried to get Molly to leave, but he would stop me—it was as if he wanted her there. He wouldn't even talk about it. I think it was during this time that he began to look around for other women. At lunchtime I would take my baby boy and run to my mother's and cry. "Mama," I said, "I want to leave him. I can't go on. I can't live this way. I'm so unhappy I want to kill myself." And my mother would soothe me, and hug me and caress me, but she was very old-fashioned and most conservative in her ways. "You are a married woman," she would say. "You must make the best of things. You must take care of your child and keep a home for your husband. No matter what."

So I went back. If not for my mother I would have left and gotten a divorce, but I could not disobey her, I wouldn't think of it. But finally I did do something. One day this boyfriend of Molly's who had caused all the trouble came around when she was out and I spoke to him. Bob. I didn't dislike him. And I said to him, "Listen, Bob, you're a nice enough young man. You're getting yourself into such a mess here. Aren't you ashamed of yourself, to come calling on a woman who is married, who has just had a baby, a woman whose mother has thrown her out, and whose sister won't have anything to do with her because of this? And here she is living with me, my husband has given up his bed so that she can stay here. Do you think that's fair? You're too nice a young man to get mixed up in a mess like this."

Well, that little talking to must have had some effect. I don't know quite what happened, but one day Phil rang the bell and took Molly and her baby and her bags and baggage away with him. And Bob was gone and Molly and Phil were back living together. And I had my husband back. But it was not easy to forget. What would happen next time? If it was not Molly with her shenanigans, what would it be? I had this family on my back. They controlled my husband, he belonged to them; whenever there was a conflict he was on their side. I counted for nothing. When you were born, and with two children we needed more space, that's when I met Mrs. Segal and we moved to the private house on Eastburn Avenue. And now Dave was doing well. He felt confident enough to go into business on his own and he was making a go of it. He sold sound boxes and then took the record concession at Vim's, a sporting goods and appliance store, part of a chain. It was on Sixth Avenue and Forty-second Street. He had the balcony at the back, overlooking the main store. He paid Vim's a percentage of his profits. We had money, we bought some furniture, it was 1931, '32, and everywhere people were out of work, but somehow, in the heart of New York, there was

91

still life. Then when you were an infant, about a year old, my
father died suddenly, and my poor mother came to live with us.
This was the last straw for her. She prayed in her room, her
health declined. And her mind was affected, my poor sweet
mama.

ELEVEN

Death was on my mind, I thought about it, brooded about it, and studied its representations. I had an old book of nursery rhymes that I hadn't looked at in a while. The letters were large, the drawings tinted in pale orange and pale green. The children and other beings in nursery rhymes were peculiar, ethereal, they inhabited nations, worlds, with which I was not familiar. Their characters were a source of uneasy imaginings. Little Miss Muffet: I would not call any girl of my acquaintance Miss anything; this one was so prissy and girlgood as to be insufferable, fully deserving her fate. I did not like Humpty Dumpty, who lacked all manly definition and was so irrevocably fragile. Georgie Porgie, Jack Horner, Jack and Jill, all seemed to me unnatural abstractions of child existence; there was some menacing propaganda latent in their circumstances but I couldn't quite work out what it was. It was a strange planet they lived on, some place of enormous fearful loneliness and punishment. Or it was as if they were dead but continued to be alive. Whatever happened to them kept happening over and over, good or bad, and I perceived a true moral in this repetition of fate, this recurring inevitable conclusion to the flaws in their beings. They suffered humiliation, damage, and shame, all forms of death or the feeling of death. They were like my dreams —birds flew out of pies, children ran with kings and queens, sheep, those most docile and slow-moving of animals, ran away, whereas the sheep in the Farm exhibit in Claremont Park in the spring didn't even move when you touched them. No human, animal or egg acted quite right in these stories. My final unalterable judgment was that nursery rhymes were for babies and I would not suffer hearing them again.

There was another kind of damage and death in the front-hall bookcase, in a set of art folios bound in flexible covers tied with colored string. Each folio had several color reproductions of the work of a great artist. I was very interested in bodies, and bodies were what these paintings showed: plump flying infants holding bows and arrows or trumpets; and naked moonfaced ladies with long blond hair and small breasts, not at all like my mother's; and scraggly bearded men almost naked and looking very pale with their eyes rolled up in their heads and their arms stretched out on wooden posts and with nails in their hands and feet. Or the same bearded, very pale, sad-faced men lying in the arms of several women who wore long veils and layers of gauzy dress and were crying, and with more of those flying babies hovering in the air above them. There were pictures of clouds with old grandfathers sitting in them with their arms extended and rays of sun shooting from their fingers, or of those scraggly bearded men again, there seemed to be an awful lot of them, they were like brothers in the same family, or members of a tribe, this time riding into little stone villages on the backs of donkeys whose eyes and facial expressions were as mournful and weary as their riders'. I wanted to paint but found the crayons I had for my use could not produce the lines and shapes or even gradations of color that I saw in those strange paintings. All pictures seemed to tell a story if you looked long enough, but these were truly mysterious events. They seemed to describe death. These pale, unhealthy-looking yellowish men with the nails in them and their eyes rolled up sometimes died in the desert, sometimes in grand palaces, they were either the fathers of those flying babies or the husbands of the crying women, it was hard to tell. They had been punished and killed but I didn't know why or by whom. How many there had been! I felt slightly queasy when I put the pictures back in the covers, I felt I had seen something I shouldn't have. They conveyed to me, whatever their intent, a kind of mental coercion which I felt as the mildest of nauseas, the slightest intimation of a need to rest.

In bed with a cold, I called loudly to my mother to bring me some orange juice. I heard her rustling about. Slam of refrigerator door. Footsteps coming down the hall. I threw myself half off the bed, my head back, my eyes staring wide, tongue extended and hands dragging on the floor. Screech. A shattering of glass. I sat up and laughed. Eventually, after sitting down on my bed to catch her breath and recover, she laughed too. "What a terrible thing to do," she said. My mother had been trained in death and disaster. She was vulnerable. She had lost two older sisters and her father. She had grieved and mourned three times, an experience I could only wonder about. She looked at Grandma every day with frowns of concern. Her blue eyes went dark. She played the piano, when she had time, almost as a form of prayer. Big chords, dashing arpeggios. My mother sat regally at the piano. Her arms reached wide.

One morning, after my breakfast of oatmeal and milk and toast and jelly, I took Grandma her tea. Carrying the glass and saucer carefully with two hands, I walked slowly down the hall to her room, next to mine, at the back of the house. In the saucer beside the glass were two white cubes of sugar—the same size Donald marked with a fountain pen to make homemade dice for one of his games. I tapped on her door; I waited for her to call "Come ahead" in Jewish so that I could push open the door with my foot and set the tea on the stand beside her bed. Grandma was interesting to me at these morning meetings. In bed she would not yet have dressed her hair—it lay in long grey braids on her pillows. She looked like a girl. Her light blue eyes were rested, and in the sun coming in the window the thin, fair skin of her face was quite smooth and you could see a little freckle here and there. She did not fear being poisoned in the morning. I enjoyed her approval. I basked in her love. In the back of my mind was also the idea of building up some reservoir of good feeling so that if she became unhappy during the day and started cursing and screaming, she would look at me and remember how she had loved me earlier and take it easy on me.

I thought now I heard her call to come in. I pushed open the door and saw immediately that something was wrong. "Grandma?" I said. I whispered, "Grandma?" She was lying in bed on her back with the blanket pulled up to her chin and her hands clutching the blanket's edge. She emitted a strange sound —like marbles spilling on the floor. Clumps of the blanket were gathered under her fingers. She was very yellow. The sound stopped. Her eyes were neither closed nor open—as if the lids were between sleep and awakeness. Her chin looked collapsed somehow, the mouth was slack. Now I felt the overall stillness of her, a declared inanimateness, the monumental event of death recorded here for me as another kind of life, a superseding condition with more visible torment than I could have imagined was possible. I put the tea down on the bureau far from her bed. I ran down the hall to the kitchen, where my mother and father were having breakfast. I thought Grandma was behind me and coming to get me. My parents saw me in the doorway and I said, "I think Grandma has died." I had not yet in my brief life been thought of as a reliable witness of anything. My parents exchanged glances as if looking for each other's assurance that what I had said could not possibly be true. But they knew something of her precarious health, and the edge of despair on which she lived and often tottered. My father pushed his chair back and hurried to the back of the house; my mother stared at me and put her hand to her cheek.

Later, with the thing officially acknowledged and phone calls made and the visit of the doctor, I felt better. That the adults had taken charge was comforting to me, and no moment since my discovery of my grandma had been quite as bad. Everyone talked in whispers. I had not yet begun to think of her as dead, only that she had died. These seemed to be two separate ideas in my mind. She still lay in her room. It was still her room. I peeked through the half-closed door and saw Dr. Gross examining her with a stethoscope. He was our family doctor, a short, round jowly man with greying black hair and a moustache who wore looped across his vest a chain with a membership badge of some sort depending from it. I had studied that little badge many times as he attended me through my wheezes and hacks and earaches. His office was only a few blocks away. He had removed the covers from my grandma and taken off her gown. She lay white and slender; I could not see her face, but her body, the female whiteness of it, was dazzling to me, not at all wrinkled and not bent but straight. I had just a glimpse before my mother saw me and told me to go about my business and shut the door firmly. I wondered if it was a thing about death that made grandmas into girls.

The next day my mother and father and Uncle Willy, all of them dressed in dark clothes, went off to the synagogue, which was around the corner and one block down on 173rd Street and Morris Avenue. Donald stayed home from school, but neither he nor I was allowed to go to the services. But we were drawn there somehow, and so we walked with my hand in his to where we could stand across the street from the synagogue and hear what traces of the music and prayer could be heard. It was a large square synagogue faced in a pebbly texture of concrete. I had touched it many times. It had white granite steps in the front that narrowed toward the top, and curving brass handrails. It had stone columns on either side of the front door, like a post office, and a translucent dome for a roof. At the very top, where pigeons sat, were two tablets connoting the Ten Commandments. Around the side where we stood, stained-glass windows were tilted open in a way that didn't allow you to see inside. We heard singing.

"Poor Grandma," Donald said. "The only fun she had was going to services."

We saw the black hearse, and another black car behind it, move slowly to a stop in front of the synagogue. "People will be coming out in a minute," Donald said and we walked back home.

I had the distinct impression death was Jewish. It had happened to my grandma, who spoke Jewish, and everyone had immediately repaired to the synagogue. A memorial candle in a glass now stood flickering on the kitchen table for Grandma, whom I had seen light similar candle glasses for her own dead. Hebrew letters were on the glass label as on the window of the chicken market where dead chickens hung on hooks by their feet, some plucked, some half plucked, some with all their feathers. Chickens, I knew, were Jewish. For days after Grandma's burial, the mirrors were covered in our house and my mother walked around in stockinged feet. We were visited by friends, who brought many white bakery boxes tied with string and put them on the kitchen table. Pots and pots of coffee were made, and women I didn't know, friends of my mother, stood strangely at the kitchen sink and washed dishes. My mother hugged me in front of visitors, drew me to her and hugged me till it hurt. She was tearful, sentimental, easy to deal with. She complimented me and told everyone how bright I was. "This is the boy who knew before any of us," she said. "He came to tell us and he knew exactly what had happened." But she also spoke Jewish to these people, just as she had to my grandmother. I went to my grandmother's room. The bed was stripped, the closet had been emptied. But in her cedar chest there were still her treasures, shawls of lace and folded dresses, and wool sweaters and knitted things all wrapped in thin white paper and with mothballs between the layers. There were also old sepia pictures of her family when she was a child, many little girls and boys standing and reclining around old men with white beards and black hats who sat stiffly in chairs, behind which stood several stern-looking women with their hands on the old men's shoulders. The little boys and girls were dressed oddly and all seemed to have drawn faces and dark hair hanging over their ears and enormous staring dark eyes. On the top of the chest was my grandma's prayer book, her Siddur, and the cover had those Jewish letters on it that looked to me like arrangements of bones. In my room I played with my pick-up sticks to see if I could arrange them in Jewish letters, but they lacked bony width, they lacked the knobby thickness even of chicken bones.

Now it was my mother who, on Friday nights at the kitchen table, placed white Sabbath candles in the wobbly old brass candlesticks, and drew a kerchief over her head and lit the candles and prayed with her hands over her glistening blue eyes.

TWELVE

More frequently now there came to the front door the old men in black who wore their prayer shawls under their coats and carried letters from rabbis and credentials from yeshivas. Now they were invited in. My mother sat them in the parlor and gave them tea. They told their stories in hushed tones or spoke only in Jewish, and so my eavesdropping didn't yield anything that specific. But I was getting the gist of things. And finally one man spoke enough English to make it clear. "The *kinder* from the schools are pushed, so now they can't go. And the business of the fathers are taken from them. Little by little. And in the street they revile them, the brownshirt heathen, and spit on them. And to the *polizei* they must report. Thousands are leaving, Missus. Their homes, their livelihood is gone. All of it gone. To Palestine, on boats, but anywhere! Where can they go! What can they do!"

My mother produced two crumpled bills from her purse, folded them, and pushed them into the old man's coin box. It was a blue box with white stripes and a white six-pointed star.

My mother joined the Sisterhood of the synagogue and began going to services on Saturday morning. She had never been religious before. "I never had the patience," she told her friend Mae. "When I was a girl, I gave Mama such a hard time because I wouldn't go. I thought it was all so old-fashioned and unnecessary. We were bohemians, Dave and I. And look at me now."

One Saturday I went with her just to see what it was all about. The women sat upstairs in the synagogue. The men, who were the bosses, sat downstairs. Sometimes there was crying, sometimes singing, but mostly Jewish death words. Jewish death was spreading.

I left and ran home by myself. Through a grate in the sidewalk on the 173rd Street side of the synagogue I could see into the basement windows. Another synagogue was down there where the poor people prayed.

I was familiar with the texture of sidewalks and the embellishments in brick at the sides of buildings. Most brick was red and of a pocked cracked surface that scraped the finger; some brick siding was yellow and was smoother. The steps of my front stoop were worn white granite, very smooth to the touch.

After this summer I would be going to school. This had been discussed several times by my parents. They were pleased about it. I was ready for school—eager, in fact—but now my mother was saying that I would also go to Hebrew school twice a week in the afternoons. She said this as a kind of declaration and she put her hand on my head. I secretly resolved to fight the edict. It seemed to me a reckless, even insane act of public exposure. I already knew that if I found myself in the wrong part of Claremont Park I could be knifed and robbed for being Jewish. I knew from the old men's whisperings in the front parlor that similar things, though even worse, were happening in Europe, especially Germany. A little boy who went to Hebrew school would live in endlessly concentric circles of danger, beginning with my park, and rippling out over the globe. Everything connected in a circle of being that, unfortunately, had assigned to us the life of prey, as on the steppes, or the veldt, where the herds of beautiful zebra or wildebeests were run down and this or that animal isolated and slaughtered for the evening meal of the predator cats. I could not have reasoned consciously that European culture took revengeful root in the New World, to which it had been transplanted. Yiddish-speaking households were not foreign to me, they were American. I did not speak the language, but I understood bits of it as spoken by my grandmother to my mother or in less purist fashion by my father's parents to him. In my comic books purchased at the candy store on the corner of 174th Street, or on the faces of the bubble gum cards, stories were told of wars between gangsters or wars between countries. Planes dive-bombed the agonized faces of screaming civilians, tanks rearing like horses on their hind legs loomed over Oriental babies crying for their mothers, and G-men and crooks, who were dressed alike, drilled each other with tommy guns. It all seemed of a piece to me, and insofar as it had something to do with the strategy of survival, I attended to it. I understood that one had as resources oneself, one's brother, one's parents and then perhaps President Roosevelt.

Of course I knew virtually nothing about religion, beyond a few of the major Bible stories and the holidays associated with them. I knew so far that most of the Jewish holidays were not as much fun as the regular ones. There was some forced insistence behind them. This was not true of the Fourth of July or New Year's or Thanksgiving. Purim, where you got apples and raisins and noisemakers and little blue-and-white flags, was sort of fun; and Chanukah, of course, where you got presents. But spinning the wooden top, to see which Hebrew letter would fall, like a gambler in death, was not to my liking. And the Purim story seemed to me not as victorious as it was made out to be. One bad man was shamed and deposed, but the king was still there who was the real problem.

Passover was the giant of the Jewish holidays and had much to say for it. The story was good and the food was good. Technically it lasted eight days, but the fuss was made for only one. It came along in the spring, but with that peculiarity of Jewish holidays of being very casual about the date of its arrival. I noticed when adults talked about Passover they said either that

it was late or that it was early, but never that it was on time. This
year it was late. My mother bought flowers for it, tulips and
daffodils. Passover involved getting dressed up and taking an
enormous journey with packages and flowers.

We were most of the day getting ready. Early in the afternoon,
an unusual time for me to be so clean and well groomed, we set
off—Donald, my mother and I—walking east on 173rd Street
over the Topping Avenue hill, and descending by degrees to the
valley of Webster Avenue. This was the East Bronx of mytholog-
ical dangers; surrounded by my family I was not concerned,
although it would have been better still were my father with us.
But he was required to work most of the day and would be
meeting us later.

We boarded a red-and-yellow streetcar with rush seats, all
occupied. It was the W car, headed north. It went clanging up
Webster, a wide thoroughfare of gas stations, warehouses, lum-
beryards and auto repair shops. The farther north we rode, the
longer the stretch between stops. One by one we found seats.
My mother, sitting first, kept all the bundles on her lap. At 180th
Street the car swung sharply right, the wheels screeching loudly
and all the passengers tilting in unison. At this point, Donald
began a sharp lookout. He was our navigator. We rode to the
stop under an elevated station that he had been waiting for, and
got off to transfer to another trolley, the A car. Now the Bronx
flattened out in blocks of empty lots, with schools in the middle
of dirt fields, and spired churches, and even an occasional
wooden house with its own yard. Finally, after a turn or two, we
broke into the peaceful suburban avenues of Mt. Vernon. Here
the car ride was smooth and we were practically the only passengers. We sat together. I liked the brown wood decks of streetcars, the walls and window frames and ceilings were of wood
too; it must feel like this in a bunkhouse or a riverboat, I

thought. And it all rested on steel carriages. It appealed to me that fast or slow, barreling along or creaking around corners, the trolley car could go only as directed by the tracks; it was all planned, all the motorman could do was crank up the power and the flanged wheels had dutifully to go the way they were led. Of course, occasionally the motorman stopped the car, got off and, with a crowbar, moved the track switch one way or another, but the principle held.

The air was cool. The streets were not of cobblestone but of smooth cream-colored seamless paving. Green parks and fields were on either side of us. Then near the end of the line, the conductor already walking down the aisle and yanking the seat backs forward for the return trip, the car reached a certain corner in Pelham Manor, where, to my mind, began the quietest, most elegant block in the world. And here we disembarked, and made our way along the beautifully named Montcalm Terrace, after a general in the French and Indian War. This was where Aunt Frances lived, on a street of raised lawns and grand homes. Her house had a sharply raked tile roof, and casement windows, and dark wood beams impressed in the grey stucco siding.

Aunt Frances greeted us with a smile at the door. Behind her was her full-time maid, Clara, a tall, angular black woman who wore a white uniform with matching white shoes. Clara took our coats and bundles. To our surprise and delight, my habitually late father was already there. He had come up from Grand Central Station on the New York Central. "You're late," he said. "What took you so long!" And everyone laughed. Then the master of this house appeared, Uncle Ephraim, horse-faced, very proper, a bit pompous, in fact—a portly man who spoke always as if delivering a speech. He gazed down at me, with critical intelligence coming like sparks of light off his eyeglasses. He had enormous teeth. "And how is Edgar?" he said. I could tell he felt superior to his wife's family. He had a patronizing air. On the second night of Passover they would have a seder for his family; the two families never met. And it was true, we were a raucous crowd. Uncle Ephraim conducted the seder down at the end of the table. Beside him sat my atheist grandfather, who was equally proper about the form of the thing. Together they prayed and directed the sacramental moments for us all, while we, our attention wandering, talked and whispered, Donald and my cousin Irma trying to step on each other's feet under the table, and my father getting into a political argument with Uncle Phil the cabdriver, who did not believe the cabdrivers should be unionized. Uncle Phil wore not the ceremonial black skull cap supplied by the house but the same felt hat with the front brim turned up in which he drove his cab. Irreverent Aunt Molly kept up a patter of remarks that made us laugh. She always looked disheveled, even in holiday clothes, with wisps of her hair not quite tucked in, face florid, bosom crooked, dress sticking to her from its own static. "Where do you suppose the Duke and Duchess of Windsor are having *their* seder tonight," she said. Even my grandmother Gussie laughed, who was pious and God-fearing and tried to shush everyone before she laughed again. When things got too noisy, Uncle Ephraim, without looking up, slapped the table with his open palm, and for perhaps thirty seconds everyone was chastened until someone broke out in the giggles, usually me, because of the funny faces Aunt Molly was making to get me to do just that.

And here we were all of us sitting around the long table in the dining room, a room where you only ate, imagine that, and even the animosity between my mother and grandmother was suspended as the sweet holiday wine, sipped at the requisite times in the ceremony, began to bring color to people's faces. The candlelight shone in everyone's eyes. There was a splendid chandelier of many crystal lights. I was asked to open the front door for Elijah, the prophet, for whom a place setting was laid and wineglass filled. It was a heavy wooden door, with a cathedral arch and black cast-iron fixtures. I peeked into the darkness of Montcalm Terrace to make sure Elijah was not there. I pictured him as one of the old bearded men who came to the door with terrible stories and a collection box in his hand. I was relieved that he hadn't come. The night sky was filled with millions of shining stars.

My brother was prevailed upon to ask the four questions the youngest male asks at the seder. He protested, was overruled and, scowling, turned to me and said, "This is the last time I do this, next year you better know how." He felt demeaned—a student at Townsend Harris High School asking why this night was different from all other nights. The answers in Hebrew to the four questions seemed, not only to me but to most everyone at the table, interminable. "Listen to them down there," Molly said of Grandpa and Uncle Ephraim. "The Jews are the only people in the world who give you a history course before they let you eat." Finally the big moment arrived—the actual dinner. Aunt Frances rang a little bell and a moment later Clara appeared from the kitchen and began to serve. I had nibbled at the bitter herbs and barely sniffed at the hard-boiled egg in salt water. Now my time had come. The chicken soup with *knaydl*, how good that was! The fish I passed over. That was my father's joke that made everyone laugh: "No thank you, Aunt Frances. I'll pass over that." Then roast lamb, baked potatoes, I even ate the string beans. Honey cake and watered wine for dessert. Then, after a brief reprise of the impenetrable ceremony, the time for singing, at which point everyone with great gusto, as much in gratitude for the finish of this exhausting event as in praise of God, sang the traditional songs as loudly as possible. The song I liked best was one of those add-on songs, like "There Was an Old Woman Who Swallowed a Fly." This song described a father buying a kid, meaning a goat. Then a cat devoured the kid, then a dog came and bit the cat, a staff came and smote the dog, and a fire came and burned the staff and then water came and extinguished the fire, then the ox came and drank the water, and finally, by the last verse you got the whole causal sequence—the slaughterer came and slaughtered the ox, which had drunk the water, which had put out the fire, which had burned the staff, which had smitten the dog, which had bitten the cat, which had eaten the kid, which my father had bought for two coins—one only kid, one only kid. I had no idea what any of this meant and I didn't want to ask for fear of being answered, but it pleased me very much.

When the time came to leave, Aunt Frances stood talking to my mother about her poor mother, and then the two women hugged. Uncle Ephraim had a gold toothpick that he kept on a fob. He held up a hand to cover his mouth while he picked his teeth. We all piled into Uncle Phil's De Soto taxi, which had jump seats. It was crowded but we fit. I sat on my father's lap and fell asleep as we went back down to the Bronx. First Phil dropped off the old folks. Then he drove us to our door. My father carried me up the front steps, I half asleep in his arms, the cool night air of spring blowing gently around my ears like an echo of the Passover songs in my mind.

THIRTEEN

School was just a half block from my house, across the corner of 173rd Street, but my whole life changed once I began there. I was six—no longer a child. I wore a white shirt with a red tie. In the morning my time was as important as anyone else's. I had to be turned out at a certain hour just like my brother and father; I ran home for lunch at twelve and back at twelve-forty-five, and when I got home from school in the afternoon I had just a few hours before I'd have to start thinking about homework. I enjoyed the seriousness of my calling. Reading came to me effortlessly. I had in a subliterate way been making sense from books for some time. The moment I began competently to read was imperceptible to me. Numbers were more difficult.

My teacher Mrs. Kalish asked me on my first day in her class if I was Donald's brother. He had been a brilliant student, she said, her favorite student at the time. This sort of comparison would eventually disturb me. Now I smiled with pride at the identification. I was a confident scholar. School held no terrors. I did not once vomit in the classroom. The janitor had a surefire system for dealing with such disasters. He appeared with his pail of ammoniated water and his mop, and a shovel and a garbage can and a bag of sawdust. He would spill the sawdust on the offensive pool, shovel it up, and then mop the whole thing with ammonia and drive the smell away. Why did children vomit so much at P.S. 70? Bathroom accidents were oddly less frequent, perhaps because the rules about going to the bathroom were fairly relaxed.

The materials of school interested me, the stiff colored paper, the jars of white paste, the sticks of chalk, the erasers larger than bars of brown soap that had to be taken outside and pounded against each other to get the dust out. To be chosen to do that, to be authorized to leave the classroom and go out in the closed yard in the sun, all alone, was an honor. Another honor was to be designated monitor of the window shades, which needed adjustment all during the day as the sun went across the sky and the light shone in our eyes or in the teacher's. Honors seemed to fall my way in school without my having to do much to get them. I was liked by the other children and they elected me class president, although neither I nor they had very much idea what the class president was supposed to do. Yet I enjoyed being president. The stair monitor had more power, but that was all right.

In the spelling bees I was the best of the boy students and invariably wound up the last of my kind to face three or four of the girls on the other side of the room. Girls were devilishly good at spelling. I might defeat almost all of them, but just as I was the boy champion, Diane Blumberg led the girls, and inevitably, when the showdown came between me and Diane, she would win. She was good at math too, and taller than I was, with fat little squirrel cheeks and a mouth perpetually primed in contemptuous judgment. Diane Blumberg was in all ways smug and insufferable.

A watercolor portrait of President Roosevelt hung above the blackboard in the front of the room. On the window ledges were various things we did for Nature, one of the best of subjects— bulbs growing in pots, or a frog in a terrarium. We had a bowl of turtles, who sunned themselves on stones, and for one or two days in spring an Easter rabbit donated by one of the mothers. Abraham Lincoln was shown on a poster and over his figure was printed the Gettysburg Address. In the long closet with sliding doors at the side of the room, on rainy days steam seemed to come from our rubber slickers and galoshes. I loved anything that got me out of the classroom. We would in two-by-twos trek downstairs to the big auditorium for the weekly movie, never something as good as we'd expect to find at the real movies, but something old and tame, like *Mrs. Wiggs of the Cabbage Patch* or *Tom Sawyer*. After each reel the lights would come on and we would be noisy and throw spitballs at one another—the discipline was less exacting at these times. The best breaks in the routine were the fire drills, because then we could march outside and stay there for mysterious endless amounts of time, the whole school standing quietly in ranks in the breeze, all the apartment buildings of the neighborhood surrounding our yard, while seemingly secret and troubled school administrative self-examination took place. On mornings of fire drills lunchtime always came quickly.

I had discovered in myself the double personality engendered by school: the good attentive boy in class, the raucous, unsprung Dionysian in the schoolyard at recess. It was a matter of expressing the dominant force—order or freedom. Other boys in the class were bigger, rougher in the mold, and their wildness was a model to us all. The quiet teacher's child in me went and sat down somewhere in the back of my brain while the hellion ran about shouting and punching. You found weaknesses and went chasing after them, like the cheetah, which I knew was, for short distances, the fastest animal in the world. The weakness of girls was their underpants. To see these or mention them or allude to them brought red embarrassment to their faces, or glances of fear, or hisses of hatred. They had an awful way of half bending their knees, holding their hands in their skirts, protecting *something*. I knew to stop, always, short of the flying fanged leap. One or two boys did not know, they had some ungoverned crudeness of spirit that did damage, bent arms back, humiliated their prey, and turned themselves into the despised among all of us, girls and boys. They were feared and detested, and went on living that way in rude derision of their unpopularity, for months at a time. When I went back into class I became serious, as if my character could only be maintained by alternations of opposites. I tried out different Edgars in the class, in the schoolyard. In transit from school to home and back in that short half block, I ran from one of my beings to another aware only of the sound of the racing breath in my ears, the scent of cold air in my brain, some pungent essence of winter and the momentary revelation of my own lengthening limbs.

School made me hungry. For lunch I loved a baked potato with butter and salt and a glass of milk. Or cabbage soup with potatoes in it and sour cream. Under my father's advice, I was developing a taste for tart things, a taste, he claimed, that was far more enduring than one for the sweet things. I was bought my first pair of knickers. They were corduroy and worn with long argyle socks. I liked my looks in the mirror, a young knickered student in his fall wool sweater, and a shock of blond hair over one eye. I liked to see my softness going away, the leanness of cheekbone emerging, a line of jaw.

There was in my second-grade class the smallest of girls, Meg. She had grey eyes and very light straw-colored hair worn short, and her mother favored more doll-like versions of the skirt and middy that girls customarily wore—skirts with stiff outward-spreading understuff and white knee socks and white-and-brown strap shoes polished clean every morning. She was the shortest person in the class, and as she was extremely quiet as well, she was clearly too delicate and inconsequential to excite the envy or malice of the other girls or the desire of the boys to inflict torture and torment. She had no apparent wish to use what she had or what she came from to make her place in our society. We all knew what a spoiled child was and she was not one. She demanded no obeisances as any of us would on the basis even of the ownership of a new pencil box. Our social life was competitive, we made alliances and broke them with the cunning of nations, but she was clearly not one of our coarse breed. She did her work well and throughtfully, without ostentation; she never volunteered an answer but always knew it when she was called on. When the school day was over she did not linger in the yard, but with her books stacked and held against her chest in that way of girls, she walked through the schoolyard gate and to the corner, and looking both ways before crossing 173rd Street, made her way along Eastburn, right past my house to the corner of Mt. Eden Avenue, where she crossed the Oval, turned left and went along the Claremont Park wall to her apartment, overlooking the park up the hill near Monroe Avenue. Although the theatricality of her mother's taste made Meg's underpants easier to see than most, she did not suffer from this. No one bothered her, least of all me. Perhaps her size made her the baby in our minds. But for the same reason, size, I may have seen in her an assumption of that titled babyhood for which I had less and less desire in myself. I was grateful to her. I was glad no one bothered her because then I would have had to reveal myself as her defender. And then it would have been said I loved her, which would be unfortunate. She had a full, inflamed-looking upper lip, which I found attractive. I was not yet bold enough to walk beside her even though her path took her right past my stoop, but her quietness, and a quality of inner certitude she had, conveyed, in the brief moments I watched her or thought about her, a similar central silence to me, and I felt as if I were looking ahead down a still corridor into my calm and resolute manhood.

School brought about an enlarged social life, generally, for I was now permitted on Saturday to go out for lunch and then spend the afternoon at the movies with one or more of my school friends. My expeditions were funded with a weekly allowance of twenty-five cents. Two hot dogs with mustard and sauerkraut and a bottle of Pepsi-Cola cost fifteen cents at the delicatessen on 174th Street; and the dime in change was exactly the price of admission to the Surrey Theater on Mt. Eden Avenue just the other side of the Concourse. The Surrey showed a cartoon, a newsreel, either a travelogue or a short, such as one of Lew Lehr's monkey pictures, where the monkeys rode bikes and wore diapers and sat in high chairs to eat baby food, one or two chapters of a serial like *Tim Tyler's Luck* or *Buck Jones and the Phantom Rider,* and finally, a double feature, an A picture and a B, the A usually about gangsters and G-men, the B a Laurel and Hardy comedy or perhaps a Charlie Chan mystery. At the end of the afternoon I came out of the theater staggering. I was shocked to see that it was still daylight, that mankind did not live in eternal darkness lit only by flashes of gunfire or the flames of car crashes, and in fact was going about its ordinary business in no visibly dramatic manner. This letdown, or perhaps it was the light, or that my skull still resounded with the unmodulated screams of joy of a theaterful of children, invariably brought me home with a headache, which, however, I could not confess to my mother lest I be reminded of it the following Saturday.

Sometimes this routine was varied with a trip downtown, if we could persuade one of the mothers or an older brother or sister to go with us. We did not choose places that were chosen by our teachers for trips on a bus during school hours—the Museum of Natural History, for instance, or Fraunces Tavern, where Washington said farewell to his troops. We liked to see radio shows. One day we got into the Babe Ruth program, where the great man himself stood in front of the microphone, although not, disappointingly, in his baseball suit but in an ordinary double-breasted suit and tie, and read from a script haltingly and ran a quiz with lucky kids picked from the audience. In fact he was past his prime as a player. But there were prizes up to five dollars and a lot of advice about clean living from the Babe. His voice was hoarse at the end, his tie loosened, his hair rumpled, but he got through it. We didn't have to be cued by the director with his placards to cheer; stopping our throats was more difficult.

On expeditions such as these I liked to drop in at my father's store, if it was within range, and show it off to my friends. "Hey, young fellow," my father would say as I walked in. Donald would be there putting stock on the shelves, Uncle Willy might be taking an order on the phone. I cautioned my friends not to make noise. I gave them a guided tour in hushed tones as we passed among the customers.

Downtown was my father's realm. In my mind it belonged to him. Every day he went to it on the subway as a diver in a big iron bell descended to the depths of the ocean; and he found things there and brought them back. His restless mind lapped our house every night like the evening tide and brought to our shores the treasures of his escapades—opera tickets, art books, magazines, papers, little badly printed magazines of radical thought, a new electric clock with an illuminated dial, a wonderful set of silver electric trains. When he took me downtown to spend the day with him, that was the best trip of all. I could then open my mind to the chaos of adult civilization, knowing that he would find the order for me. He pointed out buildings and named them and told me what was done in them, he instructed me on the difference between streets and avenues, he described the routes of the trolley cars by the letters they displayed on the front, he knew flawlessly how to get from one place to another, he knew the best shops for this or that, the best values, he knew everything. My father was an expert jaywalker walking us boldly across the streets of traffic with unerring grace. When my mother brought me downtown, she deferred uncharacteristically to his decisions, he was the master in this realm. He loved the great city of stone—it made him catch his breath and laugh. I understood, studying him, that his mind made a design of it. There was the appearance of it, which I knew, a dazzle of noise and disparate intention, jackhammers punching holes in the street, cars and trucks flowing past obstructions, yellow cabs with their skylights, double-decker buses, the great liners in the harbor blowing their basso horns; but in reality all of it was somehow arranged, it was a place of accommodation for human desire, it supported the diverse intentions of millions of people simultaneously, and he knew that and gave me the confidence to understand it and not be afraid. The heels of thousands of people drummed the sidewalk. He had been born on the Lower East Side. New York was his home, he loved its music, and through a speaker over the front door of Hippodrome Radio he sent the sound of symphonies and swing bands into the street like his own voice.

Yet when I walked from our home to the subway station on 174th Street and entered that cool catacomb through the tightly sprung turnstile, it was usually in the company of my mother, herself no mean guide. She too was a native. Holding my hand tightly, she brought me to spectacles designed for children— theatricals, puppet shows, Thanksgiving Day parades. It was to my mother I would turn in the huge air-cooled cathedral of Radio City when Snow White ran through the woods and the trees came alive to grab at her tresses and scratch her clothes into tatters; my mother was the sponsor of all that looming animated surreality.

One day she took me to the Ringling Brothers and Barnum & Bailey Circus at Madison Square Garden on Fiftieth Street. My father had gotten the tickets free. It was a weekday matinee and he could not come. My school was over, but Donald still had his high school exams, and so it was just the two of us. Far below me on the tanbark of the center ring a sad-faced clown swept the spotlight into a smaller and smaller circumference until finally it went out altogether. Another clown strode along with half a dozen baby pigs trotting after him. He pressed a button and his nose lit up. Someone doused him with water, so he opened a tiny umbrella the size of a saucer and held it by its long handle high over his head. I watched the great swinging teams of fliers doing somersaults in the air. I saw the march of elephants.

It interested me particularly that in the circus there was one wistful clown who climbed the high wire after the experts were done, and scared himself and us with his uproariously funny, incredibly maladroit moves up there. Slipping and sliding about, losing his hat, his floppy shoes, and holding on to the wire for dear life, he was actually doing stunts far more difficult than any that had gone on before. This was confirmed, invariably, as he doffed his clown garments one by one and emerged from the woeful little potbellied misfit as the star who headlined the high-wire act. In his tights and glistening bare torso he pulled off his bulbous nose and stood spotlighted on the platform with one arm raised to receive our wildest applause for having led us through our laughter, our fear, to simple awe. I took profound instruction from this hoary circus routine. It was not merely that I, the sniffler with the red nose, would someday in my good time reveal myself to be a superman among men. There was art in the thing, the power of illusion, the mightier power of the reality behind it. What was first true was then false, a man was born from himself. All the problems of my own being were not the truth of me, I knew. In my own eyes I was a man no matter what daily evidence was thrown in my face to the contrary. But that there were ways to dramatize this to an unsuspecting world was the keenness of my understanding. You didn't have to broadcast everything you knew all at once, but could reveal it suspense-fully, and make them first cry out in fear, and make them laugh, and, above all, make them applaud, when they finally saw what an achievement had been yours by taking on so well and accu-rately the comic being of a little kid.

Of course that was a hard illusion to maintain once the show was over and the lights went on. I aspired to the power of myself. My struggle went on every day but not always in my conscious-ness of it. School assisted me because I did well there, I was among peers and I was proving out. But the odds at home were against me; no matter how I grew and what I learned, I couldn't seem to better my position. Invariably there were ceremonies of my helplessness that caused me to revert to the child I had been and thought I was no longer—as, for instance, when my mother decided it was time for still another excursion downtown, but to a place I despised and detested, S. Klein's on Union Square.

I could not subscribe to whatever value it was that plunked me down, semiannually, at S. Klein's. She hated it too, or so she said, but she went about her preparations to leave the house with an energy that suggested happy anticipation. It was possible for us to communicate sensibly sometimes but not when she wouldn't admit her true feelings. So I knew all was lost, I was helpless before impending disaster, and nothing could console me, neither the long trip in the subway in which I got to stand at the window next to the engineer's cab nor the promise of lunch out. I went immediately into my passive-resisting sulk, in which my feet didn't seem to work properly, my wrist had to be held and I was by this means shaken and yanked forward, shoe-tips scuffing the sidewalk, or dragged in a kind of sideways lurch and stumble, all the way to the 174th Street subway station.

"Walk properly, Edgar," she would say. "You want me to leave you behind? Don't think I wouldn't! Oh, you foolish boy, who do you think I'm doing this for? You grow out of things as soon as I put them on. Do you know how lucky we are to have a few dollars? Other children wear castoffs and they're happy to have them."

If I persisted she would say, "I warn you, my patience is wearing thin," and give me a particularly vehement yank. I always admired my mother's metaphors. Even as they were familiar to me from much usage, they held up nicely. Patience wearing thin was very fine. A little later she would say, "If you don't walk like a human being I'm going to knock the spots out of you." That was good too, although I never quite understood the etymology of it. Some people had freckles, but I didn't, and, of course, chicken pox and measles brought spots, but no one would beat a sick child and expect to cure him in this manner, not even my mother. Besides which the phrase was *out of you,* she didn't say I'm going to knock the spots *off you,* she said *out of you,* and so that was totally mystifying. I had seen her pounding pillows or shaking blankets out the window before laying them across the windowsill; maybe it was a dust metaphor. Not that I had much time to reflect on it, because there followed almost immediately the ultimate assurance: that I would be murdered in cold blood. I never had the leisure to think about that one. Uttered in a voice loud enough to make people on the street turn and stare, it meant that unless I wanted to be physically abused, I had no recourse but to give in and allow myself to be pushed through the turnstile.

But I would not forgive her. To walk out of a brisk autumn day into a Klein's fall sale was an unimaginably perverse act even for an adult. Greeted by blasts of hot air whooshing up through the floor grates between the outer and inner doors, we passed into a harshly lit wasteland of pipe racks and dump bins hung and piled with every conceivable kind of garment for every gender, age and shape, from infants and toddlers to boys, young misses, juniors, men and women. And every single one of these garments seemed to be undergoing the imperial scrutiny of the released population of an insane asylum. Some sort of frenzied mass rite was taking place, the Flinging of the Textiles. As if in a state of hypnosis, my mother immediately joined in while I held on to her, for my life. Wriggling and elbowing her way through communicants three and four deep around a counter of sweaters, say, or scarves, she immediately began tossing them up in the air, just as everyone else was, altogether creating a kind of fountain of rising and falling colors. She did this for a while and, shaking her head to show her dissatisfaction, fought her way outward into the great flow of wandering shoppers passing across the ancient wooden floors of the place like a tumultuous migration of buffalo, hoofbeats thundering on the plain, only to find another counter to stop at and press her way toward so as to go through the same fountaining behavior all over again. Little by little as we made our way on this endless pilgrimage I slowly peeled off my clothing, like a foreign legionnaire stumbling under the merciless heat of the sun over dune after dune, my hat first, then my mackinaw, then my sweater. I held on to these items in some attempt to keep from losing them, but it was a law of life at S. Klein's that even as you were establishing loyalties to new items of apparel your old ones tried to flee from you in a kind of poltergeist of moral rebuke. Time after time I would find the cap or the sweater gone, or the jacket slipping away from me. I'd have to buck the current to find my hat under someone's foot—dangerous work: if I slipped and fell it was sudden death, there was no question about that. Or I'd find the sweater in the hands of some *other* mother looking around with a compassionate and pitying expression on her face for the owner; and then I'd have to *thank* her and suffer my mother's smiling theatrical scolding for the sake of this woman. And on we'd pass, driven like ceremonial dancers to the *plink plink* of those odd bells peculiar to department stores and to hortatory shoppers' advisories delivered like sermons over the public address systems. Stock clerks in grey jackets pushed and spun wheeled bins of clothing through the crowd with brutal élan, like the drivers of Dodgems in an amusement park. Long lines of people wound through corridors and around counters well out of sight of the cashier posts to which, arms filled with piles of ticketed clothes, they had committed themselves. And mothers were telling children to stand still and children were hanging on to their mothers' skirts and coats, and they were whining and dribbling snot from their noses, and staring at one another in slack-mouthed fascination. And people were shouting, and the occasional clerks who could be seen were denying customers whatever satisfaction they sought, and my mind was being obliterated by this population, everyone desiring in competition what we desired; I felt they were multiples of us, we had disintegrated into thousands of restless constantly moving people, a fun-house mirror of enraged and threadbare gentility, and these masses were sending up a great planetary music, harsh and dissonant like a sea wind, and it was blowing me away, eroding me, chunks of myself were flying off, soon I would be no more than a grain of sand. And then that would be swept up.

But my mother strode on. The more the scene whirled around us like a roaring inferno of human pretensions, the more steadfast she became, taking this and that, discarding one thing for another, and so gradually accumulating what she had come for. And somehow she would find some haven, some alcove, perhaps on a higher floor, where the population was thinned out and the atmosphere was quieter; and we would encamp and examine what we had. Her technique was to take from the racks several things of each kind—several shirts or coats or pairs of knickers or sweaters—and try them all on me to see which were best. So now I endured the Try-On. "Try this," she would say, and a pullover would come down over my head. "No, it's too small, try the size larger," and off would come the pullover and down come another. My role in this rite was to lift my arms on command or lower them, to endure having my head swaddled for terrifying moments in a sweater until she had found the neck hole and brought me back into light. I would have to turn around and have things held up to my back, and turn back around and have them held up to my front, or, most hideously of all, repair to some grim cubicle and behind a flimsy curtain that anyone might open, take off my pants and try on new ones. There is a kind of exhaustion that comes over you in the Try-On that is like no other. It is as if having been turned into a hothouse vegetable you have now gone into vegetable decline, or wilt. "Stand up straight, Edgar, how can I tell if something is right if you slump this way." But at this point of the ordeal it was not resistance I was offering, or intransigence, or any willfulness of any kind, because I had none; I was without volition, like a marionette whose strings are slack.

Somehow we would go through everything and come up with the selection. And then would come the Standing on Line, and lo, I was one of those miserable little children hanging on to their mothers and staring at the other beings their own size, or conspicuously ignoring them, as we moved with agonizing slowness to the register. Except that now I was sound and whole again, my mother's triumph in her purchases having reestablished in my soul the conviction that we were, after all, special human beings in all this mob, with our own secrets and superiorities. "This sweater is a wonderful buy, and it's just the right size, you'll be able to wear it with the sleeves turned up, and grow into it and wear it some more. And you'll like the knickers. They're made of the finest wool, I think they made a mistake and underpriced them, they were the only ones in the whole store.

Isn't it lucky they fit? Maybe I'll take it in a bit at the waist and then let it out when it needs it." And so on. Without doubt, she had done it again, found in this emporium of rags and seconds, and badly made and cheap clothing, just those few things that were worth buying.

And we would get out of there and find a luncheonette or a Nedick's and I would have a grilled cheese sandwich and an orange drink, and she would have a cup of chicken noodle soup; and I'd be miraculously restored, my eye keen for New York and its excitements, which usually came to a point as a new *Flash Gordon Big Little Book* at the newsstand. We took the Lexington Avenue IRT home, a subway in Manhattan that ascended into the light just south of Yankee Stadium in the Bronx, and then rocketed along northward on elevated tracks over Jerome Avenue. I sat next to her in this train, whose seats ran under the windows all the way down the side of the car, and leaned against her, my tormentor and redeemer, as she sat in her stolid thought with her ankles crossed and the Klein's bags gathered on her lap. I drew up my knees and read of the latest depredations of the wily Oriental despot Ming the Merciless, ruler of the planet Mongo, and of Flash Gordon's tough, resourceful, but sportsmanlike response. I liked Flash, and Dale, his girlfriend. They flew about the heavens in rocket ships without wearing much of anything, but they never caught cold.

FOURTEEN

I suppose I was at this time in the second grade. I was becoming more aware of my mother's unhappiness, in part because it was more explicit. Before going to work one morning my father put in her hand two fifty-cent pieces. He left and she sat down at the kitchen table. "With this," she said, indicating the coins, "I am expected to maintain a family, keep a house running, put food on the table." She was a strong woman but she wept easily. I patted her. She washed clothes using a washboard angled into the laundry sink in the kitchen. Her arms went up and down in the suds. "I used to have the most wonderful maid," she told me. "When you were an infant. A woman from Jamaica, Carrie was her name. She adored you, took you out in your new carriage and would shoo anyone away who got too close. Carrie guarded you as if you were the Prince of Wales."

Coming home from school, now I often smelled cigarette smoke, which told me my mother's friend Mae was visiting. Mae worked as a bookkeeper part time, in the mornings. It was the best work she could find. She lived with her old mother and father around the corner and got out of the house in the afternoon by visiting her friend my mother. But my mother had also come to rely on Mae, who listened to her concerns, injecting a question here or a wry comment there. Mae sat leaning forward, with her legs crossed and her hand with the cigarette up in the

air. She was totally attentive and sympathetic. I liked the sound
her stockings made when she crossed her legs. She understood
that I found her attractive and would pinch my cheek, but not
so that it hurt, or rub her hand in a circle on my back. One
evening she was wearing a silk see-through blouse with a lace
bow at the collar. Her shoulders and arms were visible and also
her brassiere. "What are you looking at, Buster?" she said with
a laugh.

I heard a lot when my mother talked to her friend Mae. "I have
exactly three dresses that I wash and iron and wash and iron,"
my mother said. "And I will go on washing and ironing them
until there's nothing left. I haven't bought a stitch of clothing
in years. And he plays cards. He knows we need every penny and
he plays cards." Mae shook her head. My mother wondered
where the rent was coming from. She was jealous of her mother-
in-law and her sisters-in-law. "Whenever he has a spare moment
he's with them," she said. "And they're always asking him to do
things for them, as if he had no responsibilities of his own. They
like things wholesale. Does Frances, who lives in Pelham Manor
in a beautiful home and sends her sons to Harvard, need things
wholesale?"

I remember hearing my mother say something that I felt like
a sudden weight in the chest: "He keeps the store open till nine
—all right, he may have to—but what does he do then? He
comes home at one, two in the morning. Where has he been?
What has he been doing! I'm struggling here all by myself,
trying to keep things going. . . . And when he *is* home he runs
to Mama." She had stood now, I was in the hall just outside the
doorway to the kitchen. She paced back and forth, "I'm a good
wife," she said. "I can make do with nothing. I've got a good
mind. I know what's going on in the world. I know music. I've
kept my figure. I don't think I'm all that bad a person to be
with." Her voice broke and she was crying, which brought me
forward into the doorway. My mother's back was turned to me
and she had lifted the corner of her apron and was dabbing her
eyes. Mae, seeing me, said with a wink, "Well, that's a pretty
kettle of fish."

On a Saturday my mother decided that we would go downtown and visit my father in his store. "And we'll get him to take us to the Automat for lunch," she said. She put on her blue hat, a sort of Robin Hood model, which she set on her head at an angle and checked in the mirror. "Do you think it looks smart?" she asked me. I said it did, it looked very smart. She was wearing her grey wool dress with a belt and shoes that she called pumps. She tucked her purse under her arm and we were off. We were taking the Sixth Avenue subway. Our station was at 174th Street, where it tunneled under the Concourse. We walked past my school and turned left and went along past the shoemaker, the Daitch Dairy, the bakery. Mr. Rosoff was in the window of his drugstore and waved to us and smiled. Ahead was the dark enormous arch of the Grand Concourse overpass. The Sixth Avenue line ran north and south under the Concourse, and so from the 174th Street tunnel we actually had to walk up to get to the subway platform.

At my urging we sat in the first car so I could stand at the window at the front end of the car right next to the motorman's cab. The train clattered through the black tunnel. The stanchions flashed by. The train headlamps cast light on the rails ahead that looked to me like two continuously shooting stars. Up ahead the next station came into view as a box of light. Closer and closer it came and suddenly the white tiles of the new station blazed forth, everything was bathed in brilliance, and we were grinding to a halt but still whizzing past the people waiting on the lighted platform. The engineer knew where to stop according to the number of cars in the train. In Manhattan at 125th Street, we became an express all the way down to Fifty-ninth. This was the best part of the trip, passing the lighted stations from the middle track, the lights rippling by, the train going so fast it rocked from side to side, banging against its own wheel carriages.

"Hello, young man," my father said when we walked into the store. Several customers were at the racks of sheet music, two were talking to Uncle Willy in the back. Lester waved at my mother. He was selling someone a radio. My father was unpacking a carton of ukuleles behind the counter near the front door. "We're having a run on these," he said. I sat down behind the counter to try one for myself. They were not serious instruments, I knew, because they were sold up here rather than in the back, where the horns and banjos and drums were. I asked my father where Donald was, because on Saturdays Donald worked at the store.

"He's out on a delivery," my father said.

My mother said to my father we were hoping he would take us to lunch. "That is entirely possible," he said. He was waiting for some calls. There was a man at Carnegie Hall he might have to meet. "Wait awhile and we'll see," he said. He did not like to be pinned down. He answered the phone and went to the back to check on some stock. Up and down the walls behind the counter were rows and rows of record albums, with dark green spines and gilt lettering, thick, heavy albums of operas, symphonies, which I hesitated to withdraw because I didn't want to break anything. Lester had sold a small radio. He saw the customer off and came to the cash register and counted several bills carefully; then he rang open the register and put all the bills inside. Then he removed a bill and put it in his pocket and closed the register. He found my mother looking at him and smiled. He adjusted his tie and patted his hair. Clearly he knew he was handsome. He took his hat from a hook behind the counter. "Tell Dave I had to go out. I'll be back in a while."

My mother had been reading some sheet music. "Did you see what Lester did?" she said to me. I had not known how to tune the ukulele properly, I could not peg the strings taut. Other people came into the store. My father moved around constantly, he was on the go. Every time the door opened the street noise flowed in as if cars and buses and thousands of pedestrians were about to come into the store. As suddenly as it had started, the sound stopped. I felt safe behind the counter. "I'm hungry," I said to my mother.

"We're waiting for your father," she said. This was a very familiar situation. He had said neither yes nor no.

When my mother spoke up he said, "You run ahead and get a table and I'll be there shortly."

"While we cool our heels?" my mother said. "Not this time." We sat and waited. Somehow my father needed pressure applied. He could not be counted upon except when pressured.

Finally, at a quiet moment, Uncle Willy said to my father. "For God's sake, Dave, I'm here and Lester will be back in a few minutes. Take your family to lunch."

The Automat was on Forty-second Street, a great glittering high-ceilinged hall with murals on the walls and rows and rows of tables. I dropped three nickels in a slot, I worked the little knob next to the glass door, and the sliced cheese and boloney sandwich on white bread was mine. One nickel got me a turn of the chocolate milk lever. This was quite fine. My parents had soup and bread and coffee. Strange people sat all about. Some of them peered at us: a little old woman with odd bumps on her face, wild red hair and a crocheted hat, and several men with unpressed clothes and stubble on their chins. The lady in the change-making booth rang the nickels on the marble counter. The busboys slapped the trays together. Because there were three of us, we thought we'd have a table to ourselves, but it was crowded and a man sat down at the fourth chair and ate his lunch from his tray. He wore his homburg tilted back on his head, he had on a dark shiny suit with cigarette ash rubbed into the lapels, his shirt collar was creased and dirty. All hunched over, he ate spaghetti and sucked in the strands like Charlie Chaplin, with little flooping noises.

My father seemed oblivious to all of this, but my mother stopped eating and dabbed her mouth with a napkin and pushed her chair back and sat with her purse in her lap, ready to go. She looked at the murals on the walls. She asked my father where Donald had gone on his delivery to be away so long. He said Donald had gone to Brooklyn.

"He agreed to do that?" my mother said.

My father laughed. "We gave him a choice. Did he want to go to Brooklyn or New Jersey. He chose Brooklyn." My mother's eyes narrowed. "Under the circumstances," my father said, "he thought he was getting a good deal." He looked at me: "Every-thing is relative," he said.

My father decided he wanted dessert. "How about some fresh fruit salad," he said. "No thank you," my mother said.

I went with him to the food counter. "They have red Jell-O, your favorite," he said. I didn't want to disappoint him because I knew the Jell-O was hard, it was cut in cubes; I liked it as it was made at home and I was able to spoon it up while it was still shimmery and easily liquefied between the teeth. That was the way I liked my desserts. I liked to take a Dixie Cup and stir the ice cream around until it was soup and drink it off. My mother tapped her fingers on the table. The old man had left. She had put her tray on another table. She said, "I saw Lester take money from the register."

"That couldn't be," my father said.

"But I'm telling you he did."

"If he did, he'll put it back," my father said.

"No wonder the store isn't making a dime, if one of the part-ners skims the cash register," my mother said. "I've seen con-soles disappear off the floor too. You won't listen to me. The man is a thief."

"Rose," my father said. "That's why I don't like to have you in the store. You're a suspicious person, you're always thinking the worst of people. You know nothing about business, why don't you just let me take care of it?"

"I know more about business than you do," my mother said.

She was very unhappy now. Icy, furious. Right in front of my eyes the day had turned bad. I knew it would be worse when my father got home. Then the true argument with the shouting and the name-calling would begin. I thought now I had probably realized everything would go this way before we ever set out the door. I was not surprised. In my mind I had traded a good subway ride for the desolate afternoon ahead, which now com-menced, my mother taking my hand and walking out, leaving my father smoking a cigarette at the table. In the swinging door I went around twice while she waited outside. I saw my father still sitting in the Automat. He smiled and gave a sad little wave.

FIFTEEN

The next day my mother refused to come on the visit to Grandma and Grandpa. Donald chose to exercise his right not to go to family things if he didn't want to, so I was the only one to accompany my father. I felt guilty doing this because it was far more fun than staying home with my glowering silent mother. She would listen to the New York Philharmonic broadcast and read and sew. That was hardly festive.

Eastburn Avenue was empty as it tended to be on Sundays once past the lunch hour. In the morning there was always a big softball game in the schoolyard, but when it was over, the whole neighborhood grew quiet. My friends had to go visit their relatives too, or stay upstairs to receive relatives visiting them. To journey up the broad Concourse with my father was to be somehow in the proper rhythm of the day, like everyone else. He cheered up, too, outside the house. He loved to be going somewhere. He insisted we get off the bus two stops early to get a walk in. He walked with a jaunty stride. He claimed a brisk pace was the only way to get anywhere and was, besides, less tiring than walking slowly. I struggled to keep up, half running when I fell behind. "Throw your shoulders back," he said. "Breathe in. Hold your head up. That's the way. Look the world in the eye!" I understood this as a spiritual instruction. But I couldn't have understood it as a self-urging, which I see it now to have been—in that way of the parent who expresses for the child in imperatives the prayers he makes for himself. From the same religion of health and hygiene, he insisted that I turn the water all cold at the end of my showers; I was still working on that, practicing by putting my head under the cold water first, then my shoulders, and so on. But I hadn't got much beyond a few seconds. He had shown me too how to rub myself down with a towel afterward, using it on my back the way a shoeshine man used his strip of cloth to buff the shoes. "Rub hard," he had said. "Bring the blood to the skin."

Immediately, when we arrived, my grandmother said, "So where's Rose?" Without embarrassment my father said she was not feeling well. Clearly my grandmother understood the situation. She shook her head. My benign grandfather was sitting in his chair by the radio. We held our hands out palm to palm and he said, "You have grown since the last time." Grandma bustled about setting out the tea things. My father had stopped at the Sutter bakery near Fordham Road. The babka he had bought was the centerpiece, a plump cinnamon loaf shaped like a baker's hat.

We stayed late into the afternoon, it was always this way with my father—to arrive late, and to stay late. The light faded, I grew bored. My grandfather smoked his Regent ovals and my grandmother, without my mother to contend with, was very happy, relaxed, freely prying into the finances of my family. She offered my father advice on running the store. My father adored her, calling her *"Mamaleh,"* which means little mother. Then he and my grandfather talked about the war in Spain. They agreed it was tragic that President Roosevelt was not helping the Spanish government fight the Fascists. My father grew heated. "Hitler sends dive-bombers, Mussolini sends tanks. I have to wonder, Pop. In the South there is still a poll tax. Negroes are lynched. Who is Roosevelt, anyway? What do we *think* he is?"

My grandfather was more stoic: "You cannot expect of a President that he should not be a politician," he said. "Even our revered Roosevelt."

Now it was late enough to hear *The Shadow,* on the radio. The

Shadow was Lamont Cranston, a wealthy man-about-town, who possessed the power to cloud men's minds and become invisible. By this means he fought crime. "Who knows what evil lurks in the hearts of men?" he said in his invisible voice at the beginning of every program. "The Shadow knows." And then he laughed a sniggling nasal laugh that made *him* sound evil. That had always slightly bothered me. When the Shadow went into his invisible mode, you could tell because his voice sounded as if it were coming through a telephone; this made sense because you couldn't see people in real life either when they were talking to you on the telephone. But there was something stunted about the Shadow's adventures. They were no contest. Typically, in a Shadow story, it would take Lamont Cranston a while to realize he was faced with a severe enough crisis to change into the Shadow. Sometimes it would happen that his girlfriend Margo was threatened. The criminals were always stupid and talked either with foreign accents or in rough gravelly voices with the diction of the Dead End Kids. They would have guns and shoot wildly, but to no avail. The Shadow would laugh his sniggling laugh and tell them they had missed. Actually I knew that with a tommy gun a smart crook could hold his finger down on the trigger and spin around in a 360-degree circle spraying bullets up and down and so have a fair chance of hitting the Shadow whether he was invisible or not, and no matter how far he threw his voice. His invisible blood would run. But they never thought of that.

Listening to programs, you saw them in your mind. From the sound effects you were able to imagine what things looked like and tell from the sound of its engine if a car was sleek and streamlined, or big like a taxi with lots of leg room and a running board. I thought of Margo, Lamont Cranston's friend, as looking like my mother's friend Mae but without her glasses, and without Mae's little jokes. Margo was an attractive woman, but lacking in humor. Cranston himself I thought a little slow-moving to take as long as he did to go into action; he was fairly sedentary, as compared, say, with the Green Hornet, who

could probably lick him in a fight if they went at it visibly. I
didn't think of the Shadow as being able to jump rooftops or
climb ropes or run very fast. On the other hand, why should
he have to? Also, I wondered about his restraint when he
could become invisible anytime he chose. I wondered if he
ever took advantage of women, as I surely would. Did he ever
watch Margo Lane go to the bathroom? I knew that if I had the
power to be invisible I would go into the girls' bathroom at
P.S. 70 and watch them pulling their drawers down. I would
watch women take their clothes off in their homes and they
wouldn't even know I was there. I wouldn't make the mistake
of speaking up or making a sound, they would never even
know I had been there. But I would forever after know what
they looked like. The thought of having this power made my
ears hot. Yes, I would spy on naked girls but I would also do
good. I would invisibly board a ship, or, better still, a China
Clipper and I would fly to Germany and find out where Adolf
Hitler lived. I would in absolute safety, with no chance of
being caught, go to Hitler's palace, or whatever it was, and kill
him. Then I would kill all of his generals and ministers. The
Germans would be going crazy trying to find the invisible
avenger. I would whisper in their ears to be good and kind,
and they would thereafter be thinking God had been speaking.
The Shadow had no imagination. He neither looked at naked
women nor thought of ridding the world of dictators like Hitler or Mussolini. If his program hadn't been on a Sunday afternoon, I would probably not have listened to it.

Hitler was on my mind a lot lately. I had heard his voice on
a radio broadcast, he shouted in German, which I heard as a
language full of spitting and gulping and galumphing, almost as
if the words were broken in the teeth; it sounded as if he were
shattering glass in his mouth, as if he breathed fire and made the
air explode in front of his face. He would say something and
you'd hear his fist pounding the speaker's platform and then a
great roar go up from the crowd, like some shrieking wind, and
then it would begin to pulsate and radio static would crack

through it, and the announcer, speaking calmly in English, would describe what was going on at this rally, the way everyone's right arm extended straight in the air as the crowd chanted and did this salute taken from ancient Rome, arms shooting up and big red-and-black Nazi flags with swastikas fluttering everywhere.

I tried that salute in front of the mirror in my room, throwing my arm forward with the elbow stiff, and trying at the same time to click my heels. Donald marched around my room holding a small black comb under his nose like Hitler's moustache and chanting German gibberish. He brushed his hair down over his forehead. It was funny. It was easy to imitate Hitler. Actually, when I had first seen his picture in a magazine I had confused him with Charlie Chaplin. Everyone seemed to notice the resemblance, they both wore these little black moustaches, and had black hair and heavy eyebrows. Charlie Chaplin himself had noticed the resemblance and Donald told me Charlie was making a movie about Hitler that was going to be really great because Charlie hated Hitler. I resolved to see that movie when it came out.

I found it disturbing, however, that they resembled each other. I loved Charlie Chaplin. We had the same taste in women, like the blind flower girl, whom we both found very beautiful and kind. He had helped her, as I would have. He was a wonderful little guy, he never got as mad at other people as they did at him, even when they were fighting, although he was often hurt by them. He just picked himself up and swung and ran. In *Modern Times* big voices telling him what to do came from speakers in this shining modern factory, but he himself, Charlie, never spoke, no matter how bad things got, he never made a sound: like the time he went after the loose nut on the assembly line and got picked up by the moving machinery and was sent winding through the gears. When he had his lunch a machine wiped his mouth for him. It seemed to me an unfortunate coincidence that he and Hitler looked alike. My father had a moustache too, they all three had moustaches. I dreamed one night my father sat with Charlie on one knee and Hitler on the other; he held on to them by the backs of their necks as if they were ventriloquist dummies, and made their mouths clack open and shut and held out each of them to me in turn, one with his floppy little legs dangling in baggy trousers and a cutaway coat, the other in a brown Army uniform with leather boots. And then my father laughed.

DONALD

Sure, I remember when we moved to Eastburn Avenue. I pushed you there in your carriage. It was great moving to a larger place. I had my own room. I was eight, a big fellow. The responsible older brother.

It's only natural that we remember things differently. I had Mom and Dad to myself for all those years before you joined us. We were prosperous. Before he got into the retail end of things Dad was in the sound box business. In those days record players, Victrolas, had spring motors, you cranked them up like you cranked cars, and the critical element was the sound box at the end of the tone arm. It was a metal cylinder, about an inch wide, three inches in diameter, with a convex grille face, and inside was a diaphragm that vibrated. You stuck a steel needle into a socket on the rim, and tightened it with a fixed screw, and put the needle on the record and that was how you got sound. Dad ran the business from an office in the Flatiron Building.

The day Lindbergh was welcomed up Fifth Avenue we saw it from the office window. I was very young, maybe four, and I stood on the windowsill and saw Lindbergh in an open car, all the confetti falling, the crowd going wild. I was so excited I leaned too far out and almost lost my balance. Dad had to pull me back in.

You say he didn't use force. Maybe he'd mellowed a bit by the time you came along. With me he was very strict and didn't hesitate to haul off when he felt it was necessary. My first day of school I refused to go. No amount of cajoling, imploring or bribing by Mom could budge me. Dad lost his temper. He picked me up and carried me to school under his arm. I'll never forget it. He carried me right up the steps and down the hall, and opened the door to my classroom and dumped me on the floor, in front of everyone.

There was another time, in Rockaway. You and I were staying with Grandma and Grandpa. They had a bungalow for the summer. The folks shipped us out there to get us out of the heat, but they didn't come themselves, Dad had to work and Mom couldn't leave her mother. So you and I were on our own with the old people. We ran around all day on the beach and played in the penny arcades, and in that time I don't think either of us bathed. So on the second weekend the folks came out to see us. Mom will tell you the story. She saw these two children walking toward her in the street, I was holding your hand, and your pants drooped and my socks were around my ankles, and our faces were dirty, she thought at first we were a pair of street urchins, she didn't realize she was looking at her own sons. She was furious that Grandma, with her vaunted cleanliness, had let things get so out of hand. There was a big argument. Dad asked me to go into the bathroom and have a shower. I refused. He was mad, everyone was mad, he picked me up just as he had my first day in school, and turned on the shower and threw me in, clothes and all.

He was a terrific athlete. He spent a lot of time with me, teaching me to play tennis, or to skate or swim. He urged me to excel. Always I was made to know what his expectations were for me. I think this explains somewhat why we had a difficult time with each other in later years. After you came along it was made clear to me that I was to help with your upbringing, and put in time with you as he had with me. And so I did. A lot of the things I taught you he had taught me. One passed things on. One worked for the family. You know that picture of Dad and me walking together stride for stride on Sixth Avenue on some business matter—where is that picture, do you have it?—I was all of thirteen at the time. I started working for him very young. Take a look at that picture when you have the chance. I have on a suit and tie just like his, but I'm wearing knickers. It's a tinted photograph, our faces are washed in this rosy color, Dad has a cigar in his mouth, he has a packet of business papers under his arm, his shoulders are back, he looks happy, we both look happy, healthy, energetic, full of beans, and the street photographer picked up on this father and son, and snapped the picture and sold it to us.

Dad liked to patronize street people. You would be walking along with him and he'd suddenly veer over to a pushcart, or stop to buy a pamphlet from someone. He did that as a matter of principle. He idealized the little man. He had a political consciousness. He rode the train to Boston for a rally for Sacco and Vanzetti. He wanted to take me but Mom wouldn't let him. The case obsessed him. He brought home Upton Sinclair's novel about it—*Boston*—it was in two volumes. He was very much a man of his time. He devoured the papers. Maybe everyone was more radical in those days. Nowadays when people protest something, they're looked on as oddities. But, for instance, Dad was talking about Hitler very early. He was onto him. That doesn't sound so unusual now, but you'd be surprised how little was known about Hitler, it took the establishment in America a long time to understand what was going on. Dad was an antifascist. He was a leftist, like our grandpa, but more of a fighter. In the big strikes—steel, coal, automobile—he was on the side of the unions. He didn't believe in minding his own business, his brain was always working. You could be sure he'd come up with another slant on things. Like when King Edward of England abdicated the throne to marry his girlfriend Wally Simpson. Well, Mom loved that story. You know, a king giving up his throne for love. It was in all the papers and magazines, the King's abdication speech was on the radio, carried shortwave from London. Everyone loved that story. But not Dad. He got angry because Mom took it so seriously. "Don't you realize," he said, "the idea of a king in the twentieth century is ridiculous?

The English king is a fossil. Like all of them in Europe now, a bunch of useless dimwits who strut around and indulge themselves at public expense. This romantic king of yours lives on the tax revenues taken from working people. I can see why the upper classes of England would find him useful, but why the American press treats this as serious news, and you fall for it, is another matter." Mom was quite miffed. "Don't you ever relax about anything?" she asked him. "I'm not the intellectual you are—all right?" They disagreed about politics as about most things.

I don't know much about Dad's life as a boy. I know he was born on the Lower East Side. Grandma and Grandpa were both from the Minsk district, they emigrated in the 1880's, I know that. They were young and married here. But where they lived, where Dad went to school, you would have to ask Aunt Frances, she would know. Dad was almost thirty when he got married. He'd already missed out on a couple of major opportunities. One was when he was training to be an ensign in the First World War. He was stationed at Webb's Naval Institute on the Harlem River. He loved the water, he used to tell me how he swam in the East River as a kid. He loved ships. He was desperate to go to sea, but the war ended before he got his commission. So that had to be a great disappointment. And then you know the story about *The Perils of Pauline.* He was a handsome fellow, and they were casting for this series, and came into the bank where he worked as a teller. I don't know, he must have been twenty-one, twenty-two at the time. And this man came into the bank who was directing the movie, I don't remember his name, but as I heard it he had a beret and a pince-nez and wore riding boots. And he looked at Dad and asked him to take a screen test. He wanted him for the male lead. Dad refused. I don't know why. Maybe he thought he had a surer thing in banking. Who knows, he might have become a big actor in the silents or he might not. But the point is, it was unlike him to back away from a challenge. He liked to gamble, take risks, he liked what was new and different. No one had a record store to match Hippodrome Music. Dad stocked black singers from down South, race records, as they were called, blues bands, ethnic music, jazz, he was really informed and it didn't matter to him that some of these things were commercially risky. One day I came back from a delivery and he motioned to me and took me into the booth and put on a record. "Listen to this," he said. "It's something new." And it was, a wonderful bouncy music, with a great clarinet solo that made you want to dance. It was Benny Goodman's first record. "Isn't that fine?" Dad said. "It's called swing."

SIXTEEN

Donald now had materials from his Townsend Harris High School courses that were beyond my understanding: slide rules, calipers, T squares. He brought home mechanical drawings that he had done and gotten good marks for, little 95's and 90's in red ink at the top corner of each drawing. They were like blueprints and showed cylinders and cones, and machine parts in three dimensions, each line measured by another that indicated its length. He explained the concept of scale to me. He knew all this and was confident with it. He had special fountain pens for drawing. All I had was one fountain pen, which I was not even supposed to use in school. But I liked to open my bottle of Waterman's blue-black ink and fill my pen by opening the little spring clip on the side and closing it slowly. You could hear the ink being sucked up. There was a thin rubber tube inside the pen that was attached to the point—that's what filled up. I borrowed his sticks of charcoal to draw with. He was generous. But if I was careless with something of his, misplacing it, or damaging it, he acted as if I had committed a great crime. Sometimes it wasn't worth the care I had to take when I borrowed something, so I didn't.

I had to acknowledge the fact that my brother was changing. He spent less time with me. High school took up a lot of his time, and then on Saturday he had his job with my father. I was left more and more on my own.

There was a candy store near Rosoff's on 174th Street—not the one I frequented, but one where the older boys gathered to horse around and talk about girls. Sometimes girls gathered there too. My brother and his friends Harold and Bernie and Irwin attached themselves to this society, sometimes stopping there in the afternoons after they got off the train. Gambling went on, boys pitching pennies against the wall or matching nickels. Inside they sold policy, a word familiar to me, though I didn't know what it meant. My brother did not talk about these things. When my mother found out why he was coming home late from school, she was alarmed. She had strong opinions about Donald's friends and never failed to deliver them. "So now they've turned into sidewalk cowboys," she said. "I don't wonder. You hang around that store and you'll end up with them in the criminal class," she said.

Donald was hurt by her remarks but did not change his ways. His green eyes showed defiance. I didn't stop to think, nor did my mother, what an estimable life Donald was leading—he was doing well in school, knocking out good grades, he worked all day Saturday, and he was studying music. Yet from my mother's vivid testimony I imagined him going to jail. I circumspectly went to see the infamous store one afternoon, being careful to do my surveillance from across the street, from the vantage point of the Morton bakery.

I saw my brother and his friends in a crowd of older boys and girls. The crowd moved about constantly. They leaned against the newsstand in front of the candy store, or sat on the fender of a car parked nearby. One boy grabbed a girl from behind and wrestled with her and put his arms around her and she screamed and laughed too. Two boys were having a boxing match but without really hitting each other. I saw Donald talking to a blond girl while ostentatiously smoking a cigarette. At that moment, for some reason, his eye caught sight of me, just a flickering glance. But even across the street I knew from the look I got that I was never to tell on him or my life would be over.

So all of this made me thoughtful. I could see my brother changing, but in no way detected any difference in myself. I didn't look taller in the mirror, I didn't feel older or anything like that. Meanwhile a thin moustache appeared above Donald's upper lip. His voice became deeper. He was moody, and his passion for music increased. He began to collect records in lieu of wages from my father. He practiced the piano now every day and without being asked. He was a better pianist, there were not those agonizing delays I remembered from the old days when in the middle of a piece all life would stop while we waited for Donald to find the keys for the next chord. When he was through practicing his lesson, he took out his music copybook in which he'd written out swing tunes borrowed from my father's stock of sheet music, and he played those. Uncle Willy had moved out of our house after Grandma died; he had taken a small apartment on the West Side of Manhattan not far from Hippodrome Music. So Donald moved back into his old room and hung Uncle Willy's banner on the wall, the purple and gold of BILLY WYNNE AND HIS ORCHESTRA taking on some suggestion of defiance or irrepressible intent, as if Donald were saying to the world that it had better get ready for him.

One New Year's Eve my parents arranged to go out and there was a big family fight because Donald no longer wanted to stay with me as he had on past New Year's Eves. He wanted to go to a party with his friends. My father wore his tuxedo this particular night, and my mother a long pale blue dress with lacy sleeves. Their eyes were alight with excitement and I felt gloomy and neglected watching them prepare themselves. My father tied a black satiny cummerbund around his waist. He let my mother carry on the argument with Donald. I enjoyed the special buttons for his shirt front and cuffs, which he showed me how to operate. But this was not compensation enough for their leaving, and putting me in the charge of my resentful brother with a moustache. "All right," Donald shouted as they were heading for the door, "but I warn you, this is it. I swear I will never, never stay home again on New Year's Eve." My mother in her long pale blue dress and her hair newly marcelled, her lips painted red, a little beaded bag in her hands, soothed Donald and with uncharacteristic gentleness agreed that this would be the last New Year's he would be called upon to take care of his little brother.

Although I would have enjoyed a game of war, or battleship, I diplomatically chose to stay in my room and play by myself. I did leave my door open to hear what I could hear. Donald was on the phone in the front hall a good deal of the time. Then he turned on the console radio in the living room to listen to the dance music being broadcast from some hotel downtown. I secretly wanted to stay up to see in the New Year but knew better than to ask. Instead I got into my pajamas and pretended to go to bed. I had my own windup clock. It had a radium dial. I could see it in the dark. At midnight I tiptoed down the hall to the living room and I found Donald asleep on the sofa in front of the radio, which was still playing. The broadcast was from Times Square. Crowds cheered, horns blew, and the announcer interviewed people who shouted their greetings into the microphone. It was 1937. I looked out the window. Eastburn Avenue was dark. I hoped my parents would be home soon. Happy New Year, I said to myself, and went back to bed.

As winter moved into spring I began to hear from the front parlor, in the late afternoons, not only Donald's swing piano but the honks and squeaks of Seymour Roth's saxophone, and the earsplitting blasts of Harold Epstein's trumpet. There was also a snare drummer, Irwin. In the kitchen my mother said, "If those boys had conspired to drive me crazy, they couldn't be doing a better job of it." The band met not only after school but on Sunday afternoons. My mother wanted to know why Harold's mother or Seymour's couldn't sacrifice themselves and their households for at least one day a week. Donald said, "We're the only ones who have a piano," and that was that. At night he listened to *Make Believe Ballroom* on the radio, where the announcer, Martin Block, played his records while pretending to be broadcasting from an actual bandstand. Of course, it was not an illusion too emphatically insisted upon. It was not, for example, as scrupulous in its representations as the broadcast baseball games in which the announcer in the studio, using sound effects of the bat cracking and the crowd roaring, pretended to be at the ballpark. Martin Block kept lists of the most popular songs of the week, and Donald wrote down the titles and made a note to get them copied.

Finally I learned what was going on. Donald and Seymour, the saxophone player, had put their first names together and invented a fictitious bandleader, Don Seymour. Don Seymour's band was known as the Musical Cavaliers, and they were preparing to audition for a summer job at a resort hotel in the Catskills, the Paramount. They had not yet decided which of them would pose as Don Seymour if they ever reached the lofty heights of the Paramount Hotel bandstand. They were too busy rehearsing. As day after day I heard them go through their repertoire I learned every song by heart. "Deep Purple" was one: "In the still of the night, once again I hold you tight, Tho' you're gone your love lives on when moonlight beams, And as long as my heart will beat, Lover we'll always meet, here in my Deep Purple Dreams." They played that well, I think, because it was slow. They were better with slow songs. "I Must See Annie Tonight" was one of their rare fast ones, and sometimes they created a double-time effect with it because Irwin's downbeat on the drums was often dissynchronous with Donald's on the piano. It was not uninteresting. And then that peculiar "Stairway to the Stars": "Let's build a Stairway to the Stars, and climb that Stairway to the Stars, with love beside us to fill the night with a song." That part of it was all right, although it was not a terribly appealing idea as I thought about it—a long climb, in fact, in cold black space. But then it went: "Can't we sail away on a little dream and settle high on the crest of a thrill, Let's build a Stairway to the Stars. . . ." and at that point I was always made nervous, just as I was when I read *Alice in Wonderland*, because sailing is what you

143

do on water, not on stair treads, and the crest of a thrill made me think of some sort of jungle bird, the Crested Thrill, so they would all be sailing up these stairs and ending up perched on the head of a bird. But it was "Japanese Sandman" that gave me the worst time, the idea of a sandman who could put you to sleep as he chose had always bothered me, that casting of grains that made your eyelids heavy and robbed you of volition was a magic I didn't like to contemplate. Added to that, the fact that the Sandman was Japanese was especially worrisome. On my bubble gum cards very toothy leering Japanese soldiers in green uniforms were machine-gunning Manchurian civilians. They were leaping over trenches with bayonets affixed to raised rifles. They cast not magic sleep grains but pure red and orange flame from the mouths of flamethrowers.

With the inclusion of a string bass and another saxophone player, Frankie, the band had grown to six pieces. On a Sunday afternoon, instead of going with my father and mother to see my grandparents, I was permitted to stay home and hear the Cavaliers rehearse. In a moment of inspiration I ran back to my room and took one of my pick-up sticks and came back and led the band with it. I stood in front of the Cavaliers and conducted. Maybe I could be Don Seymour. The light coming through the parlor windows turned the leaves of the potted snake plants a brilliant green. Donald thumped away happily at the upright, his back to the rest of the band. Next to him was Sid the string bass man, playing with eyes closed in transports of head-shaking self-approval; Sid liked to hum one octave higher than the bass notes, like Slam Stewart, a famous jazz bassist, who was his hero. Next to Sid was Irwin the drummer, now endowed with a snare, a tom-tom, cowbells, and a bass drum resting on its side, which he played with an attached pedal that catapulted a big bulbous hammer up against the drum skin. And sitting side by side in the front row of the band, just like the men of Paul Whiteman's orchestra, were the two saxophonists, Seymour and Frankie, and the trumpet player, Harold. First they played "I Have Eyes to See With," then a rousing rendition of "Bei Mir Bist Du Schoen," which Donald thought was their best number. Standing in front of the band, I waved my baton and tapped my foot. It didn't seem to bother anyone. But then I saw that the new saxophone player, Frankie, seemed not to be exerting himself. There was some hesitancy about him. I watched him closely without being obvious about it. When the moment came in the sheet music to go on to the next page, Seymour and Harold leaned forward simultaneously and turned the pages sitting on their music stands, but Frankie waited a split second before he did the same thing. Then I saw that his fingers did not depress keys on his saxophone, they only touched them. And that most of the time they weren't the same keys Seymour was pressing on *his* saxophone. Frankie was a tall, long-faced boy with sad, deep-set eyes and the shadow of a dark beard on his face. He did not live in the neighborhood. He glanced nervously at me over his saxophone. Clearly I was a danger to him. The others were making their music, and loudly. The Cavaliers were not always exactly on key but had a lot of enthusiasm. I felt the same excitement as when a parade band passed close to me on Memorial Day along the Grand Concourse, that same vault of the heart in the blare of performed music. But I knew the band members were intensely occupied with keeping up with Irwin, the drummer, who tended to go faster and faster with each passing bar, and that none of them was secure enough as a musician to really hear the others. None of them, not even Donald, knew that Frankie was making no sound.

When the number ended, Donald said, "Let's go through it one more time, and try to make the opening attack crisper and to build a little higher for the ending." As the bandleader, he had that responsibility of critique. I asked to see him, pulling at his arm as he stood in front of them. He shrugged me off and kept talking. I persisted. Finally he said, "What is it, pest!" I pulled him into the living room and closed the parlor doors.

"Donald," I said, pulling again on his arm as he looked at me with that frowning wary expression of his. A shock of hair habitually fell over his forehead, his light green eyes were the eyes of an adult, his face had not a bit of fat on it, he was a lean, not very tall, wiry big brother, a good athlete, a brain at high school, a fellow with many plans and responsibilities at age fifteen and a half. But he had hired a musician who couldn't play. He bent over and I whispered in his ear: "Frankie is faking."

He looked at me incredulously and I nodded affirmation of what I had said. "You stay here," he said and went back into the parlor and closed the door after him. I heard them go into "Bei Mir Bist Du Schoen" again, but after a bar or two they stopped. Then I heard my brother's voice. He sounded angry. Soon they were all talking. An argument began. "Shit," I heard Irwin say, and then it was quiet and I smelled cigarette smoke. A few minutes later the parlor door opened, and Frankie came out carrying his saxophone case. His shoulders hunched and he didn't look at me as he passed into the hall and went out the front door.

Nobody felt that I had been, in essence, a tattletale. The hapless Frankie was, first of all, much older than I and therefore not in the same moral universe. In the second place, he was an impostor, a fraud, who stood to gain from his imposture at the expense of the other members of the band. What would it have done to the credibility of their audition had the booker for the Paramount Hotel noticed that one of them couldn't even play? My brother was delighted with me. Everyone was. The story was told within the family and around the neighborhood how the little kid brother had turned out to be more perceptive than the musicians themselves. I was a hero. For once I had proven useful to my older brother, I had done something for him. I could make a fair claim now to be taken seriously. There was also a new awareness in me that size wasn't everything, that wit was a strength in the world, the exercise of one's brain.

Nevertheless a shadow lay on my mind. My mother now wondered why a boy—meaning Frankie—would be so desperate as to pretend to be able to play the saxophone. Did he so badly need a job? Where did this Frankie come from? she wanted to know of my brother. Where did he live? What did his father do? These questions and my doubts were overwhelmed, fortunately, by the news of a successful audition just a few days later: Don Seymour and the Musical Cavaliers had been hired for the following summer. Five dollars a week per man, plus room and board. For this they would also have to do lake duty as lifeguards, in the afternoons.

SEVENTEEN

Happy with my brother's accomplishment I was slow to think of the result—that he would be gone for the whole summer. I would be alone with my parents. Things were changing, and, as usual, in the spring, a season I was beginning to appreciate as the mysterious menacing time of the cycle, I became uneasy. Almost in confirmation of my feeling, we were told that we had to move. Our landlords, the Segals, who lived above us, had sold the house. The people who had bought it, German refugees named Loewenthal, wanted the ground floor for themselves. The Segals had been genial friendly landlords, generous with the heat in winter. The new owners were a dour couple, not gracious at all. My father said they lacked style. There were arguments about painting the upstairs apartment and replacing the antiquated refrigerator with the gas cylinder mounted on top of it, and, after we moved upstairs, about the piano playing and even the noise we made walking across the floor. I didn't like their daughter either, a small, skinny dark-haired child, a spy and a snitch who whispered in her girlfriend's ear as I walked by. On a particularly raw day when my mother asked Smith to put some more coal in the furnace, Mrs. Loewenthal stopped him and told my mother to wear a sweater if she was cold.

My mother declared to me that German Jews, even newly

arrived ones, were arrogant and heartless. We were descendants of Eastern Europeans, a more natural, more humane people, who knew what suffering was. "They thought they were Germans," she told me, "and look what's happening to them now. With their snobbish highfalutin ways. You'd think, barely getting out with their skins, they would change."

But the apartment upstairs was clean and light. I looked down at the backyard now from a safe distance, I was above the clothesline strung across to the back fence, and the sheets on washdays flew in my mind like pennants below the king's tower. From the corner of the window of my room in the back I could see over our side yard and through a tantalizing window of an alley to a rhomboid of green grass in Claremont Park. The whole apartment did seem smaller. Because of the front stairs there was one less room. On the other hand, with Grandma gone and Uncle Willy moved to Manhattan, the family had shrunk. In some way the new light in these rooms illuminated for me the degree of our family's struggle. The Sohmer upright had to be hauled upstairs by piano movers with block and tackle hanging from the roof; the piano came in through the living room window. That was exciting, but I saw now the chips in the lacquered mahogany I hadn't seen before. My parents' bedroom furniture with its romantic olive color and frieze of rosebuds looked old and scratched.

At P.S. 70 we were now deemed of an age to be sent once a week to the below-ground swimming pool, a vast chlorinated cavern of tile, where first the boys and then the girls were set to swimming if we could, or taking instruction in waving our arms and holding our breath. The boys' teacher was old Mr. Bone, the Poseidon of the place. He didn't speak, he roared. His deep voice bounded over the water in echoes of itself. He was the school's swimming coach and lord of this underworld, a fat bald

man with steel-rim spectacles who wore a white cotton undershirt stretched taut over his enormous belly, and white ducks
and rubber sandals. He also had a gimpy leg. But that he was
fit we all understood by the size of his arms, rounder and thicker,
even, than my father's. And that he was dedicated, there was no
question—he spent his sunless life down here, whereas we had
to endure the pool and showers only once a week.

The girls were instructed by his associate, Mrs. Fasching, as
skinny as he was fat, with red hair curling from under her bathing cap, and in a black-skirted swimsuit, which successfully hid
her person except for the freckled legs and arms. It was common
knowledge that the girls wore bathing suits to swim, while we
did not. Even during their showers they wore suits, which
seemed unjust. How could you take a real shower while wearing
a bathing suit? Brown soap was available at each position, big
hard cakes of it, and if we were not seen by Mr. Bone to be
adequately scrubbing ourselves, he would warn, in that voice
like a whale's call, that we had better get to it properly or he
would come into the shower and show us how.

That weekly visit to the realm of water tested my courage. I
was not ready to swim and didn't care to shower in public. There
was no air to breathe down there, only a fetid mist that seemed
to turn to oil on your skin. It did no good to tell Mr. Bone you
had had a bath the night before, or that you bathed at home
twice a week: under the shower you went. And it's true, for some
children the P.S. 70 shower was the only water they saw from
one week to the next. It was because of those same children we
had to endure health checks in the nurse's office, where our
scalps were examined for lice and ringworm. The nurse also
turned up the children who were discovered to need eyeglasses.
It was my mother I always went to for explanation of the com-
plexities of money and class. "Some children are from families
too poor to have their own doctors," she said. "They don't come
from good homes and school showers are the only water they
see. They are the same children who need to stay in school for
lunch because there is no lunch waiting for them at home."

On the other hand, she told me, some of my teachers were getting quite rich. "They've kept their jobs in the middle of the Depression," she said. "They have done quite well on their salaries. Prices have gone down and they can afford things no one else can who hasn't that security. Some of them are buying cars and houses. They've become landlords."

I appreciated this information but found it of no use in dealing with my fear of swimming underground. There was one exercise in which we boys were sent into the pool to hang with our hands on the pool's tiled rim while we let our bodies drift backward and then kicked our feet. Since that didn't involve putting my face underwater I could handle it all right. But we were a string of fifteen or so boys along the edge at intervals of three or four yards, and some of us were inevitably in water that we couldn't stand up in. My friend Arnold was next to me and he lost his grip and went under. I looked for Mr. Bone, but he was down at the end of the line yelling at someone. Arnold came up gasping and went under again and was flailing, so that he was putting himself farther and farther from the edge. He was getting out of reach. His arm came up. Letting go the edge with one hand, I grabbed his arm and pulled him toward me and put his hand on the tile. Arnold came up red and sputtering and spitting water. His eyes were red. We looked at each other, too terrified to acknowledge the seriousness of what had happened. You came up, you went down, you took in water like air, and in a few quiet moments you could die.

The schoolyard, also, was a realm of mythic dimensions. It was the site of games and ceremonies of enormous meaning. It was an immense yard fenced in chain link. The Eastburn Avenue end was level with the street, but since 173rd Street went uphill, the Weeks Avenue end was a couple of stories below street level. On

Sunday mornings I watched grown-up softball games with such towering Ruthian hitters as could power the ball from home plate, at the Eastburn Avenue end of the yard, over the fence atop the concrete wall two stories high a block away. I rarely played in the yard after school, it was too vast, an enormous concrete plain with that high fencing around it and beyond the fence the attached apartment houses looking down through their windows. I always thought of windows as eyes, I always saw animate intelligence in them; I saw cars that way too, cars had faces when you saw them from the front, they had eyes and noses and mouths with teeth.

On a school day a Chevrolet coupe ran up the sidewalk on Weeks Avenue and knocked a woman through the chain link fence atop the high wall. With her bag of groceries she fell the two stories to the schoolyard below. She had been carrying bottles of milk. They had broken and the milk spread in pools about her body. Then her blood seeped into the milk. The front half of the car stood pushed through the fence, its wheels hanging over space and spinning. One of the children happened to be at the window of our classroom. She cried out. Everyone, including the teacher, ran to the window. I saw the thing in that moment of peace and stillness when the disaster has occurred but not yet resounded.

Then all at once the street was in a commotion. I heard a scream. Cars screeched to a halt. My teacher ran out the door to the principal's office. As we watched, the mixture of milk and blood spread over the concrete. In moments people were running from every direction, as if the street had never been empty and the event had occurred in front of an audience. Our teacher had called the police, but others had too. Two green-and-white police cars arrived. Police attended to the driver. Then one of the cars raced down 173rd Street to the Eastburn entrance of the yard. The police drove right into the yard. An ambulance from Morrisania Hospital came. This was our morning's class. The ambulance could not get into the schoolyard, and so the two attendants in white came on the run. They examined the

152

woman. she was quite still. They put her body on a stretcher and put a blanket over it. It lay there while police and doctors consulted. Then the attendants carried the body to the ambulance. I watched the woman's arm, which had slipped off the edge of the stretcher: it bobbed in rhythm with the unhurried pace of her stretcher bearers.

All of us jostled about the windows and looked. I felt the vibrancy of the heated bodies around me.

I would have been glad then to go back to work, but my teacher was too upset. She let us out a few minutes early for lunch. Everyone was talking about the accident. I went home the regular way but saw up on Weeks Avenue a crowd of children standing looking at the Chevrolet coupe, which had still not been extricated from the fence. The police were keeping them back. The schoolyard itself was closed off in case the car fell into it. When I arrived home my mother was on the phone; she had heard the news. She was quite shaken when she came into the kitchen, where I sat over my tomato soup and peanut butter sandwich. She knew the family. The dead woman was the grown daughter of a member of the Sisterhood of the synagogue. My mother sat down across from me. "Right there in the schoolyard where children play," she said. She was pale. She ran her fingers through her hair. "What a terrible thing. How awful. That poor woman."

Yet from my vantage point high over the schoolyard, in the sunlit classroom windows, I had felt not fear but enlightenment. Air was like water. You could fall into it. From this height the spectacle of the event was magnified, the whole field of circumstance could be seen. The human figures were small.

At night, before sleep, I remembered the arm of the dead woman bobbing up and down as she was carried in the stretcher, the hand limp, palm up, as if the dead arm were pointing to the schoolyard, indicating it repeatedly—so that I should not forget —as a place of death. For weeks afterward the stain of her blood was visible on the schoolyard ground, a darkening of meaningless shape on the sun-bleached cement.

I found it very pleasurable to rub color comics onto waxed paper. You laid the waxed paper over the comic and rubbed back and forth with the edge of a ruler or a wooden tongue depressor. The color would attach to the waxed paper like a decal. It was never as vivid as the original but was all there, quite legible, the characters and the words they spoke. I had resumed another practice, soap carving, which I had learned from my brother. This required my mother's cooperation because soap cost money. But if you could cadge a bar of white soap, you could work at it, shave away at it with a kitchen knife or a pocketknife, and carve animals or human figures. I made a man in a bowler hat. The shavings could be wet and molded into a kind of vestigial soap bar.

A peach pit could be hollowed out: if you did it right, and left the seed inside intact, you could make a real whistle. But it took a while. If you started in the summer you'd be finished in a year, because it was dreary work.

Donald was busy all the time, but I could still get him to help me build a model airplane, because it was really exacting work. He couldn't resist. You taped the diagram to a table and then built the wings or fuselage, pinning the struts of balsa to the paper. You cut them to size with a single-edged razor blade, and then attached one strut to another with a drop of clear airplane dope. Predrawn templates of flat balsa automatically provided the curves. If I made a mistake and ruined a piece, Donald could make a template copy out of a blank piece of balsa scrap. When I had all the parts constructed—wings, fuselage, rudders and elevator—he took over the assembly and then the covering of thin colored paper.

I had my eye on one model advertised in a hobby company catalogue: it wasn't just a plane, it was an airship. To me airships, or zeppelins, were the most amazing things in the sky. You saw them occasionally from a distance. They were so big they could be seen even on the horizon. They floated gently, like clouds. They moved so slowly they were visible for a long time, as airplanes were not. One evening on the radio, the newscaster said that the largest airship ever built, the *Hindenburg,* was sailing from Germany to New York. Its route would bring it to the eastern seaboard over Long Island. It would head due west to a landing tower in New Jersey, which meant it would be visible over the city sometime in the afternoon. I might then be through with school. Yet I didn't dream I would see it, it did not occur to me that something on the news would be something I would witness. I didn't think of the Bronx as a place where anything happened. The Bronx was a big place with miles of streets and six-story apartment houses attached one to another, up hills and down hills it went, every neighborhood had its school like my school, its movie, its street of shops built into the sides of the apartment houses; it was tunneled with subways and bound together with trolley lines, and elevated lines; but for all of that, and for all of us who lived here, myself included, it was not important. It was not famous. It was not central to the world. I thought the *Hindenburg* would more naturally fly over Manhattan, which was central to the world. I talked on the phone to my friend Arnold, who lived in the apartment house across the street. Would his mother let us go on the roof after school? I thought from Arnold's roof, six stories high, it might be possible to catch a glimpse of the *Hindenburg* way downtown, over Manhattan the next day, if it was flying at a high enough altitude.

But Arnold's mother said no one was allowed on the roof, so I gave up thinking about it. When I woke up the next morning I had all but forgotten about the *Hindenburg.* I went to school. It was a warm clear day. I walked home after school with my friend Meg. Then I played stoopball. I flipped bubble gum cards. The leaves were pale green on the hedges. Harry, the fruit and vegetable man, pulled up along the curb with his wagon. He called out to the windows. He tethered the reins to the big brake on the side of the wagon. Harry had a wrench for opening fire hydrants. He opened the fire hydrant in the middle of our block

and filled a pail with water and put the pail on the street in front
of his horse. The horse drank. The wooden poles that connected
him to the wagon dipped toward the ground. For good measure
a leather harness was chained from its braces to the front of the
wagon. The leather went around the horse's hocks and up over
its back. The harness itself looked enormously heavy, like a big
leather tire around its neck. The wagon had spoked wheels
rimmed in steel. Leaf springs sprouted from the axles. All the
fruits and greens were wet. Harry had sprayed them with a hose
to make them clean and shining. I could smell the wet greens.
He twisted off the green stalks of a bunch of carrots for a lady
and fed the greens to his horse.

I went to the small park, the Oval, in the middle of Mt. Eden
Avenue. Here, as it happened, one had a clear view of a good
deal of sky. I don't remember doing much of anything. Perhaps
I bought a Bungalow Bar. Perhaps I was looking for Meg, who
sometimes came to the Oval with her mother. Over the roofs of
the private houses that bordered the north side of Mt. Eden
Avenue, across the street from the park, the nose of the great
silver *Hindenburg* appeared. My mouth dropped open. She sailed
incredibly over the housetops, and came right toward me, just
a few hundred feet in the air, and kept coming and kept coming
and still no sight of the tail of her. She was tilted toward me as
if she were an enormous animal leaping from the sky in monumental slow motion. Some sort of line lagged under her, like a
halyard, under the cupola. Then, as I blinked she was visible in
her entirety, tacking off some degrees to the east, and I saw her
in all her silver-skinned length; the ribbed planes of her cylindrical balloon, thick in the middle, narrowed at each end, reflected
the sunlight, flaring sunlight in striations, as if a deck of cards
were being shuffled. I heard her now, the propellers alongside
her cupola whirring like fans in the sky. She did not make the
harsh raspy snarl of an airplane, but seemed to whisper. She was
indeed a ship, a real ship in the sky, she moved like an airship.
The enormity of her was out of scale with everything, out of
scale with the houses and the cars on the street and the people
now shouting and pointing and looking up; she was like a scoop

of sky come down to earth, or a floating building, or a populated cloud. I could see little people in the cabin, they were looking out the window and I waved at them. The *Hindenburg* was headed over Claremont Park now, toward Morris Avenue. I was not supposed to go there alone. I looked both ways and ran across the street, and up the stone steps into the park. Cars had stopped in the street and drivers had gotten out to see. Everyone was looking at her. I ran through the park following the *Hindenburg,* she was going so slowly, so grandly, I felt I could keep up with her without trouble. I saw her through the trees. I saw the length of her passing through an opening of blue sky between the trees. I waved at the people in the cupola, which was the size of a railroad car. She was going over treetops. I ran into a grass meadow to get an unobstructed sight of her, but now I realized she was going faster than I thought, she seemed to drift in the wind, I heard a rising pitch of her engines, she was changing course, she was over the street, over the trees, and slipping behind the apartment-house roofs of Morris Avenue. I waved and called. I wanted her back. I had been laughing all the while, and now, as the tail of her disappeared, she was gulped up by the city as if she had been sucked out of the sky. I ran as far as the park wall, smiling and red-faced and breathless, unable to believe my good fortune that I had seen the mighty *Hindenburg.*

I hurried home to tell my mother. When Donald came home he said he had seen the ship too. He had still been in school for some special exam and had looked out the window and seen her. Everyone taking the test and the teacher, too, had run to the windows. "We should get a model of the *Hindenburg,*" he said. "We should save up and get it."

And then in the evening she crashed. We did not hear the radio broadcast describing this, it was the hour for *The Answer Man* and *I Love a Mystery.* But then a news bulletin came on. At the mooring tower in Lakehurst, New Jersey, she had caught fire. She collapsed, the steel twisting and curling up like paper. I could not imagine something the size of a flying ocean liner going up that way. Many people had died. They fell out of the sky in flames. I didn't understand how it could happen. "You see," Donald said patiently, "airships are really lighter-than-air ships. They couldn't fly unless the gas inside the balloon weighed less than air. You see that, don't you?"

"Sort of," I said.

"The gas they use is hydrogen, because its density is so much less than the density of air. On the other hand, it's a very volatile gas, which means it ignites easily. That's what happened. Maybe someone lit a cigarette. I don't know, it might even have been static electricity." I was impressed with his explanation. So was my mother. She beamed at him. He was taking chemistry at Townsend Harris. He had a chemistry set in a wooden box—not a toy but a real set, with vials of powdered chemicals stoppered with corks and their scientific names on the labels, and beakers and test tubes, and rubber hoses and clamps and measuring spoons, and a little scale with two dishes.

I did not think of the dead people, I thought only of the fall of the *Hindenburg*. My mother had said she was a German ship, sent over by Hitler for his own glory, and that if those people had to die she hoped they were Nazis. But none of that mattered to me. All I could think of was that the ship had fallen out of the sky. They were not supposed ever to touch land, they were tethered to tall towers, they were sky creatures; and this one had fallen in flames to the ground. I could not get the picture of that out of my mind. In the Saturday cartoons, one, about Popeye, showed Popeye's ship sinking. He swam away and the ship stuck its nose up in the air and went straight down, like a knife, making a funny *glub glub* sound and sending up a stream of bubbles. But a real ship going down, I knew, was a terrible sight, like a great animal fallen; she would lie on her side, or maybe turn upside down, and go under by degrees, faster and faster, creating a terrible whirlpool in the sea as she went. My father had told me he had once seen newsreels of an ocean liner foundered on a beach in Jersey. She lay in flames on her side. Even on water ships could burn. Everything around me was going up and down, up and down. Joe Louis hit Jim Braddock and Braddock went down. I had seen paintings in books of knights fallen from their horses, or horses fallen, and in *King Kong* there was the terrible shaking of the earth by the falling of the great dinosaurs in battle. And, of course, Kong himself had fallen. Just recently I had seen an old man in the street suddenly drop to his knees for no reason at all, and then topple to one side and sit on the sidewalk leaning back on one elbow, and I had found that terrifying. In bed, trying to sleep, I imagined my father stumbling and crashing to the ground, and I cried out.

EIGHTEEN

Of course I fell all the time, but that was different. I lived in proximity to the pavement, in front of my house I knew the topography of the stoop and the cement sidewalk, and the cracks in the sidewalk and the chips in the grey blocks of the curb. I had a best friend now, Bertram, who lived a block away on Morris Avenue and took clarinet lessons. He was short, and tubby. I directed our games. Pretend I'm this. Pretend you're that. Pretend I say this and you do that. The latest serial in the movies was *Zorro,* a kind of Lone Ranger in black with a black horse, and in our games I was Zorro and Bertram was everyone else in the cast. I was more agile than he, and therefore the hero. We had laths we had found in the ash can which we used for swords. Bertram, in our duels, represented many soldiers or a whole posse, and I'd no sooner stab one of them and see him fall, than another would pop up and challenge me. I leaped up on the stoop, I raced past him down the brick stoop and jumped to the ground. I fell and dueled with Bertram while on my back. He danced around me. Our game was a long-running serial and took us down the alley and into the backyard. Here, as Zorro, I now had the daring to climb the stone wall patched with cement that divided my yard from the back of the apartment house on the other side of it. The wall held up a rotting wooden fence that tilted over it and impeded passage. The cement was cracked and crumbling. Colonies of brown ants lived in the holes. My friend couldn't quite handle this wall. I raced along my dangerous parapet and he ran alongside, below me, in the yard. Loyally, he huffed and puffed. He could never win these adventures because I was always Zorro. He died and died again. He might, during our dueling, touch me with the end of his sword and say he'd gotten me, but I always insisted it was a flesh wound even if his sword hit me square in the middle of the chest. He'd try to argue but I'd draw him back into the duel, lifting my sword, nicking him and dancing backward with a merry laugh. He'd start to chase me and we'd be back in it. Truly we were not playing. It was understood life was cheap. People fought. Blood flowed. Honor and justice were at stake. We went on with it hour after hour. The invention was endless. I told him what to say, then I answered. We replayed the scenes when I thought of something better. The dirt and grit of crushed stone was embedded in the flesh of our palms. Our eyes glistened from exertion, our cheeks were red. Once or twice a day Bertram cried real tears and I was close to them. When we reached some grim exhausted end to all this, with someone's mother calling, dusk sending a chill down our sweated backs, we emptied our pockets of the things we had collected in the course of the day's adventures—clothesline, flinty chips of rock, empty cigarette packages, ice cream sticks—and went each to our home.

After the last day of school Bertram and I had all day to fight it out. But then his mother took him away for the summer to a cottage in the Catskills. Donald left for his job at the Paramount Hotel. My father was away at work most days and nights, and so my mother and I were each other's companion a good deal of the time. Once, I reflected, our house had been full and something was always going on. Now there were just the two of us and it was not much fun.

My mother sat at the window of the sun parlor and looked out. I understood it was not something she preferred to do. It was what she did. She sat there, with her arms on the windowsill. Sometimes she drank a cup of coffee, sometimes a cup of tea. She was not so strict with me. I could stay out after supper. The exact hour of my bedtime was not now of the utmost importance to her, perhaps because I didn't have school in the morning and could sleep late, perhaps because she had other things on her mind. I took advantage of the situation readily enough. I listened to programs that would have been unthinkable during the school term: *Gang Busters,* the crime-story show written by Colonel H. Norman Schwarzkopf, which came on at ten o'clock; *The Kraft Music Hall* with Bing Crosby and Bob Burns, and even *Jimmy Fidler's Hollywood Gossip* at ten-thirty. Adding these to my regular shows, which I had won from hard and protracted negotiations—*Easy Aces,* and the *Chase and Sanborn Hour* with Charlie McCarthy, and *The Royal Gelatin Hour* with Rudy Vallee, and the *Green Hornet,* of course, and *Jack Benny,* and *Eddie Cantor, Mr. Keen, Tracer of Lost Persons, Horace Heidt and his Musical Knights,* plus all my afternoon adventure shows—I pretty much had free rein with the airways. Listening to a full day's radio programs exhausted me, but it was a nervous sort of exhaustion, lacking real physical discharge, and my limbs hurt and my mind clamored. Bed at night was a stale place, the pillow grew clammy despite my plumping it and turning it so that I could feel its cold side. I reheard bits and pieces of the radio programs in my mind. I concentrated on the serials. I analyzed how they achieved the realistic sounds of horse hooves at a gallop, airplanes in dogfights, chairs breaking over people's heads, creaking ropes at quayside in mysterious Oriental ports, and so forth. Mostly I imagined the geography I had been taught, the backgrounds of these programs being barely indicated by a descriptive line, or a remark in the story or a trace of a sound effect, but which shone in my mind in colorful detail. There was a West, there was a vast deep sky to fly, there was the Orient, there was Europe, and dangerous seas between. Occasionally I realized that the pillow under my head was one of the very malefactors who populated these exotic realms; somehow he had gotten to the Bronx. I wrestled him, punched him, grunting and grinding my teeth in appropriate fashion; sometimes it looked as if he had me, but with my last bit of strength I flung him from me up into the air, and took him out with one beautiful sock as he came down.

Oddly, on those rare evenings when my father was home some discipline was reinforced. He felt most of the shows I liked were trash. "You'd be better off reading a book," he said, although he knew I read books all the time. He himself listened to the news commentators, like H.V. Kaltenborn, although I couldn't see why he did, they irritated him so. He turned them off in anger when he could no longer stand what was being said, but he always tuned in again the next time.

The only program the whole family could agree on was *Information Please,* the quiz show in which the questions were really hard and the board of experts who answered them were really learned. The joy of the show was in hearing questions asked the answer to which no one could possibly know, and then hearing one or another of those fellows answer in a shot, and make it all sound simple. Each of them had fields of expertise the others did not, and altogether it was pretty hard to trip them up. If you did, if the question that you sent in *did* stump the experts, you were awarded a set of the *Encyclopaedia Britannica.* We all sat and listened to this program. Sometimes, if the subject was music or politics or history, my father guessed the answer before the experts did.

I loved it when the three of us all did something together. If my mother and father were fighting, our going out and doing something was the way they called a truce. Everyone could be angry and not talking, and I would nag each of them in turn until I got them up and out, my father going along with what he pretended was my mother's idea, and my mother pretending it was my father's. But it was mine. I'd get them to the movies this way. Going to an air-cooled movie on a hot evening was a necessity. It didn't even matter to me what the films were, my mother seemed to like love stories and musicals, my father dramas. I would sit through Jeanette MacDonald and Nelson Eddy singing to each other just to be cool and just to know that in the dark on either side of me sat my parents and that they might actually talk to each other afterwards on the way home. Most times they did, but sometimes even the evening out wouldn't do any good; I would have heard my mother laughing during the movie, but when we came out she still wouldn't talk to my father. Sometimes my father fell asleep during the movie, sometimes when he was restless he went out for a while. He knew how to leave the movie house and go have a soda or smoke a cigar and then get back into the theater without paying another admission. I myself would never try that.

His business was not good and this seemed to make him quieter and more serious. He did not bring home surprises as often.

My one reliable friend this summer was the little girl Meg, whose family, like ours, had no vacation planned. I played potsy with her in the Oval if I had previously checked to see no boys I knew were in sight. This was a girl's game of hopping around in numbered boxes and it was quite easy. You threw your skate key or something into a particular box you had to reach, and if it stayed in, you hopped and jumped your way over to it, picked it up while standing on one foot, reversed your direction without touching a line, and hopped your way back. Certain boxes had to be avoided if the other person had previously claimed them. Sometimes it got complicated. My mother thought Meg a sweet child, that's what she called her, a sweet child, although she was critical of her name.

"What kind of name is that," she said.

"It's short for Margaret," I said. "But everyone calls her Meg."

"Well, that's no name for a girl, that's a scullery maid's name. I fault the mother."

She did not look approvingly on Meg's mother. I couldn't understand why. The woman had always been nice to me, she was a pretty woman, slender, with short reddish-blond hair and a nice smile. She seemed always to be listening to a pleasant song inside her head. Her name was Norma. I knew this because

this is how Meg addressed her, it was very unusual not calling
your mother Mother, but Norma did not seem to mind. She had
a good way of making a cold chocolate drink, she took a spoon-
ful or two of cocoa, and added milk and sugar; then she crushed
some ice cubes in a dish cloth with a hammer; then she poured
the ice cubes into an Orphan Annie Ovaltine Shake-up Mug,
which was a cup with a domed lid; and she shook it up till it was
cold and served it with the crushed ice. "I'd make a good bar-
tender," she said. She did nice things like that.

They were not particularly well off, this family. They lived in
a tenement house without an elevator, on the fifth floor, a long
walk up. The stairs were dark, the hallways were tiled in little
six-sided tiles, like a bathroom. Their apartment was small, but
very light, since it overlooked Claremont Park at Monroe Avenue. In the basement of the building was a little grocery store
with a window that looked up at the front sidewalk. In that store
you saw people's legs as they went by, as if they were chopped
off in the middle. I sometimes went there for my mother.

Meg did not have her own room. There was only one bedroom, so she either slept in her mother's bed or in the living
room on the sofa. Things were broken down in the living room,
the sofa's springs were coming out the bottom, and a standing
lamp with one of those upside-down glass shades to direct the
light to the ceiling had a piece of the shade missing as if
chomped out by something that ate glass. It was not a clean
house by my mother's standards. The bedroom was overpacked
with things, bureaus piled with folded clothes and perfume bottles, boxes stacked in the corners, newspapers and junk everywhere. It was just those two rooms and a kitchen. On the kitchen
ceiling was a wooden rack with clothesline strung up on it; you
let it down like a shade by means of a rope attached to the wall,
and you dried your clothes that way. So pink silk underwear
always hung from the kitchen ceiling. There were roaches in the
bathroom, and a red rubber hot-water bottle and a trailing
enema tube hung from the shower rod over the bathtub. There
was a bathroom tray for a cat, although Meg told me their cat
had fallen out the window and died. I remember this apartment

so clearly because I spent so much time there, especially on rainy days. It was interesting to me that from the mess of this house both Meg and her mother could come out looking so clean and nicely dressed, as they always did. Meg's white summer one-strap shoes were always newly polished. She had very many of the latest toys and games. Of course, they would be of more interest to girls; she had several dolls, for example, including a Shirley Temple model complete with different outfits to dress her in. These were contained in a miniature trunk, just like the trunks people took with them on ocean voyages. Inside, on hangers, were a Shirley Temple nursing uniform with a red-and-blue cape of satin, a horseback-riding outfit with riding boots, coats, sundresses, shorts, and so on. Meg loved Shirley Temple. I myself could not abide her, but said nothing. I had seen Shirley Temple in just one movie—I knew that kind of spoiled girl. Buttery, overly cute, a teacher's pet, a real showoff. Meg herself was not like that or I wouldn't have been her friend. She was a serious, thoughtful child, very quiet and trusting. She never got mad and never left the game no matter how badly it was going for her. We were playing in the park one day and it began to rain. I went to her house and called my mother to let her know where I was. "You're up there?" my mother said. "You come right home." "But it's raining," I said. "It's letting up," she said. "This minute!"

When I got home I was angry. My mother said I was not to go into that house ever again and I said I would if I wanted to. She called me a foolish child. "But what's wrong?" I said over and over. "I will not discuss it," she said. I had to reason this out for myself. I knew she liked Meg and never put up an objection when she came to our house. So it had to do with her house. Or her mother. In the mysterious way of our family conversation, whenever something was not quite right I was left in the dark about it, although smartly feeling its consequences. When my mother was angry at my father, I could never exactly pin down her reasons. It was like that. I would learn more by listening to them argue at night when I was supposed to be asleep. Now I eavesdropped on a phone conversation my mother had that evening with her friend Mae. Our phone was in the front of the house, and I was in the kitchen having supper. I heard just one phrase: *ten cents a dance.* I don't know how, but I knew my mother was talking about Norma. I didn't know what she meant, exactly, but it was such a weighted comment, delivered in her tone of moral authority, part disgust, part sarcasm, that I immediately decided it was unjust. I resolved to continue to go to Meg's house. I was not willing in this case to accept the humiliation of being told what to do. My mother had a way of telling you what to do that left you with no honor. Once I showed her an advertisement on the back cover of a comic book, it was for an air rifle that shot BB's. I wanted it and proposed to save up for it. "Don't be ridiculous," she said. "Stop bothering me with such nonsense."

But the episode did suggest to me something I had not been prepared before to recognize. When I went upstairs to Meg's I always hoped Norma would be there. I had to acknowledge that to myself now, and with a weird feeling in the chest, some breathable excitement, as if I had done something terribly wrong although I didn't know what it was. When the mother wasn't home, or when she went out while I was there, I was disappointed. The visit became less interesting. She always smiled when she saw me. She had large eyes, widely spaced, and a wide mouth. She was very kind. Sometimes she joined us in our games. She would sit on the floor with us, and we three would have a good time.

NINETEEN

We received our first letter from the Paramount Hotel in the mountains. "Dear Mom, Dad, and Edgar," wrote my brother in his orderly way, assigning to each the places we had in his mind. I admired Donald's handwriting. He wrote in ink on unlined paper, and there were no blots and the lines were straight. One of my bad subjects in school was penmanship, and so I studied his letter and copied it out. I could hear his voice as I read, he was very good at explaining things—and I heard him now explaining how things were at the Paramount Hotel so that we would understand. He told us he was working hard and enjoying it. Some of the guests had requested tunes other than the ones the Cavaliers knew how to play—that was the biggest problem. People were getting tired of hearing the same songs every night. Could my father send up sheet music for a list of songs that was attached to the letter as quickly as possible? He would try to find time to rehearse, although it would be difficult because the management wanted them down by the lake during the day. Anyway the food was good, and he was getting a nice tan. It was a characteristic of the mountains that no matter how hot the day was the evenings were cool. My parents laughed over the letter, although I didn't find anything particularly funny in it. My father said he would mail up some sheet music immediately, before the Cavaliers heard the gong.

This was a reference to the *Major Bowes' Original Amateur Hour*, a radio program. Aspiring musicians were contestants on the program, and if they were no good, Major Bowes would ring a bell to stop their performance. It made you laugh even though it could not have been funny to whoever it was who might have been rehearsing for weeks to be heard on the radio and hoping to win a professional contract from the appearance. But it was funny. People played glasses of water each filled to a different height to make a different note; they played big ripsaws by bending the blade and stroking it with a violin bow; they played spoons, and even made music by tapping their teeth and slapping the sides of their face while their mouth was open. They always got the gong. One-man bands, my favorite, always got the gong. But I thought some of them were amazing—strumming guitars while blowing on harmonicas held on neck braces, or cornets affixed to their chairs, and beating bass drums with their feet, and playing organ chords with their elbows, and hitting cymbals with sticks taped to their foreheads. It was not real music they produced, these one-man bands, but something else, a mechanical not-quite-in-tune-music, like calliopes or music boxes; whenever I had the chance to listen to a one-man band I did.

My father explained to me that in the old days of vaudeville on the Lower East Side there was a fiddler named Romanoff who was famous for playing "The Flight of the Bumblebee" while holding the violin behind his back. "The immigrants loved Romanoff, they thought he was the best violinist in the world because he could play the fiddle behind his back," my father said. "Not even the great Heifetz could do that. Not even Fritz Kreisler." He looked at me with a big smile on his face, his eyebrows poised while waiting for me to get the point. I understood what he was saying, but I still liked one-man bands.

A more serious matter arose regarding my brother when our former landlady, Mrs. Segal, came by to visit. As it happened, Mrs. Segal and her husband had gone to the Paramount Hotel for a week's vacation and had been delighted to find Donald there. "But you wouldn't believe the hovels they have those boys in," she said. "Shacks, with mattresses on the floor, like dirt farmers. No running water, they have to use the outside shower beside the boathouse."

My mother was speechless.

"Ordinarily I wouldn't say anything," Mrs. Segal said, "but I know how particular you are."

"He didn't tell us," my mother said.

"Of course not," Mrs. Segal said, "You know boys, it doesn't matter to them. They wouldn't bathe if they lived in Buckingham Palace." Mrs. Segal held my chin in her hand as she said that. She thought the whole situation very funny. "Of course Donald is having the time of his life," she assured my mother. "He's a big shot. All the girls adore him."

When my father came home my mother told him what Mrs. Segal had said. "I want him home this instant," she said. "He's living in filth. Send him a telegram. I'll go up there myself if that's what it takes to get him out of that pigsty."

"Rose," my father said, "if you bring that boy home in the middle of the summer, he'll never forgive you."

It was difficult for my mother to control herself. After a day or two she wrote Donald a letter and said she had heard from Mrs. Segal about the living conditions of the staff. "Stand up for your rights," she told him. "You're just as good as the finest guest. Professional musicians have a right to expect sheets on the beds, at least."

TWENTY

I had a theory about death in its various forms—for instance,
drowning, being run over or burned alive, which were death
by accident, or something like infantile paralysis, which was
death by germ: It was simply that if I thought of it, if I imagined
it, it would not happen to me. I would be guarded against it,
made immune, merely by an act of thought, foiling this or that
particular death with a mental inoculation against it. And it
didn't matter how the thought entered my mind, if I had heard
of something terrible happening to someone else, or seen something bad, or just idly dreamt of the word describing it, I was
safe. Perhaps it was not so much theory as a working hope, but
it was holding up nicely.

In the fall of my eighth year I woke up one morning with one
of my stomachaches. I was pleased to be allowed to stay home
from school. I had a new comic book about Frank Buck, a real
person. Frank Buck went to Africa and Asia and trapped big
game; he didn't kill animals, he brought them back by ship to
the zoos and circuses. He was kind to the animals, which I liked.
He had wild adventures.

My illness brought no theoretical thoughts to my mind. It
didn't seem at all consequential. Exhibiting the same aplomb
with which I handled death, I regarded myself as an expert on
illnesses, at least as they made their appearance in me. I knew

my colds, my grippes, my earaches. I knew their characters and the courses they might take and the treatment they called for. They posed no fears for me, although they did for my mother. I had learned how secretly to avoid the worst treatment. Mustard plaster for chest colds for example: once it was applied and my mother had left the room, I would insert a towel between my skin and the brown bag paper in which the clammy English mustard had been spread. Then I would pull the covers up to my chin so I didn't have to breathe the acrid fumes of the cursed detestable stuff. When I heard her coming back, I would remove the towel and suffer the burning sensation for as long as it took her to leave again.

This time I had a low fever, which was no particular inconvenience. I just didn't eat very much. Everything was fine. But on the second day the mildly annoying ache was still there and I stayed in bed more of the time, a fact noted by my mother. In the late afternoon Dr. Gross came over and had a look at me. As usual he made me a present of some tongue depressors. He pressed my stomach and looked down my throat and in my ears while his vest chain swung with its hanging badge.

"Well," he said in his genial growly voice, "it doesn't appear to be much of anything. Let's wait another day or two and see what happens." This was not my mother's usual inclination in the face of illness, she liked to know what it was and to deal with it firmly. But the symptoms were vague and I seemed to be active enough even though in bed. I drew, listened to my programs, I demanded tea and toast and Jell-O with annoying regularity, and so she acceded to the doctor's advice.

A couple of days later my stomach was still hurting and was tight as a drum. I went to bed early. When I awoke the next morning my stomach hurt no longer. I told this to my mother with a smile. She regarded my flushed cheeks. "I don't like the way you look," she said. When she read my temperature on the thermometer she gasped. It was a hundred and five degrees.

My mother cursed the name of Dr. Gross and called Aunt Frances in Westchester. As a well-to-do matron, Aunt Frances knew numbers of specialists. At her behest we received a phone call very soon afterward from a Dr. London, a friend of her family's. I heard my mother describe the situation to him. She came back to my room with an alarmed expression on her face. "Dr. London is a Manhattan doctor," she said. "He's sending around an associate of his who has an office near here. He said you are not to move but to lie quietly with a pillow under your knees." She placed the pillow very gently as she spoke. She was pale.

A short while later the associate arrived. I did not get his name. He scared me. He was not genial like Dr. Gross, but severe and unsmiling; he did not prod me about in Gross's friendly way, kneading this and that, but touched me gingerly with the tops of his fingers and peered at me with a worried frown. He wore a dark blue pin-striped suit and vest. His hair was grey. "Dr. London's suspicion was correct. This child must immediately go to the hospital," he said to my mother. She put her hand to her cheek. They went out of the room together. I resented being left like that when it was me they were talking about. I heard them in the hallway.

The strange doctor spoke on the phone in the front hall and then spoke to my mother outside my room door. "You are not to waste time calling for an ambulance. Get a taxi. Take him to Poly Clinic hospital. It's on West Fiftieth Street. Here is the address. Dr. London will be waiting."

He explained to my mother how I should be carried, wrapped in a blanket, in a folded position, with as little room for movement as possible. Then he left.

My mother called her friend Mae for help. "His appendix has burst," she said.

I was alarmed now because in my registry of self-protective thoughts I had never entered a burst appendix. How could I have, not knowing what it was! I felt light-headed. My fear dissolved and I became angry. The pain was gone and *now* was when I had to go to the hospital. I decided I would not go to the hospital. I complained bitterly while my mother put me in fresh pajamas and wrapped me in a blanket. She was uncharacteristically gentle but simply ignored what I had to say.

By this time Mae had arrived and was ringing the bell. A yellow De Soto cab was waiting at the curb in front of the house. My mother carried me down the steps and Mae ran ahead to hold the cab door. To my mortification there was the landlady's little girl from downstairs, whom I hated. She was there in front of the house carrying her schoolbooks, watching the whole thing. She had no regard for my feelings but kept looking and looking, she hadn't the decency to go about her business. I ignored her, but was furious with this wretched brat. Oh my awful luck, to be seen carried wrapped up in this way just at lunchtime when the children were coming home from school. How she *knew*. She would tell her mother. And my humiliation would be public knowledge.

That was the reason I cried in the taxi, not because I was feeling ill. "Shh," my mother said. "Don't worry. Everything will be all right." I could tell she was not entirely sure this was so. The cab was going very fast. The driver blew the horn repeatedly. I knew where we were, we were going down the Grand Concourse. I saw the tops of the trees on the center islands, the framed blue-and-white street signs attached to the lampposts, I saw the tops of the apartment houses. I was seeing the Bronx upside down. We kept going and crossed the bridge into Manhattan at 138th Street. I smelled the cracked leather of the cab's upholstery. I saw the back of the driver's head, his soft cap. I heard the ticking of the meter and tried to count the clicks, to keep time with them in my mind. I must have dozed. We were coming down Madison Avenue now from Seventy-ninth Street, there is a hill there and I twisted to look out front at the cars and buses. The driver blew the horn. The cab turned into Central Park and headed to the West Side of Manhattan.

I found myself on a stretcher in the hospital. My blanket was taken away. I was very thirsty. I twisted my head looking for my mother but I could not see her. I was being wheeled down a hall, the overhead lights ticking past like the ratchets of the taxi meter. "I am very thirsty," I said, "I want some water, please." Someone said, "In just one minute we'll give you water."

And then I was in an elevator with several people smiling at me and saying reassuring things. I didn't know them. I didn't believe them. Then we were out of the elevator in some dark room, and many people were there, indistinct shapes in the darkness, and the stretcher was being positioned in some way, and the movement back and forth was nauseating me. I was terribly thirsty and asked for water. Instead, straps were fastened around each of my wrists and my ankles and chest.

A doctor with a white cap on his head and a long white apron like Irving the Fish Man's, appeared. I couldn't see his face, he had on a mask covering everything except his eyes. He was saying something but his voice was muffled by the mask. He wore rubber gloves. I realized he was saying I was going to be all right. How could I trust him! I had no control over what they were doing to me. They had tied me down. They did not seem to hear when I said I wanted something to drink.

Another doctor in a white cap sat down next to my head and said he was going to put a mask over my face and he wanted me to breathe very deeply when he did. "Let me see the mask," I said. He held up not a white cloth mask such as he wore, but a conical rubber device, colored black, whose sides were collapsed on each other, the narrow end attached to a tube. It looked more like a balloon than a mask. I knew beyond question that I wanted nothing to do with it. He saw the alarm in my eyes. He lifted the mask toward me and turned away at the same time and turned a wheel on some kind of machine I had not noticed before that was sitting next to him. I heard a hissing sound. The mask as it came toward me was now a perfect circle. I knew I could not avoid it but turned my head from side to side anyway. I wanted a moment to compose myself. "Just breathe deeply," he said. "Can you count? Count from one hundred as you breathe, but backwards, see if you can, ninety-nine, ninety-eight and so on," and he clasped it over my face. I was shaking my head no. I tried to tell him I was thirsty. I wanted two things, a glass of water and a moment to compose myself, but I could not speak because the hideous rubbery mask was clamped over my face and held there. I couldn't breathe, I was trying to tell him. A cold sweet poisonous gas was what this man wanted me to breathe. I tried to get him to stop. I had something to say. I began to struggle and felt hands holding me down. Whichever way I turned my head the cold sweet suffocating poison stuck to me. I was breathing it, I couldn't help it, I tried to hold my breath but it was impossible, and with each breath I took, more of this unbreathable sweetness was coming into my lungs and choking me. I gagged. It was not air. It was cold, it smelled like the hiss of gas in a cellar, it had echoes in it, it rang like metal footsteps, it hissed, cell doors clanged shut, I heard my voice calling to me down long stone corridors, I could not breathe. I knew I must not lose consciousness. I fought. I shook my head, I could not free myself.

And now great swirls of colored light advanced toward me, spinning like pinwheels, revolving so fast they seemed to scream. And then the light was splintering and flying toward me, needles of it stinging me, flying past me, yellow and red stings, and now a roaring sound filled my head and began to pulsate. And all this swirling light and roaring screaming noise popped into Donald Duck looming up from a point, and he spoke and clacks came out of his mouth, and then Mickey Mouse loomed up in front of me and made horrible faces, and spoke in clacks or roars, and they were laughing at me and shaking their fists and showing their teeth. And I couldn't help it, now I was breathing in this terrible gas in a white tiled swimming pool or corridor whose walls moved in toward me and then outwards. I was falling through my *Compton's Picture Encyclopedia* article on the sea and these underwater animals were laughing in my ears, but the laughter pulsated like a machine, and I couldn't stop breathing even though I knew it was the machine breathing. The smell was cold, the hiss grew softer. I felt as if I were under the sea but breathing under the sea somehow this air that was the only thing left to breathe in all this cold floating. And then, with a certainty that made me scream, I knew I was being cut, I felt the knife go into my belly and cut downward. I tried to tell them to stop, but water hissed into my mouth and I saw myself drifting away and they cut and cut, and I wanted to cry but could not, the tears remained in my throat and in my throat I grieved, and felt such despair of death that I gave up and I let it come floating. And it all floated away.

Then, much later it seemed, I saw things for a while and then no longer saw them. It was quiet. I heard voices but could not distinguish words. My mouth was dry. When I called for water, a wet piece of cotton was brushed across my cracked lips. I was angry and came into consciousness kicking. That they would tie me to a table and force me to breathe what I couldn't breathe! I was held down, Donald was holding my hand, he was saying, "Take it easy, take it easy!" I went to sleep and awoke, quite clear in the head now. I was in some sort of room with curtains. Others were outside the curtains. They had their own concerns. Children were crying. The curtain was pulled back and a nurse showed me how I could have water. She took a tongue depressor with cotton wrapped around one end and dipped it into a glass of water and then let me suck the water from the cotton. It was not enough, but she would only give me it that way.

I felt very bad, as if things were sticking in me so that I could feel the insides of me, what my insides felt like. I was told to lie still, which I was glad to do because of this wet sticking feeling in my stomach. Then my mother stayed with me awhile. She was angry at the nurse about something. She told me I had my feelings under the covers like that because I had drains in me, the operation was over, I didn't have to worry that that would ever happen again, but meanwhile where they had made the incision there were rubber drain tubes to see to it that all the poison left my body. The idea was to keep those drains in me for a while and not to close things up to make sure all the poison came out. That was all. I didn't want to know about it. I didn't want to see.

Whenever the doctors changed the dressing I kept my eyes closed because I didn't want to see. I was not well. I was not happy. I was very tired and injured, I felt I had been badly treated, I had been cut, I had stitches in me and drains, and at night when no one was there and I woke, I heard another child crying and I couldn't help it, I wept too.

Then my grandma came to visit me. She walked through the curtain. So she hadn't died after all. I was glad the curtains were pulled around my bed because none of the others could see her, she embarrassed me speaking in Yiddish and looking very old and shabby in her black dress, and with her grey hair pinned up in her braids but scraggly around the edges, she was not as neat as she usually was and she smelled of her sour grass. But I was thirsty and explained to her how to do the water, and she did this properly. Then she felt my head with her dry ancient hand and she thought I was too hot, she found a washcloth at the foot of my bed and went outside the curtains to the sink along the wall and rinsed the cloth in cold water and came back and put the folded cloth over my forehead. "You are a dear precious boy," she said to me and I understood this clearly even though it was in Yiddish. She took a penny from her old change purse of cracked leather. In her forefinger and thumb she held this penny and with her other hand opened my hand and pressed the penny into my palm, just the way she always did. "I bless you, my beloved child, I pray for good health for you. You are a good boy and I love you," she said. "God will protect you."

When my mother and father arrived, I told them Grandma had come to see me. They exchanged looks. My mother excused herself and left the room holding a handkerchief to her eyes. My father sat down at the side of the bed.

"I brought you some books," he said. "It's something new. They have these pocket-sized books now, wonderful books for twenty-five cents. I know you like Frank Buck, don't you?"

I nodded. He was very serious. Dark circles were under his eyes.

"Here is his own book about going after big game," my father said. *"Bring 'Em Back Alive.* It's not just a comic book. It's his autobiography. And here is a story about a young deer called *Bambi,* by Felix Salten," he said. "Just to get the animal's point of view."

That didn't interest me as much, but I didn't say that to my poor father. I realized how worried he was, how I had worried them all with my burst appendix.

"And here is a famous book, a classic that you might not find interesting just now but you may in the future. It's a wonderful book, *Wuthering Heights,* by an English writer, Emily Brontë."

"Thank you," I said, although I was too tired to do more than look at the covers.

"I'll put them here on the table next to you. You see them? You can just reach over when you want to look at them."

Much later I found out what happened at the end of the hospital corridor outside my room. After visiting me, my parents met with Dr. London, who had performed the surgery. He told them I had a fifty-fifty chance of pulling through. Then he left to go about his rounds and at that point my mother attempted to throw herself out of the hospital window. The odds the doctor had quoted did not seem to her favorable. My father held her, wrestled with her at the open window. He held her until she went limp in her despair and broke down crying.

If they had only asked me, I could have told them I wasn't going to die. I knew I would not because of my theory. My theory held that if I thought of something before it happened, it wouldn't happen. I had experienced a ruptured appendix before I had thought about it and that was unfortunate, but I had thought about dying from it before it had had the chance to kill me, so now it couldn't. It was very simple.

I was no longer frightened. I may not have liked the drains in me, the profoundly uncomfortable foreignness of tubes lolling about in my guts, but I did not fear for my life. The time of terror for me was before I was put under as I wrestled the deadly sweet ether that filled my throat and my lungs with its terrible chemical chill. But it is apparent to me now that my parents interpreted the visit from my dead grandma as a sign of my own impending death. That particular day I was very close to death. Nobody could have persuaded me that it was not a palpable visit Grandma had made, a real event, and that was the point. My dear hollow-eyed family, these great framers of my existence and gods of my thought, had a way of coming into my room so hesitantly, with grim and fearful glances from the door, and lips pressed tight in pale faces as if awestruck by what they saw; I had to turn my head and smile at them before they would come in, before they were satisfied that I was still alive. They would suppose, in the delirium that produced my occult meeting with my Grandma, my own terrible passion,with my eyes turned into the past as if rolled up in my head, and I seeing what was dead and gone in the disconnection from my own forwardness through time, as if, becalmed and drifting to stillness, to inanimation, the mind sees death as life.

These horrors of meaning were for my family to understand. I was only ill with peritonitis. My conviction was not shaken even when I was moved into another room, a bigger room, with no curtains around my bed, but with a kind of railing, like a crib's. I was very insulted. It was a children's ward, and there were many such crib beds, each with a child either younger than I or older, and there were many of us now regardless of age in these humiliating beds and all of the others were looking at me. Some of the little ones stood up to look at me. I still had to lie down. I could see out a big window to a windowless building across the street. It was the north side of Madison Square Garden, which pleased me. At night I imagined I could hear a sports crowd cheering at a basketball game.

When Donald came to visit he was angry because nobody had told him that I had been moved to this special ward.

"I went to your old room and the bed was empty and the mattress was rolled up," he said. "Nobody I spoke to knew anything. I ran all over the place trying to find out what had happened."

He sat down beside my bed and rubbed hs eyes with the back of his hand. "Can you imagine a hospital full of doctors and nurses and not one of them knew where you were?" He began to laugh with tears in his eyes. "Finally, I saw one of your nurses, and she told me you were here." He shook his head. "Jesus, what if I had called Mom when I couldn't find you!"

I introduced Donald to the other children nearby. There were four or five of them. I wanted them to know I had an older brother. He waved and some of them said hello but most just stared. They were all dying. I knew that, it was clear to me. One girl, Miriam, who was several years older than I, had had her leg sawn off. She was on the bed next to mine. A couple of kids were in wheelchairs during the day and had to be helped into their beds at night. One of them was very yellow and skinny. They were all dying. I knew that because I had heard the doctors and nurses talking. Also the toys here were very elaborate, the toys and games these children had were the most glorious I had ever seen, but they didn't seem to care; each day their parents or grandparents came and brought more toys and games but they were not thankful. Some of the children had been here for months. They did not enjoy visits, they only enjoyed talking to one another, and teasing one another. I was not one of them, I could see that. Though I had been put in among them, I didn't think that I was dying. They didn't think I was either, because none of them wanted to be my friend. Except Miriam, the big girl in the bed next to mine. She liked me. "Your brother's very handsome," she told me after Donald had left at the end of the visiting hour.

What pulled me through was a new drug, sulfanilamide. My impression then was that it was a kind of yellow powder that had been sprinkled all around inside me before I had been sewn up. I think now it was administered after the operation as well. In a few weeks I was released from the hospital and brought home wrapped in blankets. It was winter. In the early spring I was allowed to get out of bed for a while each day, and after that I was taken to the country for my convalescence, the country being Pelham Manor, on Montcalm Terrace, the home of Aunt Frances and Uncle Ephraim, hosts of the yearly Passover dinner.

Their three children were grown and away at college, two boys at Harvard and the youngest, a girl, Lila, at Smith. Here, in the stillness of this elegant home, with its low ceilings, carpeted stairs, casement windows and wine and velvet smells, I stayed for a week and took my ease. There was a backyard with a large rock and a profusion of forsythia in bloom. Aunt Frances had undoubtedly saved my life by finding for my parents a doctor who understood what had happened to me. She really liked me and I liked her, she was gracious and kind, a very pretty woman with prematurely white hair and a quiet aristocratic bearing, like a good queen in a fairy tale who still bears some of the loveliness of the princess. She did not raise her voice, which endeared her to me. I was given the bedroom of her daughter, Lila, a single room, with Lila's awards and honors all over the walls. She had raised dogs in her early youth, and various ribbons, many of them blue, testified to her skill. Her champion dog, Vicky, a Kerry blue terrier, was still in residence. I was invited to browse through her books, a largely disappointing collection of science texts and dog-training manuals and, from her childhood, Nancy Drew mysteries. But she did have all the Oz books, by L. Frank Baum, and I read these and found them to my taste.

I was still slightly afraid of my uncle Ephraim. He was the kind of intimidating adult who thinks of children as naturally imperfect beings that have to be constantly instructed against their own worst natures. He had a deep voice and he asked questions that awaited answers. An oil painting of himself stood over the mantel in the large living room. I studied that painting in the day, when he wasn't home. It portrayed him as thinner and handsomer than he was, it showed him without his glasses. He was a portly man, with frameless eyeglasses and large teeth, a big nose and a double chin, and he wore dark suits and went off to take the New Haven line to his lawyer's office with the somber mien of a cabinet minister proceeding to affairs of state. At dinner once I put a green pea on my knife and received a ten-minute lecture on why this was not right. I was asked if I understood the points he had made and was then asked to repeat them. I thought he liked me but that I had a long way to go before he could respect me or admire me. He looked on our family, all of us, I thought, as woefully flawed and probably tempered his judgment with the reflection that not many people could be expected to achieve life's heights as he had. He was a right-wing Republican and liked to argue with my father in a Socratically baiting manner that was condescending.

Yet, of course, he was kind. He had assumed the role of overseer of the entire family's legal welfare, even though we were connected to him by marriage only. He was everyone's lawyer, without fee, charging neither my uncle Phil the cab-driver, when Phil needed to be incorporated for his protection as a medallion owner, nor presumably my father, who probably had needed some legal work in starting up his record business. Uncle Ephraim had more money than anyone else in the family and so probably contributed greatly to the support of my grandma and grandpa. I couldn't have known that a man as proper and august as this had his own deferences: he had not been allowed to marry Aunt Frances until he had given up his job running a magazine subscription business and gone to law school and gotten his degree. That ruling had come from my grandma and put him in her debt for the rest of her life. His three or four years studying law at night while he supported himself in the day taught him a discipline for which he was grateful; the frustration of going unmarried until he proved himself able to support the woman he loved brought him out of the Jewish lower-middle class into a life of wealth and self-determination. Money, propriety and responsibility were his and he wore them all like a judge's robes.

I knew my father detested Ephraim's politics, and his conservative values and pomposity. I assumed my uncle Ephraim disapproved of my father's leftist politics, his impulsiveness, his impracticality, his romanticism. They were like the Aesop tale, the ant and the grasshopper, and I could not for long decide for either existence because I would find it by itself insufficient, though I was all for my father. I always wanted him to win. I did not want that carefree singing grasshopper to come begging when snow covered the ground and he had nothing to eat. This feeling governed me in the week or so I stayed at Pelham. It was like Heaven for a good child, muffled and beautiful. I sat wrapped in a blanket, the sun coming through the parlor windows behind the kitchen; outside was a composition of grass and flowers and trees. Everything was in its place, even the Japanese beetles, which dutifully flew into the lamplike trap to quietly crawl over one another and die. Aunt Frances made her will known quietly, and courteously; even her live-in housekeeper, Clara, the tall black woman with a stony face and a sweet, low mellifluous voice, had a stately grace. Everyone in this house seemed to move in a kind of self-assured regal calm. I contrasted this with the chaos of my home, the intensity of our lives, the extremity of our emotions. In the mornings I drove with Aunt Frances and Uncle Ephraim in their enormous black Buick Roadmaster to the Pelham Manor railroad station. There at exactly the same time each morning the train came along its gravel bed—not a subway but a real train pulled by a locomotive —and chuffed to a stop, and Uncle Ephraim climbed aboard and waved to us. There seemed to be no errors in this life, it moved with a picture-book perfection, at least as it was presented to me in my convalescence.

But I disliked the charitableness of it, it was a life of dangerous propaganda, the more so because it was so quiet. I felt guilty for enjoying myself and the peace of this privileged household. I had to be someone else here, I couldn't whine or complain or make demands, but only show my gratitude. I felt coerced here in Heaven, and I was happy when at last it was time to leave.

Now I recall the present Donald brought me when I was still very ill and lying in the children's ward. It was actually a gift from one of his friends, Seymour or Irwin, or Bernie, I don't remember which. It was a lapel pin shaped like a pickle. It was funny. It was a Heinz 57 pickle, which people got for visiting the Heinz Dome at the New York World's Fair.

"When you're all better," Donald said to me as I turned the pin over in my fingers, "we'll go to the World's Fair."

"Have you been yet?" I said.

"No," my brother said. "We wouldn't go without you, you know that. We'll all go together. Mom and Dad and you and I. The whole family."

AUNT FRANCES

I don't know what to tell you about your father. He was a free spirit. As children we were not that close. I was older, I had different friends, different ideas. I spent my time at the downtown Ethical. The downtown branch of the Ethical Culture Society was for Jews. The Upper West Side Ethical was for the Irish. I learned table manners, music, how to behave, all the better things. The Ethical made my life.

But Dave was not interested in that. He was wild. He was handsome and bright but very trying. He teased my friends. He chased them when they came to visit us. Or he held the door closed against them. One day one of my friends was wearing her first pair of heels and he was chasing her down the stairs of our building and her heel caught on a step and snapped right off. How she cried. He was sorry then, although he pretended not to be.

One of my friends was Felix Frankfurter's sister. The Frankfurters were poor too, as poor as we were.

We lived on Gouverneur Street. Every week, with my group of girls, I walked from the Lower East Side to the Academy of Music opera house on Twenty-third Street. We each had fifty cents for the occasion. Seats were twenty-five cents. The other twenty-five cents were for carfare, but instead we bought bunches of violets, so we walked both ways and sang the songs we'd heard on our way home, with our pretty violets. I remember seeing *Babes in Toyland* at the Academy, but that must have been later, when I was in high school.

Dave was a dreamer, he was always late to school. When he was getting dressed in the morning he'd be putting on his shoes and socks and he'd forget what he was doing and sit there, he'd forget he was supposed to be pulling on his sock.

As a teenager he spent most of his time at the Socialist headquarters. That was our father's influence. Your grandpa was a wonderful man. He read three papers a day. He was a great reader, he loved books, the Russian authors were his favorites. He had a remarkable memory, he remembered books he'd read thirty-five years before, he could quote from a book and talk about it as if he had it in front of him. He was a dyed-in-the-wool Socialist. But he never pressed his ideas on us. He would explain things and let us make up our own minds. Dave loved him, he adored him.

When my father first came to America, this would have been 1886 or 1887, he was a young man not yet married. In fact he and Mama had not even met. He worked at whatever they gave him, they made him a cutter, but he was terrible at it, he was terrible all his life at business, he had no head for it. Years later he became a printer. He had a little shop on Eightieth Street east of Third Avenue. Before that he worked for your father in the sound-box business. But as a young man he immediately enrolled in school and learned everything he could. He went to the Eastside Alliance every night after work to learn English. And he studied socialism. Morris Hillquit was his teacher, the famous lawyer. And at the end of the year Morris Hillquit gave my father a dictionary because he was the best in the class.

My mother was better at earning a living than my father. She did piecework. For a while she had a tea shop. Later she ran a resort, a kind of boardinghouse, in the country. I was fifteen or so. The resort failed. She was strict with us girls, with me and Molly, the baby. But Dave could do no wrong. Dave she adored. Dave was the apple of her eye. And he loved her.

From Gouverneur Street we moved all the way up to 100th

Street, where the hospital is now. Then there were tenements. There was a farm on Park Avenue at Ninety-eighth Street. My mother would hand me ten cents and I'd go to the farm and pick the things we needed. Everything was a penny. A bunch of radishes, a penny, a cucumber, a head of lettuce. One penny.

Dave and I were not close until many years later when we were each married, with children. I married much earlier. When he married Rose they made the handsomest couple I had ever seen. Rose was a beautiful girl.

Ephraim and I began to court when I was sixteen. Dave was thirteen or fourteen. There is a family story that Dave threw Ephraim down the stairs, but that is not true. What he did was lock him out, hold the door to keep him from visiting me. Dave made Ephraim's life miserable. There was friction between them. They never liked each other.

Ephraim and I had a wonderful marriage. We never argued. He was a conservative Republican, a member of the Liberty League. He knew I felt differently. I voted for Norman Thomas one year and simply didn't tell him and he didn't ask. He trusted me to handle all the household accounts and make the domestic decisions while he attended to his law practice. He never questioned my judgment. The system worked beautifully. Ephraim was a remarkable man. You know, by the twenties we had a household staff of five—housekeeper, cook, maid, a nurse for the children, and a chauffeur. But when the stock market was booming, Ephraim advised many of his clients to take out second mortgages on their homes and invest in the market and so after the crash in '29 he felt responsible to those people and made good on every one of those mortgages. He didn't have to, but that's the way he was. He wiped out his fortune. We had to let the staff go, except for Clara. We had to struggle to put our boys through college.

Dave should have done better than he did. But he was a dreamer. When we lived on the Lower East Side, he liked to go down by the docks and look at the sailing ships. In those days the ships came right up to the street. The prows extended over the sidewalks. You could hear the ropes flapping in the wind, you could hear their masts creaking. He loved that. he stared at the sailors. My mother told him not to go there. She thought he would run away to sea. He was unpredictable. He was a trial to us all. Papa had a wonderful sense of humor! When they were retired and living up on the Concourse, Dave would call on the phone and say he was coming to visit on Tuesday, for example. Tuesday would come and he wouldn't appear, and wouldn't appear, and my mother would fret and Papa would say, well, he didn't say *which* Tuesday.

I loved Dave, we all did. When he was so sick, the last year of his life, I drove him around Manhattan to his accounts, to the stores he sold to. He could hardly walk, he was on crutches, but he couldn't afford to stop working.

I do remember one story about your father when he was a little boy. There was a wonderful family, the Romanoffs, who had taken my mother and father under their wing when they were first married. They were an older couple with no children. Mr. Romanoff enrolled me in school because at that point my parents' English was not that good; he knew English and could speak to the authorities. Anyway, they were delighted with us. Mr. Romanoff had a successful business, a drugstore up in the hundreds somewhere. That was the country. And he especially loved Dave. So the Romanoffs invited Dave to stay the weekend with them, they had no children of their own, you see, and so my mother, wanting to show her little boy at his best, bought a beautiful new suit for him with a hat. Dave turned red when they dressed him up for the visit. He hated the new suit. The hat was a little top hat, I think. When Mama brought him to the Romanoffs, Dave went upstairs and while the adults were downstairs on the street in front of the house, the suit came sailing out the window and landed at their feet. He would not wear it. And to emphasize the point he came outside in his underwear, this four-year-old, and came down the steps and in front of everyone threw the hat down in the dirt and stomped on it. He jumped up and landed with both feet on the hat again and again. Stomped it into the dirt. So they would know what he thought of it.

TWENTY-ONE

For several months I would sleep badly. I was afraid to go to sleep: in my dreams I smelled ether and felt a knife cutting into my belly.

When I went back to school, I was for a day or so treated as a returning hero. We all smiled shyly at each other. My classmates had sent me a big homemade get-well card with everyone's name painstakingly autographed. My friend Meg's hand was very clear and round and firm, which had not surprised me —as a girl she would be good at penmanship. My friend Arnold wrote like a spider.

All along my teacher had been sending me the lessons and I was almost caught up.

At home I learned that my father was moving his store to another location. The Hippodrome theater was being torn down and all the businesses there had to leave. He had found another site a few blocks north on Sixth Avenue, up near the new Radio City Music Hall between Forty-sixth and Forty-seventh streets and was hopeful about it. It was a large space, which meant he could display more stock; on the other hand, the rent was more and there would be inevitable losses of sales from the move. So everything was at a risk, including the money he and his partner had borrowed to build the shelves and the cabinets for the display of merchandise. There would also be a loss of selling time while this work went on.

One day my mother took me downtown to see the new store as it was being renovated. We found my father in his shirt sleeves, which was unusual, he always wore his coat and vest and tie, even at home on weekends. He was running around with a cigar in his mouth and stacks of records in his arms; he and Donald were stocking the shelves with albums. Lester, his partner, was unpacking radio consoles, and in the back a man on a ladder was still painting the wall and two carpenters were building the listening booths, of which there were to be three. I was tremendously excited by what was going on. The store was much bigger than the old one, half again as wide. The floor was carpeted. A wide staircase halfway back and in the middle of the floor led to a basement level that was to be devoted entirely to musical instruments. Uncle Willy was to be in charge of this section. My father's face was flushed with excitement. He put his cigar down on a counter for a moment and his partner, Lester, said, "Dave, don't you know better than to put a lighted cigar on a new piece of furniture? We haven't even opened the store yet!" We all stopped what we were doing. My father said very firmly, "Lester, this cigar won't burn the counter. Don't you know anything about tobacco? A cigar is a rolled leaf, it is not shredded like cigarette tobacco. A cigarette will continue to burn, a cigar goes out when you put it down." He was very scientific in his explanation, and I was relieved. "Put that in your pipe and smoke it," he said to Lester, and everyone laughed.

Outside, crowds of people moved along the sidewalks. I was excited that my father's new store was so close to the Radio City Music Hall. Only a block away was the Roxy. We were at the heart of things. Occasionally people stopped to peer through the locked doors. They pressed their noses up against the windows. They were very curious.

Some days later the store opened, and the following Saturday we again went down to see it. Everything was finished now and shining. Red, white and blue bunting was draped across the top of the windows and the front door. In the windows were displays of radios and electrolas, and photographs of Paul Whiteman and George Gershwin, Benny Goodman and Fats Waller, and Arturo Toscanini and Josef Hoffmann, as if somehow they all knew my father and had gathered to celebrate the new store. The inside was hushed and remarkable. Standing on slightly raised platforms were the latest models of console radios, all the famous makes, like Stewart-Warner, Grunow, Maytone, Philco, and Stromberg-Carlson. Attached to each was a small tag with the price and description of the radio's feature. I liked particularly the RCA Victor model in heart walnut that went for $89.95. It had eight tubes, two of glass, a magic eye, an edge-lighted dial and a phono connection. Also there was a Crosley with fifteen tubes, five of them glass, an autoexpressionator, a mystic hand, and a cardiamatic unit for $174.50. Smaller table radios were grouped on counters and shelves behind the counters in the radio section. I liked very much a new-model Radette that featured telematic dial tuning. It was a telephone dial set right over the circular station indicator so that you could dial your station as you dialed a telephone. I thought that was really fine for only $24.95.

There were many different kinds of phonographs as well, and one or two units that combined radios and record players, although these were very expensive. A glass cabinet held packets of steel needles and books on musical subjects, including *The Victor Book of the Opera.* We had that at home. The walls were lined with shelves filled with record albums, and in the listening booths there were standing ashtrays and record players built into the counters with electric pickup arms, the kind you didn't have to wind, and soundproofing panels on the side walls and ceiling. I liked the way the doors to these booths clicked shut.

Downstairs all the musical instruments shone in their cabinets, golden saxophones and black clarinets, and silver trumpets, and accordions with gleaming ivory and black keys. There was even a card with batons of different sizes with tapered cork tips. A set of drums sat on a pedestal lit with special spotlights. Uncle Willy let me sit up behind this rig and play for a minute or two, but with the brushes only, so that nobody would be disturbed. Of course, there were no customers down here, so it didn't matter that much. And when I went upstairs just one or two people were on the premises, one in a listening booth, the other studying the rack of sheet music. Lester stood behind the radio counter, his arms folded, a cigarette in the corner of his mouth. My father awaited customers at the classical music counter. Behind him was a whole wall of record albums of symphonies and operas and concertos. Their bindings were dark green. He stood with his hands flat on the glass countertop, he was dressed in his blue serge suit with the vest and his dark red tie, he looked impressive to me standing there leaning slightly forward, attentive to the occasion and awaiting for whoever it was would come in needing assistance.

We had not yet been to the World's Fair, but all around were signs that it was going on. Kazoos and ocarinas in their cards had World's Fair emblems. Next door was a souvenir shop where Trylon and Perisphere pins were on sale, and banners with pictures of them painted on the cloth. The Trylon was a skyscraping obelisk; the Perisphere was a great globe. They stood side by side at the Fair, and together they represented the World of Tomorrow, which was the Fair's theme. Almost every day in the newspaper was a picture of Mayor La Guardia welcoming some dignitary or movie star to Flushing Meadow, the site of the Fair. I did not pester my parents, I knew we would go eventually. Everyone was very busy. Besides, the truth was I had misgivings about it, it seemed so vast, such an enormous place, with so many things going on simultaneously, shows and exhibits and people from foreign countries, that I did not know where I wanted to go first. It was difficult to visualize. I was not even there yet but had fallen into the habit when I thought about the World's Fair of worrying that I would miss the best things. I didn't know why I felt that way.

My father had predicted the Fair would be good for business. He explained that people were coming to see it from all over the country. They would have to stay in hotels, they would have to have dinner, they would spend money going to Radio City and they would pass the shop and see records and electrolas they wanted and they would come in and buy something. People on trips always set aside money to buy things. Besides, in his store they could find things you couldn't find anywhere else. He was very optimistic.

Nevertheless, as the year moved into the winter, and the year 1940 began, the Fair closed for the season and business had not been what he had hoped.

At home in the evenings earlier now, my father was in the habit of listening to all the news commentators to find out what was going on in Europe. I knew, even before it was discussed in my class during current events, that a terrible war had begun— Hitler and Mussolini against England and France. He listened to every one of those news commentators; they didn't just read the news bulletins, but analyzed them too. Then my father analyzed their analyses. His new theory was that you had to listen to them all to figure out what the truth was. He liked Gabriel Heatter and Walter Winchell because they were antifascist. He detested Fulton Lewis and Boake Carter and H. V. Kaltenborn because they were against the New Deal and against unions and made comments verging on fascist, America First sympathies. He hated Father Coughlin, who said the Jewish bankers were to blame for everything. I grew to recognize the voices of these men and the products that sponsored them. Gabriel Heatter talked about gingivitis, which was a fancy name for bleeding gums; he passionately described the advantages of Forhan's toothpaste for this condition in the same fervent tones with which he described democracy's battle against fascism. If you didn't listen carefully, you might think that fascism and bleeding gums were the same thing.

My father sat in a chair near the radio and the newspapers opened in his lap to news stories with maps about the very same events being discussed by the commentators. He bought most of the papers—the *Times,* the *Herald Tribune,* the *Post,* the *World-Telegram,* even the *Daily Worker.* He would not read the Hearst papers.

In the movies on Saturday afternoons, after the cartoons, the Fox Movietone newsreels showed scenes from the war in Europe: big cannon muzzles afire in the night, German dive-bombers with angled wings coming out of the clouds. You saw the bombs falling. You saw burning buildings in London. You saw people swinging bottles of champagne against the sides of ships and diplomats getting out of cars and walking hurriedly up the steps of palaces for meetings. The war was talked about everywhere and shown in pictures. I liked to draw, I had made up my own comic-book stories and drawn them and colored them with crayon. I had a hero modeled after Smilin' Jack, the comic-strip pilot. I called my man Daring Dave. He had a moustache and wore a leather helmet with goggles and a lumber jacket and he had flown racing planes—like Smilin' Jack. I loved to draw these planes, snub-nosed daring little machines with checkerboard designs on their wings and ailerons. I drew them trailing exhaust in the sky so you could see what looping maneuvers they were capable of. They flew around courses measured by pylons. They flew over hangars decorated with wind socks. I wasn't sure exactly how something as vast and immeasurable as air could be used for a closed race course but I trusted that it could. I drew all sorts of those racing planes, some with cylindrical engine cowlings, some with enclosed cowlings pointed like index fingers. I drew cockpits that were open to the wind and cockpits that were enclosed with Plexiglas covers, but whatever the plane, whatever the design, I always put those streamlined wheel covers on them that were like raindrops coming along the window sideways in a windy rain. I liked streamlining, I liked those Chrysler cars that looked like beetles because their wheels were almost completely covered over and all their surface was rounded to get through the wind more easily, and for the same reason I liked those rear tapered airplane wheel covers. But now that World War Two had come to Europe I

decided to get Dave into a fighter plane. I put him into a Spitfire
flying over London for the Royal Air Force. The English insignia
was a bull's-eye colored red, white and blue. I liked the colors
but wondered if it wasn't a mistake to paint brightly colored
targets on the wings and fuselage of your planes for the enemy
to shoot at. I showed Nazi Messerschmitts going down in smoke.

I did not think the war was anything but far away. I did not
feel personally threatened. But my mother talked about the war
with worried references to Donald. He had graduated from
Townsend Harris High School under a rapid advance program
and now, age seventeen, he was enrolled at City College. My
mother was afraid Donald would draw a low number in the
Selective Service registration and be drafted into the Army and
taken off to fight in Europe. This seemed to me an outlandish
worry, inasmuch as America wasn't even in the war. I could not
quite make the connections adults around me were making. One
day I saw a headline in my father's copy of the *Post:* WAR
CLOUDS, it read. The article went on to speculate about how
and when the United States might have to become involved in
the war against Hitler.

In the same Madison Square Garden where I had seen the
Ringling Brothers and Barnum & Bailey Circus with that family
that rode bicycles on high wires and the little clown who swept
the spotlight at his feet, the American Nazis, called the Bund,
had held a rally. They had put up a flag with a swastika next to
an American flag, and marched in their brown shirts and with
belts like Texas Rangers going from their shoulders down slant-
wise to their waists. They gave the fascist salute. There were
thousands of them. Charles Lindbergh and Father Coughlin had
spoken to them and they shouted and screamed just as the
Germans did when Hitler spoke to them. "They are everywhere,
this rabble," my father said one night at dinner. "Two of them
came into the store today and I kicked them out. Can you imagine the temerity—coming into my store in their uniforms to try
to sell me a subscription to their magazine?"

Donald told us about one of the boys who had been in his
junior class at Townsend Harris. His name was Sigmund Miller.

He lived in Yorkville, the German neighborhood on the Upper East Side of Manhattan, and he was a fascist. "Considering that the school was almost one hundred percent Jewish, he was pretty brave about it," Donald said. Sigmund Miller would explain in class discussions why he was for Hitler. He got beat up repeatedly after school. But Donald was telling this because of what happened subsequently. Donald and Bernie and Irwin and Harold Epstein and Stan Mazey all went together to high school every morning. They met at the corner and walked across the Concourse and down Mt. Eden Avenue to the Jerome Avenue El. One morning on the train a man was reading the *Daily News*. Sigmund Miller's picture was on the front page. He had murdered his girlfriend. He had made a suicide pact with her, but after he killed her he had not been able to keep his part of the bargain. "Excuse me," Stan Mazey said to the man reading the paper, and yanked it right out of his hands. "I think a friend of ours just killed someone."

"Why would they want to commit suicide, your friend and this girl?" I asked at the dinner table.

Donald looked at my mother. "She was pregnant," he said.

My mother said, "I don't think this is appropriate conversation for dinnertime."

I was offended. "You think I don't know what pregnant means?" I said to her. "I can assure you, I know exactly what it means!" Then I was doubly offended because everyone laughed, as if I had said something funny.

TWENTY-TWO

It was winter now and the sky grew dark early in the afternoon. My father came home from work in the darkness with the cold blowing off him like the breath of his coat and hat. Donald came home each night with his books under his arm, his nose red and his eyes glittering with the cold. Even now I had pains where my scar was—lesions, the doctors called them. I played out of doors very little. I was not supposed to exert myself. My scar was long and I examined it every day. It was a thick raised welt slanting from my side down toward my testicles. At the top of the scar and at the bottom were depressions, dips in the skin, where the drains had been placed. These were the tenderest spots of all, and when I touched them I could feel my insides cringe. So people who went out into the world of German war, fearless of the Nazis on the dark streets of New York, had my admiration. I had changed physically since the operation; I had been a lean wiry little boy, very well coordinated, I was never a fast runner but I could throw gracefully and catch and get some fair hits in punchball or stickball. All that was gone. I was shaped like a pear, I was overweight from all those weeks in bed, and physically shy of my own movements. I was always afraid of tearing something, I did not like to jump around or leap down from the wall in the backyard as I had once done in my Zorro games with my friend Bertram; it was as if I still had stitches in me, I could sometimes feel them, and the terrible awful feeling when they had been removed, I could feel them as they had been snipped by the doctor and I could feel the gut string pulling through my flesh. I had nothing to counteract my tendency to fat. If I wasn't afraid to run around, my mother was afraid for me. She had very quickly gone grey at the temples. She looked at me worriedly and fed me as if I were still convalescing even though I had long since gone back to school. I ate lots of junket desserts and lots of eggs and slices of buttered bread and thick soups of chicken stock and beef with potatoes and cabbage and vegetables of all sorts. I drank lots of milk, it came now homogenized, which meant you didn't have to shake the bottle to distribute the cream evenly. I had to eat hot cereal in the morning, Cream of Wheat or oatmeal, even though I preferred Post Toasties or Kix. And since I didn't move around very much, my whole being was changed, I had grown taller and bulkier, I still had a sunny smile and a handsome countenance, but also a double chin. I tried to compensate for this by combing my hair in a way Donald combed his, with a pompadour in the front. Mine didn't stay up for very long, I was never allowed to let my hair grow long enough to make it really work. Donald as a college freshman grew his hair longer and combed it carefully each morning and in the evening too when he came home from school. In fact, when he didn't have anything else to do, Donald went to the mirror to comb his hair, running the comb through it, and propping it and patting it with his other hand till it was the way he wanted it. He was these days dignified and soft-spoken and serious, as befitted a college student. He no longer wore knickers, he wore long trousers pleated and with slightly pegged cuffs. He wore a chain from his belt to his side pocket. Outside the house he affected a straight briar pipe, which he clenched in his teeth on one side of his mouth. He never smoked it, that I knew, he just clenched it. Our relationship was changing. At seventeen he now hovered at about twice my age, and took on the coloration of a father rather than an older brother. He showered every day. He offered me less instruction because our interests no longer coincided, but appeared more and more in my eyes as a model to be emulated and studied. In the evening, when he got home, he listened to the fifteen-minute sports broadcast of Stan Lomax, who with great thoroughness rattled off all the minutiae of collegiate sports with heartening references to the New York city colleges and institutions that were disdained by the other sports news authorities. Stan Lomax dealt with the football fortunes of Brooklyn and City colleges with the same judicious objectivity as he mentioned the University of Michigan or the Minnesota Gophers or the Duke Blue Devils. Donald liked that. He had the fervent pride of the assimilationist, as we all did. Listening with him, I envisioned gothic campuses of idyllic rusticity, as if the sports scores were stories being told. Elegant young football players with names like Tommy Harmon strolled across tree-lined quadrangles in their slacks and argyle sweaters and two-toned shoes with pretty coeds in pleated skirts and angora sweaters by their sides. In their conversation they quietly admitted to having scored the winning touchdown. There were no books and no lectures in these visions of mine. What was essential to them was that same dusk of winter, that late afternoon of cold hard air and leaves spinning down from the plane trees of the Bronx streets, produced by the clouds of World War Two. I liked in my house circles of lamplight surrounded by rings of darkness that grew in depth the farther out they went. I liked the shelter of a desk lamp, feeling toward it Bomba the Jungle Boy's affection for his campfire in the roars of the dark surrounding night.

TWENTY-THREE

Yet actual football, as opposed to the symbolic game, we preferred, as it was performed by professionals. This was a trait we learned from our father, who had discussed how much better and livelier the pro game was than the collegiate version. There were two teams in New York, the Giants and the Brooklyn Dodgers. They had the same names as the baseball teams but were not related. For some reason my father liked the Dodgers, he admired their quarterback, whose name was Ace Parker, and two linemen, Perry Schwartz, an end whom he thought almost as good a pass catcher as Don Hutson of the Packers, and a terrific tackle named Bruiser Kinard. Donald and I made the Giants our team. We had Tuffy Leemans in the backfield, along with Ward Cuff, Hank Soar, and the passer, Ed Danowski. On the line was the iron man Mel Hein, at center, and two great ends, Jim Lee Howell and Jim Poole. That was a team. Everyone played both offense and defense, Mel Hein usually played the whole sixty minutes without a substitute, Ward Cuff dropkicked field goals and Hank Soar could be counted upon for at least one interception when he was back at Safety on defense. When the Giants played the Dodgers, fans of both teams showed up at the park.

One Sunday at about one o'clock my father decided to take us to a Giants-Dodgers game. Donald said, "We'd just as well not even try, we'll never get in, people started lining up for seats early this morning."

"Let's just give it a shot," my father said. My mother made us sandwiches and a thermos of hot chocolate. She claimed she was tired and would not mind being by herself for a few hours by way of placating Donald's and my guilt at leaving her alone on a Sunday. We knew Sunday was the only day my father was at home. For his part he seemed to have no cares leaving her.

Wrapped up against the cold November day, the three of us boarded the subway and rode down to 155th Street, and came upstairs in the shadow of the El outside the great steel-girded Polo Grounds. My heart sank. The streets were packed. The game was less than an hour from kickoff and immensely long lines of people were in front of the ticket kiosks. My father told Donald and me to get in line, just to keep a place, even though we knew it was likely the game would be sold out before we ever got to the booth. Saying he would be right back, my father disappeared.

All around us hawkers were selling pins and pennants, and bags of roasted peanuts. I really wanted one of those football pins, miniature footballs painted golden brown with painted laces attached to a ribbon with each team's colors, blue for the Giants, silver and red for the Dodgers; but I didn't want to be thought of as a baby. The footballs were made in Japan and you could pry them, like walnuts, in half at the seams. We could hear the crowds roaring inside the stadium as the teams warmed up. Occasionally we heard the sound of a punt. Our line inched forward with tormenting slowness. What could be worse than being on the outside and hearing cheers rise from behind the ballpark walls? The El pulled into the station overhead, and people came running down the stairs. The sidewalks overflowed; people ran and walked in the streets between the cars. I developed that specific prayerful longing that went with these situations: If we got into the game, I said to myself, I would do my homework every day for a week the minute I got home from school. I would help my mother when she asked. I would go to bed when I was told to.

Taxis kept pulling up and discharging passengers. Occasionally I saw a limousine polished to a black shine, with one of those open driver's seats and with white sidewall wheels and glittering chrome radiators and headlamps, and a running board trimmed in new grey rubber. The chauffeur would run around to the sidewalk door and out would step elegant women in fur coats and men in belted camel-hair coats, the collars turned up. They carried leather cases, which I understood were filled with flasks of whiskey and picnic delicacies, and they carried plaid blankets to keep warm, and some of them were recognized by people in the crowd, who called to them. They waved, smiling, as they passed through the gates. One or two older men in black coats and homburgs were saluted by policemen on guard. I saw in these sportsmen, I derived from them, information of a high life of celebrity, wealth, and the careless accommodation of pleasure. I understood that these people were politicians and gamblers first and sportsmen second. Something in their attitude appropriated the occasion. It was theirs. The team was theirs, the ballpark was theirs, and I, standing with my runny nose and muffled to invisibility in a buffing crowd of heavy-coated football fans on the outside and waiting to get in—a momentary swatch of color at the edge of their field of vision—I was theirs too. I felt all this keenly and became angry. Someone jostled me and I pushed back with my elbow.

Then there was a commotion in the street. One of the ticket booths had closed its window and put the SOLD OUT sign behind the little iron bars protecting the opaque window glass. The crowd at this kiosk dissolved noisily, there was shouting, and people invaded the lines at the other windows not yet shut down. Policemen were running toward us from the street and from under the concrete stands. Another elevated train thundered in.

"It's almost game time," Donald said, and just then another roar went up and our line dissolved into a swirling pushing angry mass. He was exasperated. "Where's Dad," he said. "We've come here for nothing."

At this moment, as we stood bewildered and feeling bruised

with disappointment we heard a voice—"Don, Edgar, over here!" My father was waving to us at the edge of the crowd. We pushed our way toward him. "This way," my father said, his eyes alight. In his hand he held three tickets spread out like cards. "What!" we said, finding it hard to believe. He'd done it! From one moment to the next he led us from despair to exhilaration through the turnstiles and up the ramp into the bright sunlight of the stadium.

Ah, what a moment, coming out into the raked tiers, seeing with my own eyes the green grass field, the white stripes, the colors of the two helmeted teams deployed for the kickoff. Tens of thousands of people roared with anticipation. Pigeons flew into the air. The game was about to begin!

Incredibly, my father had gotten tickets for the lower stands on the 35-yard line. We couldn't believe our good fortune. It was magic! His face was flushed with delight, his eyes widened and he pursed his mouth and puffed his cheeks like a clown. We were no sooner seated and the game was under way than he looked around and spotted an usher; five minutes later we were in even better seats, farther back in the section, where with some altitude we could now see the whole field clearly. "What do you think of this," my father said, smiling at us in triumph. "Not bad, eh?" He loved this sort of situation, the suspense of getting in just at the last moment. The game meant more now, more than it might have if he had purchased the tickets a week in advance.

There was no question we were witnesses to a momentous event. The two teams struggled back and forth on the field. We groaned or cheered as the pass was caught or the punt dropped.

Donald and I followed the game intensely, cracking peanut shells and chewing and frowning and offering each other extended critiques of the action. My father was more calm. He smoked his cigar and every now and then closed his eyes and turned his face up to the afternoon sun.

The Giants were in blue jerseys and the Dodgers in red and silver, and both wore the sectioned leather helmets that came around the ears, and the buff-colored canvas pants, and the black high lace-up shoes. When the sun went below the roof level of the upper stands, long shadows fell across the field and across our faces. The changing color of the day brought new moods to the game, new fortitude and desperation to the embattled lines, as the backs slashed off tackle or did their line bucks, as the centers hiked the ball and the backfield ran in box formation and compacted into their handoffs and laterals and blocks, and ran and threw from their scattered single wing. They were well matched, you could feel their effort, you heard the thudding leather of their shoulder pads. The dust flew up in the planes of sunlight as they fought on the dirt part of the field, the baseball diamond. My father did not passionately root for the Dodgers. It seemed more important to him that the score remain close. Donald and I wanted the Giants to pull ahead and win without any equivocation. Something happened to the sound of the game; the dimming light seemed to give it distance. Ace Parker punted the ball for the Dodgers and it rose in a looping spiral high over the tops of the stands; then I heard the sound of his shoe hitting the football.

In the late afternoon, dusk falling, the game ended, with the Giants winning by one touchdown. Everyone cheered. The two teams walked together toward the small bleachers at the end of the field and climbed the stairs under the scoreboard into their locker rooms. They held their helmets in their hands. Fans leaped over the bleacher walls and called to them. People flowed onto the field. We made our way down. It was awesome to tread in the black grass, with the marks of the cleats visible like traces of battle. It seemed to me a historic site. It was a hard cold ground. A wind blew in from the open backs of the stands, which now stood silhouetted, a great horseshoe-shaped shed, little light bulbs glittering dimly in each section of the upper and lower tiers. The air down here on the field was pungent with the cold. It smelled electric. I apprehended the awesome skill and strength of the football player. Boys ran through the crowd, dodging and dashing about like halfbacks, with invisible balls under their arms. I walked with my brother and father to the field gates, passing under the scoreboard and out to 155th Street. Here the milling crowds, the gabble, the horns of taxis, the rumble of trains, and police on horseback blowing their whistles brought my mind back to the city. We were hoarse and tired. The day was over. We pushed our way down the subway steps into the crowd on the station platform. We jammed into the train, the three of us forced together, packed tight in the train and barreling toward the dark Sunday night, when even the arguing stopped and there was stillness, and a cessation of all striving, my night of unnameable dread, that most mysterious night of the day of rest.

TWENTY-FOUR

The winter was to be a bad one. I woke up one night to hear my mother and father arguing. They were all the way at the other end of the house but I could hear her clearly. She was saying he had lost the store. I heard his voice then, but not the words, only the tone of earnest entreaty. He spoke a long time.

"Undercapitalized, my eye," she answered. "You've gambled it away. When you should have been taking care of business, you were out playing cards, running around and being a big shot. And Lester meanwhile was stealing from you."

"You don't know what you're saying, Rose," my father said.

"I know full well," she said. "Yes, of course these are bad times, but other people survive. They're competitive. They pull in their horns. They cut costs, they do not give credit, they buy on consignment—don't tell me how to run a business. If I were in charge you wouldn't be in the trouble you're in now."

I fell asleep while the argument went on. But in the morning everything was as it had always been. My father went off to work. Donald went off to school. My mother gave me my breakfast and asked me if I had done all my homework.

The issue I understood as the way each of them thought. Something was wrong, but my father seemed to think he could set it right and my mother was telling him it was too late to make things right. I heard pieces and bits of this argument over several weeks, sometimes late at night, sometimes allusively, right in front of me at the dinner table. My mother's voice rang with prophecy. She spoke as if something had already happened when it hadn't. This I resented especially, as I knew her to be more realistic. He still had hope. He insisted things were to be done and I couldn't entirely believe him, but I resented that she would not honor his intentions, she would not take them seriously. "Don't hand me any of your cock-and-bull stories," she said. "What bank is going to lend you money with the books you've kept."

This terrible event loomed larger and larger as it did not happen. It was the subject of all our lives. Donald continued to work in my father's store on Saturdays, just as he had since the age of thirteen. He was not paid, it was his family responsibility, which he dutifully met. I campaigned to help too. On Saturdays I went downtown to be Donald's assistant. As I grew stronger I accompanied him on his delivery rounds. Stores on Sixth Avenue adjoined residential neighborhoods. All the little brownstones and residential hotels between Sixth Avenue and Ninth, on both sides of Broadway, provided a small town's population for any shop or service. Donald delivered records that people ordered by phone, and radios and phonographs that they had left for repair. Sometimes he journeyed south to the Fourteenth Street area, where one or another of my father's jobbers supplied him with spare parts or record stocks. These were interesting trips for me, my courage held in tremulous tension by the presence of my older brother at my side. We walked in the dappled shadows of the El on Third Avenue, under the structure of black steel trestles that shook and sounded into the depths of the street bed the thunderous but unseen passage of the trains. There was no louder noise. It was like a tornado of sound; you could not, as the train passed overhead, hear what was said to you. You could see in some places the crossties laid under the tracks with nothing but air between them. People lived in tenements whose third- or fourth-floor windows looked out on the tracks, so close they could jump right onto them if they chose, so close the headlamps of the clattering trains would shine into their windows at night. We passed Christian missions with men in soft caps and shabby black coats standing about gazing at everyone who walked by, we passed electric tattooing parlors and barbershops that advertised fifteen cents for a shave and haircut, there were pawnshops with wooden Indians out front, and shooting galleries, ten shots for ten cents. Men with sandwich boards hung over their shoulders and flyers in their hands walked along advertising "Best Price for Old Gold," "Gaiety Follies." We stood under the marquee of a theater showing a triple bill with movies and movie stars I had never heard of. Men sat in there all day for ten cents, Donald said, just to have somewhere to sleep. Pushcart peddlers at the curbs sold everything—shoes, notions, fruit, even books. Men slept on their sides in the doorways, their hands under their heads, they were grown men but they slept curled up as I did. The doorways were their homes. How could I not with these sights in my eyes understand the meaning of a business? It was not an obscure lesson. Donald took us through gatherings of people poised at the corners waiting for the lights to change, he jaywalked us between jams of yellow cabs and trucks, streetcars running in the shadows of the elevated lines rang their bells at us, and he got us unerringly to our destination, into lofts or offices where we were expected and where packages marked with my father's name were waiting for us. My father still existed in business, and this encouraged me. My brother knew his way around town. Back at the store, people were buying things. Hippodrome Music looked busy. Why was all of this not sufficient?

I thought neither my father nor my mother was the one to whom this question should be put. I asked Donald.

"It's hard to understand," he said. "But it's not your problem. It is not anything a kid should worry about."

"Everyone's always hiding things from me," I said. "We weren't allowed to go to Grandma's funeral, which was really stupid when I was the one who found her dead."

"What are you talking about that for?" Donald said. "This is business. When the store moved they lost customers. It's taken them longer to build a clientele. Reliable customers who come in again and again are called a clientele. They can't get enough money from what they're selling to pay their salaries, and their bills, and to buy more things to sell too. Now, do you understand?"

Then while all this was going on Donald quit college at the end of his first term. He told me it was boring and that was why he was getting out. But that didn't make sense. He had joined a fraternity and I knew he loved spending time with his frat brothers, as he called them. They even owned their own house. They all smoked briar pipes there. Snooping around Donald's room when he was out, I found a letter from the college in his bureau drawer and it gave his marks, two D's and two F's. I knew what these grades meant, he had explained to me that in college they didn't mark with numbers, they marked with letters. I could not believe that my wonderful brother, who had been held out to me all through grade school as a wonderful student, was failing courses at City College. He was becoming like my parents —an adult to be observed and worried about. All these strange things were going on, everyone was unhappy and the three of them got into all sorts of arguments now, nobody liked what anybody else in the family was doing, my father was angry at my brother, and my mother was furious with both of them. All of it together pushed me down into myself, I wondered if I was to blame because of my operation; people didn't just leave the house, they slammed the door, dinners were silent, I felt small. I felt my ears were flattened along the sides of my head. My friend Arnold, from my class, had ears that grew that way, tight against his head and very tiny, and that's the way I felt my ears were now. I was feeling all hunched up into myself.

In this terrible time some basic practices were maintained, including the Sunday afternoon visit to Grandma and Grandpa's house on the Concourse north of Kingsbridge Road. Once again

I was the only representative of the family to accompany my father on these visits. It was Grandma's feeling that extravagance at home had contributed to the financial fix he was in; Rose had not been as economical as she might have, she was careless with a dollar, she liked good things too much.

"Please, Gussie," my grandfather said. "The man is talking business. If you have nothing intelligent to say, say nothing."

Even my father was piqued by his mother's inability to think of anything but his wife's spending habits. "Papa," he said, "why are all women like this? It's as if we don't exist. Whether they love or they hate, they think only of each other, they are alone in the universe," he said with exasperation.

"You talk," my grandma said in an ugly spiteful voice, hobbling across the room with the tea things, and slamming them down. "And she spends."

On one of these trips our visit coincided with the visit of Aunt Frances, who for the first time heard all the details of our family's troubles. She looked very fine, with a dark blue suit and a black hat and a white blouse. She wore white gloves and put them down on top of her leather handbag when she came in. She took off her hat and ran her fingers through her beautiful white hair. She calmed everyone down, she could do that, calm people down because she spoke so softly and with such grace. "I will talk to Ephraim," she said.

I respected Aunt Frances because she was so soothing. My parents had relied on her to get the right doctor for me. My mother hated my grandma but disliked Frances only on occasion. However, she liked Aunt Molly, the funny one who was so sloppy, and she felt they were friends. My father loved both his sisters as well as his mother, but disliked Frances's husband, Ephraim, although he would not tell me that, I knew it for myself.

But Frances and her husband Ephraim had powers over us all. I didn't know why. I knew they were wealthier, but I didn't know if they were wealthier because they had these powers, or if they got them from being wealthy, but they were not troubled people, as far as I could tell; even when they had had troubles such

as my cousin Lila's getting polio when she was a little girl, before
I was born, they would not have doubted their powers to do
something to save her, as they did, or to know what to do to save
me, which they knew. It was hard for me to understand exactly
what I perceived of my aunt and her husband, but they were a
degree or two above us, although I couldn't have said what I
meant by "above." People wouldn't talk to them in a way they
wouldn't want to be talked to. They had power over situations,
they could command things, they could run things, and especially impressive in my beautiful aunt's case, they could do so
without raising their voice.

Donald had been looking for any kind of a job he could get,
he did not want to work for my father now because he would not
be paid. He would put in part-time hours while he was looking,
he said, but he wanted a real job of his own. One of Uncle
Ephraim's connections, it turned out, was the owner of a large
printing firm, B. J. Warriner. This firm was so important it
printed the ballots for all the elections held in the City of New
York. It printed documents of all kinds for the city and the state,
and the man who owned this firm was Uncle Ephraim's friend
and legal client. One day Donald received in the mail a letter
from Uncle Ephraim and another letter under it addressed to
the Employment Manager of the B. J. Warriner firm. I studied
this letter over Donald's shoulder as he sat in the kitchen. "Be
careful," my mother said, "or you'll get it wet. Keep it off the
table." At the top of this letter, which looked almost like parch-
ment, was the name *Ephraim Goldman* in raised letters, you could
feel them with the tips of your fingers—*Attorney at Law.* In the
letter Uncle Ephraim called the attention of the Employment
Manager to Mr. Donald Altschuler of 1650 Eastburn Avenue,
The Bronx, as a young man known to him for many years, whom
he could recommend as being of sterling character, commenda-
ble intelligence and great promise, and who was now looking for
suitable employment.

Donald got a job with the Warriner firm as a messenger boy
for fifteen dollars a week. It was not a job he could take satisfaction in, he found it demeaning after having led a band and

attended college. "Uncle Ephraim's influence isn't what he thinks it is," Donald said. He left every morning very early, because Warriner was far downtown, on Hudson Street, and the subway ride was very long. When he came home he smelled faintly of ink. He said the presses were interesting to watch. He said he liked the men in the pressroom but not the executives in the office. They sat at phones and sold people printing and thought they were hotshots. He liked getting out and making the deliveries. Regularly he took proofs of things to police head-quarters on Centre Street and to the Municipal Building on Chambers Street. He liked the far downtown; when he had a free minute he liked to go to the piers. He could steal a few minutes from delivering something on Whitehall Street to watch the ferries at Battery Park. Or if a delivery ran into his lunch hour he could go to the Aquarium.

But his disposition had changed, he didn't see his friends now, he didn't want to play with me at all; when he got home from work, he didn't talk to anyone but threw himself across his bed and went to sleep.

In my memory I now think of this time as sunless. It was a harsh winter with snow always in the street, accumulating through several snowfalls despite the Department of Sanitation snow-plows, which were really water wagons with plows attached, and despite the sanitation men who with long-handled flat-bladed shovels pushed the slush and snow into the sewers. Snow built up in banks along the curb, and lay against the sides of buildings grey and crusted. The sun never seemed to come out and light left the sky not long after school was over for the day. I huddled near my radio and listened to my programs. I read my Richard Halliburton book that Mae Barsky had brought me in the hospi-tal: *The Complete Book of Marvels*. Richard Halliburton went around the world exploring its marvels. He swam the length of

the Panama Canal, and climbed to the top of the George Washington Bridge while it was being built. He slept secretly one
night in the Taj Mahal, and he had his picture taken sitting at
the top of the biggest pyramid in Egypt. He climbed the mountain to Macchu Pichu, the ancient hidden site of the Incas of
Peru. He went places by ship and sometimes flew the flying
boats.

I also found myself deeply attentive to movie serials. It was a
matter of serious discussion with my friends how closely the
heroes of the movie serials resembled the originals of the comic
strips. *Dick Tracy* was one of the more effective in bringing the
comics to life. I believed Tracy was Tracy, his chin wasn't as
pointed as I'd hoped but he had that look about the eyes. *Don
Winslow of the Navy* was another good one. Don Winslow got into
fights on speedboats as they were running along out of control.
At one point he was captured and taken by motorboat into a
secret cave hidden inside a cliff; there were landing docks in
there and steel doors in stone walls and sailors in black sweaters
under the command of an evil Oriental. Anything with caves
fascinated me. The caves in Missouri that Mark Twain describes
in *Tom Sawyer* I had never forgotten: When Tom and Becky got
lost in those caves, and they shared their pitiful piece of cake and
Becky lay down to die and Tom went on in the narrow lightless
passageway with only a string to bring him back to her, I could
almost not bear to read. The worst moment of all was when they
heard the voices of rescuers come closer and closer only to
recede and leave them alone once again, in the silence. I could
not breathe reading that. I thought in that situation I would not
be as brave as Tom or resigned, however piteously she cried, as
Becky. In sheer terror, like someone buried alive, I would exhaust myself screaming and trying to break through the cave
walls with my bare fists, I would run around in circles and stumble into deep clefts in the rocks, I would gasp and moan and die
of apoplexy. But Don Winslow, who habitually found himself
imprisoned in caves, did not worry me. They were very well lit
caves, they were electrified, steel doors rose and fell silently, a
mark of civilization, and it was far preferable to be a prisoner of

someone, no matter how evil, than to be alone in the darkness miles underground. In fact, it wasn't until Tom Sawyer saw Injun Joe's candle around the corner in one of the dark rock corridors that I knew the children would escape. As mean and frightening a villain as he was, Injun Joe was life. For me he was a sign of the way out, a hint from the author that he would relent and give his children back to the ordinary concerns of good and evil.

But, generally speaking, the movie versions of comic book heroes were great disappointments. Flash Gordon, for example, was too thick around the middle. He didn't seem to be as quick-witted as he was in the panel drawings, there was some sinuous capability lacking there. Of course, Zorro was better on the movie screen than in the original. And *The Green Hornet* was best of all on the radio. My friends and I were thoughtful critics of these conversions of life forms. Arnold—the boy with the peculiar flattened ears and handwriting like a spider, in addition to strangely large eyes behind his eyeglasses and a wet sort of speech that produced a kind of spray when he was excited—was the most astute of all of us. He knew everything about serials, he could tell us who produced them—Republic Studios or Universal or Monogram—and the names of the actors who played in them. He even knew the genealogy of Britt Reid, the Green Hornet: Britt Reid, he said, was none other than the Lone Ranger's grandnephew. We were skeptical, and hurt Arnold's feelings by laughing at him, but he drew himself up and marshaled his facts. "One, the Lone Ranger's real name was Reid, and he had a nephew, Dan Reid." We gave Arnold that—Dan Reid was in several of the radio stories. "Two," said Arnold, "Britt Reid, who is the Green Hornet, has a father named Dan Reid. Three, this Dan Reid who is Britt Reid's father is an old white-haired man, which proves enough years have passed for him to be the same Dan Reid, the boy, whose uncle was the Lone Ranger. Four—Britt Reid is the Lone Ranger's grandnephew!"

Wiping my face, I grudgingly accepted Arnold's analysis. I thought privately that if it was true, it was disappointing. The Lone Ranger was one thing, the Green Hornet was another.

One rode horseback, the other drove a Lincoln Zephyr with custom wheel covers. The Green Hornet moved about the city, a modern city, he wore a hat with a snap brim and a belted raincoat with the collar up. I didn't want to know that he was related to the Lone Ranger. Also I didn't like to believe that families through generations tended to wear masks and dedicate their lives to fighting crime. Each of them would be presumed to eliminate all crime forever. There was a loss of the idea of perfection. The Lone Ranger was *lone,* and that was the way he should have been.

But then one night when *The Green Hornet* radio program came on, my mother happened by and heard the opening theme music. It was very fast and full of tension. " 'The Flight of the Bumblebee,' " my mother said. "Why do you suppose these junky programs all use classical music for their themes?" She was thinking also of *The Lone Ranger,* which used the overture from *William Tell,* an opera by Rossini. That led to my revelation. In school the next day I sought out Arnold. "Arnold," I said, "it's not that the Green Hornet and the Lone Ranger are related. It's that their writers are related! I bet you we will find out that both stories are written by the same person. Both programs use classical music, both the heroes wear masks, the Lone Ranger has Tonto at his side, and the Green Hornet has Cato driving his car."

Arnold looked at me. His favorite subject was Science. He wanted to be a scientist when he grew up. He already had the objectivity of the scientist, which is the willingness to give up one hypothesis for another that is more reasonable. His eyes widened. "And they both leave calling cards!" he shouted.

"A silver bullet!" I cried.

"A hornet pin!" he screamed. And we pounded each other and jumped up and down and laughed.

I found out that my father had lost his store one morning when I met him at the breakfast table. He was cheerful. "How are you, young man," he said. He had brought home a radio that you didn't have to plug in. It worked on a battery. It was covered in alligator skin and had a leather carrying handle. It was like a small suitcase and you flicked the switch and it lit up on the dial just like a regular radio. You could carry it anywhere, to the beach or picnics, but I found it heavy. Then I noticed a cardboard box with many packets of needles and also a microphone, the kind used by radio stations, except that it wobbled on its base. And finally there was a pack of records in green envelopes. Some of them were old with grooves only on one side. "These are rare recordings by Caruso and Gigli," my father said. "If we hold on to them long enough they'll be valuable." While I ate my oatmeal he opened his newspaper. I saw the headlines. The other bad news was that France had fallen to Hitler.

DONALD

I didn't actually flunk out of City College, although I was called before the Dean—the late Dean Morton Gottschal. He said I would have to improve my grades or I would be out. But I wasn't ready for a full-time college career, I knew that. I quit City and enrolled in night school and went to work as a messenger at Warriner during the day. I wouldn't go back to school full time till after the war, when I racked up straight A's and got my degree in two and a half years. At Warriner I made twelve dollars a week, not fifteen, as you said, although I could hope to supplement that with what I could clip on the expense account. You'd charge for a bus ride, a nickel, but you walked—that sort of thing. You walked fast. I didn't feel I was cheating. They paid me nothing. I worked hard, I did what I was supposed to. Maybe they paid so low because they knew all messenger boys padded the expense account. But anyway I worked all day and then went to night school. I was still seventeen and a half. I was a kid. I'd always worked. I started working for Dad when I was thirteen or fourteen. I know I was that young because I couldn't go to lunch myself, he had to take me. I still wore knickers. Now, maybe eighteen, I was keeping the family going. Dad had lost his store, he was out of work, and my crummy twelve dollars was keeping the household in food. I turned my pay envelope over to Mom every week. I was the breadwinner. I was very disturbed by that.

It didn't last long, a couple of months till Dad got a job as a salesman with Home Appliance Distributors. But it wasn't good. I was tied down to them, I was doing what he should have been doing. Mother always complained about not being given enough to run the household, although there was never any time when we didn't have food or clothing or were threatened with eviction. But that was the big problem in the family, never having enough money. We all lived with that idea, it was the thirties, it conditioned everything—teenage kids were expected to help out, there was no question about it. But it was getting to me, I suppose. Harvey Stern, whom I'd known since first grade, had found out about an interesting opportunity. The Signal Corps was accepting applications for a civilian trainee program. They taught you how to be a radio operator, how to transmit and receive in Morse code, work a transmitter, repair radios, all of that; and they paid you besides. When Dad got his job at Home Appliance and began to bring money into the house, the folks didn't need my salary anymore. The great thing about this job was that it wasn't even in New York, it was in Philadelphia. Harvey and I went down and took the exam and a few weeks later we were told we had passed, and we were hired. We would live in a dormitory there and study radio and get paid and be on our own. So that was a big break for me. The folks gave me permission, it seemed the wisest course for several reasons. We all knew I would be drafted. When the time came it would be better to enlist. If I had experience in radio, I could hope to get a technical rating in the Signal Corps.

So I was free. I was leaving the house. I would not come back for several years, until after the war. I went down there and started to live for myself. It was a remarkable feeling. In Philadelphia we met some girls and went to bed with them. That was the first time for me. Life was speeding up. Everyone believed war was coming, nobody knew how or why, but everyone felt it. People wanted to live and enjoy themselves while they could. It was a strange feeling living for myself, on my own, with nobody to tell me what to do, and with nobody's welfare to worry about except my own. I did well in the Signal Corps school, in fact I finished first in my class. I was a very good radio operator. I bought my own bug. That's what the telegraph key in its modern form was called. It was semiautomatic. You could transmit faster than you could with an old-fashioned key. We each had our bug and developed our sending styles so that they were as recognizable to other operators as our handwriting or our voice. I wanted to go into the Signal Corps when I enlisted and become a radioman on airplanes, I wanted to get an assignment to the Army Air Corps, which is what the Air Force was called then, it wasn't a separate branch, it was part of the Army. The word "radioman" had glamour attached to it. You were on the leading edge of technology. I thought I was getting out, getting away from that intense family life we lived, I couldn't have realized it or articulated it but we were all too close and everything was terribly intense. There was no letup. Partly it was everyone's struggle for survival, partly it was the enormous difference in the personalities of Mom and Dad. Dad went off in all directions, he was full of surprises, some of them were good, some not so good. But it kept everyone on edge, Mother especially. You know, once I was working in the store when it was at the Hippodrome, and, you remember, Dad kept these record catalogues on the counter by the cash register, catalogues, and invoices, all that sort of paperwork. And stuck among these one day I found a photograph of a woman. A very glamorous woman, it showed her head and shoulders, it was a formal portrait theatrically lit. She had long hair flowing over her shoulders, which were bare, she was wearing some sort of costume, I suppose she was some kind of singer, I don't know why I thought that. But, anyway, in ink at the bottom she had written, *To Dave, Always.* And it was signed *Irene.* I didn't say anything, but I was enraged. I found it unforgivable that he was fooling around. He was the kind of man to fool around, to philander. He was errant. He had a wild streak in him. He was generous to us and we all lived together as a very close knit family relying on one another, and that was all true, but he had his secrets and they came out of the same part of his character that made him dream big impractical dreams that he couldn't realize. I mean he was a scrapper and he kept us going somehow. But something really broke for me when he accepted my messenger's salary for Mom's allowance. Why didn't he say something about that? Why didn't he say he'd pay me back? Why didn't he say he'd keep an accurate record, and account for every dollar and make sure I got it back when he was on his feet again? But he didn't. And Mom came to depend on me. I mean I think of it now, I started working very young, I always did something, I was always trying to get ahead, get myself a summer vacation by putting together a band with my friends. That wasn't a bad thing to do, at age sixteen, posing as a nineteen-year-old professional musician. Where did I learn that enterprise? It was part expediency, of course, partly the spirit of the time, but I had some drive to bring to it that was all my own. Dad was a good model in one way—he didn't like working for anyone else, he liked to be on his own, he had ambition, he was always cooking up deals, even though most of them didn't come through. But that would have impressed me. He was a good salesman too, and knowledgeable about what he sold. Even though he wasn't really the hustling salesman type, he had a refinement about him that would not let him hard-sell. But he was never satisfied to be what he had chosen to be. Do you know what I mean? You could not define him by what he did. There was no security in him of definition. You could never imagine his finding one thing to do and making a success of it and not try to do anything else. I don't think he ever found what it was that would make him say, "This is me, Dave Altschuler, and I am forty-eight years old and I live at such and such address and I do such and such for a living and I am satisfied with my life and my work." You couldn't pin him down. And the funny thing is I thought I was getting away from him. And what did I go and do but get into a radio business of another sort, just like my father, riding the airwaves for a living.

TWENTY-FIVE

I still had my Heinz pickle pin from the World's Fair; lots of people had them, there was a currency in these things and some kids didn't care for them, they went from hand to hand; and so I now had not only the Heinz pickle but the Planters nut company's Mr. Peanut, who wore a top hat and monocle, and I had a DC-3 charm from the aviation exhibit. I found out that my friend Meg's mother had a job at the World's Fair, although she didn't say doing what. But as a result Meg made me a present one afternoon of a full-color map of the Fair, and it was the kind of map I liked, with the drawings of the buildings in three dimensions, and in color, as if you were looking down from an airplane, but it was like a cartoon too, with little flags and people walking, and the very clear overhead view showed you immediately where the attractions were and named each one right on the roof. Meg had already been to the Fair several times and was able to tell me what was good. I got a hang of the layout this way, and by studying the map carefully—it had an index, which located things for you by means of a simple grid, A to K and 1 to 7—I was able to plan just how I would go about seeing the Fair, where I would start, and the best way to proceed, step by step, until I felt that I knew what to do, I could see everything I wanted to see and not become confused or miss anything. That had been a worry of mine.

It was peculiar living in the house without Donald, it was not the same as his being away for the summer, I felt the distance of our ages keenly, that I was a boy and he was now a grown man. Somehow I had not kept up to my original rate of lagging behind. When he did come home from Philadelphia for a weekend, I found I was shy, I didn't know what to say. And he was reserved too, he asked me about school as if he didn't remember what it was like.

He had a snapshot of himself standing in front of a car with his arm around a dark-haired girl in a belted wool coat and they were both smiling at the camera. Behind the car was a red brick building, which was the apartment house where he lived.

And then as time went on Donald came home less and less on the weekends and the house was very still. I couldn't seem to make the noise to fill it up, even when I asked a friend over. When I came home from school my father would not be there, of course, he worked now for a distributor, selling appliances to stores around Manhattan. As often as not my mother would be out shopping, or doing work for the Sisterhood, and so I would be alone in the house. I would have instructions from my mother to turn on the light under the three-sided iron pot in which she baked potatoes. Or there would be some change for my ice cream. Alone in my house after school, I sometimes became desolate. On one afternoon of rain my mother was late coming back and I began to imagine she had been hit by a car. Maybe she had fallen on the subway track. I cried. I don't know why her absence affected me so.

When she came home I hugged her, which made her laugh with surprise.

There was some sort of chastened peace between my mother and father having to do with the changed circumstances of our lives. Donald would be called into the Army if war came. That was very much on their minds. And then this new job of my father's had done something to his spirit. He had not worked for anyone else for many years, he had become used to being his own boss, he did not easily acclimate to his setback. On the occasions when I stayed home from school with one of my colds I saw that he did not leave the house eagerly. He found excuses not to leave, he would clean up the kitchen or offer to do some shopping for my mother before he left for work. He claimed that, as a salesman calling on accounts, he had to give the stores time to open their doors and get going on their day. This reasoning did not persuade her, she felt he was losing out to his competitors. But my father could not be budged, he took a long time over breakfast and then washed all the dishes, and then even on the way to the subway stopped to do errands.

He was not attentive to me, at home he read the newspaper or listened to music. He was thoughtful. He was always a robust man but now seemed to be stolid and portly and losing his joy of things. I would not think of mentioning the World's Fair to him. Nor to my mother, who was out of sorts most of the time and afflicted with various aches or pains. Her shoulder was giving her trouble, she had some sort of inflammation of the shoulder and sometimes wore her arm in a sling. She rested on the sofa a lot; she could not easily play the piano with her bad shoulder.

And then I was told that we would be moving out of our house. The reasoning was that, with Donald not living at home anymore, the three of us didn't need such a large place. The landlord was intending to raise the rent when the lease was up, and it just wasn't worth the money.

My mother had found just the apartment for us and she took me to see it while it was being painted. It was up on the Grand Concourse. She met me after school. North of 174th Street, Eastburn Avenue became a hill. We trudged up Eastburn past apartment houses of the walk-up variety, four or six stories around small courtyards and with dingy front halls. Our new house was at the top of the hill where Eastburn met with the

Concourse and also 175th Street—a six-story edifice of ocher brick triangularly shaped to the corner it was on, like the famous Flatiron Building in Manhattan. My father had made this comparison by way of encouragement when he knew I'd be going to have a look.

The apartment was on the second floor, one flight up. You entered a narrow windowless corridor that led into a foyer. The foyer opened in one direction into the living room and in the other to a small kitchen and dinette. A painter was on his ladder in the kitchen. A second painter was doing the bathroom next to the dinette. Then down another narrow hall, exactly at the triangulated end of the building, was the bedroom. There were three big windows, one on each wall. We overlooked the stop where we had always waited for the bus going up the Concourse to my grandma and grandpa's house.

"You see," my mother said as I looked out the window, "it's a wonderful view. When there's a parade on the Concourse you can stand here and see the whole thing. Everything's so light and airy. You're not much farther from school than you were. A nice wide street, with trees, the Grand Concourse. This is the place to be. We're very lucky."

But I knew what she felt. It was painful to me that she was making the best of things, finding reason to be thankful about this and that when I could tell she was miserable. We no longer had the means to maintain ourselves as we had. It was a degree of the seriousness of our decline that she would not articulate it. "The only thing is, we'll be a little bit pressed for closet space," she said. I liked my mother to be tough and realistic and to call a spade a spade, as she always had. As she went around now, pointing out why this tiny apartment would be such a wonderful place to live, I was truly glum. It felt as if you could barely turn around in it. I had never lived anywhere but in a private house near the park. The Concourse was a wide six-lane thoroughfare with pedestrian islands to help one cross, the outer lanes being for local traffic, the four inner lanes for express traffic. The pedestrian islands were planted with trees. Way over on the far side was an unbroken bank of apartment houses, north and south, as far as the eye could see. I didn't know anybody who lived in them, or if there were any children.

When the move actually occurred, I was in school. That morning I had gotten up from my own bed in my own room as usual, I had my breakfast in the kitchen, where I'd always had it, the morning sun coming in the windows that looked on the alley, the old wooden table with the oilcloth, and the wooden chairs with the spoked backs, just where they'd always been in the middle of the large kitchen. On one wall the refrigerator with the cylindrical motor on top; on the other, the big enameled cabinet my mother called a "Dutch kitchen" with a slide-out ledge, lots of little closet doors and a flour sifter built in. "Here's your lunch," my mother said, handing me a paper bag. "Tuna salad sandwich, which you like, and an apple. Here's ten cents for your milk. At the end of the day, don't come back here. Come to the new apartment. Look both ways before crossing."

I left the house walking over bare floors and through cardboard cartons of packed things. Pulling up to the curb was a moving van.

At the end of the school day, as instructed, I turned right as I came out of the schoolyard, crossed 174th Street, and took the long walk up the Eastburn Avenue hill to the new apartment on the Concourse. It felt strange. I kept turning around to look down the hill. I saw children coming out of school and going my old way home.

The door was open. My steps resounded on the bare floor. I found my mother sitting alone among many of our things, which now looked strange in these new rooms painted cream, the latest color, she had told me. She sat on the sofa and looked exhausted. She gave me a wan smile. She had managed the whole move herself, my father having gone off to work as I had to school.

In the new kitchen I drank my milk as I always had. The refrigerator was a new model with round corners and the motor hidden in the rear. White metal cabinets hung from the walls over the sink. Everything was very close together. The kitchen floor was little more than a space between the fixtures. It was all neat and compact. The kitchen was divided by partitions that came to my shoulders. The partitions created the dinette. We had a new oval table with a shiny, marbleized top and four matching chairs.

The modernity of everything was what we talked about; that and the reasonable rent and the concessions given by the landlord as a reward for our having moved in.

The new living room was filled to capacity with our upright Sohmer and sofa and chairs and lamps, and console radio and record player and carpet and end tables and knickknacks. Against the wall at right angles to the old sofa with its curved Empire back was a new square two-cushion sofa with high square arms that could be converted into a bed. My parents would sleep here. Gone was the olive bed with the frieze of flowers on the headboard. I would have the triangular bedroom looking out over the bus stop. There were two new single beds here. When Donald came home, he would share the room with me.

Each day when I returned from school I explored more of the neighborhood. The Concourse, I saw, was actually built along a ridge; if there were no buildings, if all the land were returned to early times, the Concourse would be a plateau overlooking valleys to the west—that would be Jerome Avenue—and, less precipitously, those to the east. The light was different on the top of the plateau. A bit colder. There were no green hedges or plots of grass. We were suspended one story above a great impersonal street, with a lot of sky visible, and the constant hum of traffic. Across 175th Street, on our side of the Concourse, was the Pilgrim Church, whose bell rang on Sunday. And directly on the other side of the Concourse and one block down, was the new Junior High School that I would be going to when I finished the sixth grade, at P.S. 70. And so my last connection with

Claremont Park and with my old street and schoolyard would be gone.

Understanding the isolation I felt, my mother relaxed the rules about my coming home immediately after school was out. She even consented to my visiting my friend Meg. I had only to advise her in the morning if I intended to stay on in the old haunts with my friends and play. I played stoopball or punchball in the same clothes—white shirt, red school tie—I wore for my classes. I came home with shirttails hanging, my sweater tied by the sleeves around my waist, and my knickers drooping. My mother, who had to scrub the clothes on a small washboard in the sink in the little kitchen, did not complain. She missed Donald and had softened her discipline of me. She too found things to do in the old places, taking on the direction of the Mt. Eden Synagogue Sisterhood choir two afternoons a week.

TWENTY - SIX

In the spring, with the days getting warmer and the light lasting, I spent as little time at home as I possibly could. On rainy days I went invariably to Meg's and drank milk with her. Meg had grown a bit, she was still petite, but she had filled out some. I was aware of the faintest golden down on her forearms and legs. She was very graceful and held her head high when she walked, her hair was thicker, which made her look older; and I happened to notice at times when I was behind her that her skirt moved in the rhythm of her moving backside, which was round enough now to push out the cloth that way. I couldn't have said what I felt, but all the children in the class now considered me Meg's boyfriend and believed that when we grew up we were going to get married. If someone teased me about this, I had to throw my books down and jump him. But most of the time I was not directly confronted in this manner and so did not have to deny anything. She and I never discussed these things, recognizing the danger of entrusting such delicate matters to words. If either of us had said anything, the other could no longer have sustained the relationship. It could only continue unarticulated, tacit, in the pretense of ignorance. We felt loyal to each other and calm in each other's presence. We shared things: she gave me cookies and, outside, I would buy two ice creams with my money. We played in Claremont Park a lot, where we were by ourselves. I sometimes found her looking at me with a grave expression on her face. I liked her mouth, especially the upper lip, which flourished in a thickened curve toward its corners so that at any moment you would think she was about to cry. She had light grey eyes, which had grown larger. We were nine years old now.

Meg's mother, Norma, worked every day at the World's Fair from four in the afternoon to closing time. This meant she went off to the subway in the early afternoon, before we were out of school. Norma had to take a subway to Manhattan and then transfer to the Queens IRT. When I saw her she was very weary, but said she was lucky to have the job. But that meant Meg and I were left alone most of the time. We did our homework together. She still liked to play with dolls, to serve them an imaginary tea on little tin plates and cups, and talk to them. One of her dolls was a very popular model called a Didy-Doll, as ridiculous a bit of cutesyness as everything else having to do with girl culture. The feature of this doll was that a small nippled bottle of water could be applied to its mouth and a moment later the water would come out of a hole between its legs. I found my friend's attentions to this doll embarrassing. One rainy afternoon we were sitting on the floor in her living room and she insisted that I administer the water. I didn't want to. The doll was lying there on its back with its legs spread out and no clothes on. Meg insisted that I push the little nippled bottle against the doll's painted mouth. The blue glazed-button eyes of the infant doll stared up at me. Meg kept saying, "Go ahead, she's thirsty, can't you see she's thirsty. Please, do it, she is very thirsty." Her voice grew constricted as she repeated these words, and my own pulse was loud in my ears and I felt my face flushing. The intensity of her belief, as if this toy were really alive, I found both disgusting and thrilling at the same time. But I was determined not to give in, but to torment these feelings of hers and be cruel to them. I jammed the rubber nipple not into the doll's mouth but at the hole between the legs. I pushed down until water spilled over the doll and onto the floor. Meg cried out and threw her small self at me, knocking me backward from my sitting position. In the next moment she was on top of me and using her whole body to pound me, rearing up and dropping down flat, as if trying to pound the breath out of me, doing that again and again while I lay there on my back. Each time she fell on top of me I could feel her warm breath chuff in my ears. I felt the warmth of her, I smelled her sweet soap smell, I put my arms around her and found myself holding her backside with my hands. Her dress was up around her waist and I felt her thighs and her cotton underwear. She tired suddenly and lay still on top of me. Then she became aware of something that was not too familiar to her, although it was to me—my stiffening. She struggled back from it in alarm, the prod of it was uncomfortable to her. I wouldn't let her go but pushed up and rolled her over and lay on top of her as she struggled. Her eyes were lowered. Just for a moment I held her pinned like this and then got off and sat up, as she did, and a moment later we were playing as if nothing had happened. The little puddle of water became spilled tea in her game and she sponged it off the floor with a paper napkin. Later we did our homework and then I went home.

In a confusion of thought I saw my friend in my mind as I went to sleep that night. I was restless. I could not get the pillow right. Finally I lay on my side, curled, with the pillow turned length-wise so that it was between my legs. I experienced a diffuse sense of urgency all through my body, my limbs, my fingers and toes. I found that I was angry. And then all at once I was feeling sorry for myself. I heard no sound in the house. My father was not home. My mother was reading in the living room. The corner street light shone on the ceiling. I heard a steady hum of traffic. I didn't know where I was. We had new venetian blinds, of which my mother was proud, but no matter how they were adjusted the bright light of the Concourse shone through.

Yet it gradually came to me that I now had a private life. Nobody in my family saw Meg and Norma, only I did. I liked that. Living in a new neighborhood had made me independent. I ranged now. I did not run right home after school. I could see Meg without even telling anyone. This was an unusual household, this mother and daughter. It had no father. It brought out in me a certain feistiness. My loins stirred with protective feelings. This was my secret life of adventure. Norma was nothing like other mothers I had known, including my own. There was some carelessness of spirit about her, which I perceived in the way she pushed at her hair with her fingertips, or looked at herself in her living room mirror over the sofa. She did not represent author-ity in my mind. Once, on her day off, she and Meg and I sat down to play a board game. I started to read the rules just as Donald always did. "Let's not bother with that," Norma said. "Let's just play."

I could not envision my mother sitting down with Meg and me on the floor and playing one of our games with us. Maybe that was the sort of thing that made my mother dislike her. Both daughter and mother had got down on their knees, and sat back on their legs the way girls do. Except that Norma was wearing a housecoat and it fell back over her thighs, which looked very white and soft to me; she kept pulling the material over herself and it kept falling away, and I noticed that. Then she noticed me noticing and she smiled and tousled my hair.

With my new freedom I was developing a certain confi-dence. I was reading more than I ever had, three or four books a week, sea stories and boys' stories, and sports and adventure novels; and I began to feel hampered having to wait for an adult, my mother particularly, to find the time to accompany me to the library. The library was in the East Bronx, on Wash-ington Avenue. It was quite far. I applied now and received permission to go to the library myself. After the first or second time, I had no fear of getting lost. I went every Saturday morning. It was May, the weather was warm, and I walked along in the sun of the season holding two or three books in each hand at my side. I developed a modest shortcut or two, walking east on 176th Street past an old people's home, where they sat on rockers on a porch and looked at me, and then down a steep grade curving to a junction with Tremont Avenue, a main thoroughfare, just at the site of an Eye Hospital. At the bottom of the hill was Webster Avenue, with its trolley cars and cobblestones of Belgian block. Crossing Webster at Tremont could be dangerous, trolley lines bisecting and branching off, trucks rumbling along, you had to keep your wits about you. Then I passed over the New York Central tracks at Park Avenue, and with the Third Avenue El in sight, I turned right on Washington Avenue and only one block away was the library. It was an Andrew Carnegie branch library. Across the street was a company that sold stones for cemeteries. A big display room was filled with these immense granite monuments with names of imaginary dead people carved in them. Around the corner was the Pechter Bread Company. The whole neighborhood smelled of delicious bread baking. They baked those hard-crust rye breads with the little postage-stamp union labels stuck on them. Our family bought the Pechter breads and here was the very place they were made.

I never made this trip carelessly. These were still dangerous precincts. The East Bronx turned out not only criminal boys but, as I now knew from the kind of history children collect in schoolyards, major big-time gangsters. My library was not far from the late Dutch Schultz's old beer barns. He'd owned taverns on Third Avenue, under the El. I knew I had more to fear from the boys than from the grown-up gangsters, but altogether there was a culture here that was not mine. No, the East Bronx was not a place to take lightly. I had to admit to myself to being slightly relieved when I reached the front steps of the Washington Avenue branch and passed into the quiet rooms with the oak bookshelves.

It was at this library that I learned about the contest for boys sponsored by the New York World's Fair Corporation. An essay contest. A poster on the bulletin board told all about it. The topic was the Typical American Boy. You had to write in two hundred and fifty words or less what you thought were the qualities that best exemplified American boyhood. You had to submit a signed photograph of yourself and you had to write the essay clearly in your own hand and on one side of the paper. The paper could be lined or unlined but it had to be eight by eleven in size.

I had a keen eye for contests. Many were false and ridiculous, and only the innocent would enter them. They usually required you to say what you liked about a product in twenty-five words or less and send in your remarks with a boxtop or label. The contest was really designed to get you to buy the product. My friend Arnold had made up a contest for Castoria, the laxative. "I like Castoria because it's foul-tasting and gives you terrible diarrhea, and we all know what fun that can be."

But this was different. This was run not by a company but by the World's Fair. I read the rules carefully. They wanted original thought. Whoever won would have a statue made of him by a famous artist, and the name of the statue would be "The Typical American Boy." There were other prizes too, including free trips to the Fair, all expenses paid. My mind began to race.

In the old days Donald and I had collected coupons from newspaper promotions of various sorts. Enough coupons and you collected your premium—in one memorable instance the *New York Evening Post* offered a set of ten volumes called *The World's One Hundred Best Short Stories*. That had taken a year of coupons. We had been very methodical and efficient, cutting the coupons out on the dotted line, keeping them in order in packs, slipping rubber bands over them and storing them in a cigar box. But there were contests too of an intellectual sort, puzzles, rebuses, tests of vocabulary and grammar. With success you could earn subscriptions to magazines or even money. All these were means of entry in my mind to a just and well-regulated world of carefully designed challenges to boys. By accepting these challenges you advanced yourself. So I recognized this World's Fair essay contest. I recognized it. In my early days I had joined secret organizations run by Tom Mix and Dick Tracy, among others. I had in the depths of my desk drawers numerous artifacts of entry, a Jack Armstrong whistle ring, little lead Buck Rogers rocket ships with wheels, water pistols, magnifying lenses, badges, secret code cards, and so on. For each of them I had once eagerly awaited the mail. The mail was very much a part of all this. There were rules of postmark to consider and specifications as to format. Wherever you were, at whatever far edge of the world's consciousness, one three-cent postage stamp could vault you into the heart of things.

Under the printing of the contest rules were the palest, most meaningful shadows of the Trylon and Perisphere. Only gradually did I perceive them. They emerged in my mind as a message just for me, a secret summons, wordless, indelible.

I fully understood why our family hadn't gotten to the World's Fair. Nobody had said anything, but I knew. Boldly I asked the librarian if I could borrow a pencil. I asked also for a piece of paper. I didn't care if she smiled. I copied down the information on the poster. My heart was beating wildly. I worried that the old people trying to read their periodicals would hear it and the derelict men nodding in their hard chairs would wake up, and all of them would give me dirty looks.

Setting out for home, I thought past the sentences I would compose for my essay, and saw my own noble head in bronze gazing into the sky over the New York World's Fair. One day

Meg and her mother would arrive at the Fair and see it promi-
nently displayed. Their mouths would drop open.

I decided not to return home the way I had come but to walk
past the Pechter Bread Company to Park Avenue and go north
along the railroad tracks to Tremont. I wanted to see the trains
in their wide trench below the street. This was the line my
stately uncle Ephraim rode to and from his mansion in Pelham
Manor. Park Avenue was split down the middle by the tracks
and each narrow half was cobblestoned, barren of people, bordered on one side with windowless red-brick warehouses and
on the other by a fence of black iron spears. I walked along
this fence in weeds strewn with garbage and imagined myself
doing a tightrope act on the grid of electrified wires over the
tracks.

At this moment I was confronted by two boys with knives.

They were on me before I even saw them. They pushed me
up against the fence, prodding me with the tips of their knives
until I was pressed fast. I felt the fence imprinted on my back.

My terror afforded me a stunned clarity of mind. These boys
were big, they were my brother's age. The thinner one had the
lightest, deadliest eyes I had ever looked into; they were close
together in a narrow, lopsided face. There was a loutish droop
to the small mouth, the lip turning outward at one side, the
lower teeth showing.

The heavy one was taller and he had very black hair combed
back in a pompadour, and he had pimply skin and a roundish
jowly face with a snout for a nose. His black nostrils made almost
perfect circles. His knife was not held as precisely to my stomach
as the other's. He was nervous and looked up and down the
street.

"You Jewish?" the thin one said.

"No," I said.

He grinned, reached forward with his free hand, and stripped
my books from me. The books lay in the weeds. "Jewboy," he
said, "I'm going to cut your ears off. What do you say at confes-
sion?"

"What?"

"Let's see you cross yourself." I did not know what this meant. "You're a Jewboy," he said. He pushed the knife point into me. I could feel it. One shove and it would go right through me.

"Where's your money."

"Come on," the fat one said. "Hurry it up." He was really nervous. I produced my money, a dime and two pennies. The fat one scooped the coins out of my palm. "Let's go," he said to the other one.

"First I'm gonna slice up this lyin' Jew."

"My father's a cop," I said to the larger boy. I stared at him as resolutely as I could, knowing him to be scared. "He works in this precinct," I said. "In a patrol car."

They were both staring at me now. I gave no more evidence. In an instant I could be dead or free as the deadly shorter one casually drifted from one side of his impulse to the other. I felt the point of the knife. The pressure increased.

"Come on, let's go," the fat one said.

The thin one grabbed my jaw and banged my head against the fence. "Fuck you, Jewboy," he said.

They ran across the street, laughing. They turned the corner and were gone.

I picked up my library books. The sheet of instructions I had copied had fallen out of a book and lay crumpled in the grass with a footprint across it. I could still feel the knife point. I pulled my shirt up to see if it had drawn blood. There was the smallest red dot, like a pinprick, just at the top of my scar.

I decided not to tell anyone what had happened. I walked home quickly, turning every block or so to see if they were following me. The affront increased with every step I took until I was hard pressed not to cry. I found myself trembling.

Why had I mentioned my father! He existed now in their minds. I thought this put him terribly at risk, even if I had portrayed him in a uniform. A policeman! It was the weakest of ploys, if they had been any smarter they would have remembered how infantile a claim it is: My father is a policeman. It is what four-year-olds say to one another.

I was supposed to be on guard in the East Bronx. I had smugly assured myself that I was. All my life I had known about boys like this, and here I had foolishly wandered into their lair. I had come to their attention. If I hadn't been busy daydreaming, I would have had the sense to stay away from the railroad tracks. Edgar, I heard my mother saying, your head is always in the clouds. Come down if you know what's good for you.

The last block to my apartment house I ran. I stood inside the street door, in the shadow, and waited for them to appear. When they came in the door I would run out again. I did not want to lead them to my mother.

No one came. Standing in the dark hallway, I played and replayed the scene over in my mind, looking for some small moment of honor, something I could find for the pain. But it came out the same way every time: "You Jewish?" "No." Humiliation broke over me in waves, like sobs. I was enraged. At this moment if those boys had appeared I would have killed them. I felt ill. Then I began to sweat and grew suddenly cold. I leaned against the wall. A film of cold clammy sweat covered my face and neck and back.

For weeks afterward, whenever I went out, I looked for those two boys, and the fact that I never saw them did not remove them as a threat from my mind. I could go about my business only by the accident of their not being there, a matter entirely of their choice, and so even when absent they had me. But at the same time I knew it wasn't even these two in particular, because Christian boys were like this all over, and you were free only at their collective whim, only if they happened not to walk down your street or lope through your backyard or otherwise see you. I struggled to understand Christianity as something that would shove a knife into my belly.

I was not to resume my Saturday trips to the library for some time. But my resolve to enter the World's Fair contest for boys was unshaken. In fact, writing an essay on the Typical American Boy had now the additional appeal of an act of defiance. I, not those miserable louts, would propose the essence of American Boyhood. They were no models for anything. I doubted they could even read. If, by some accident, they were to hear of the contest, they wouldn't know the first thing about how to go about writing for it. The best they could hope for was to go along the streets and stick up someone who had written for the contest and to steal what he had written. Well, it wouldn't be me.

I knew I was in for a lot of work. I had not only to compose the essay and copy it out neatly, but to find an envelope and buy the stamps for it. I decided to write my essay in secret, at night, after I did my homework. I would confide in no one. First of all, the writing was supposed to be done without help. But also I didn't want anyone confusing me with advice. I especially didn't want anyone telling me what the odds were against my winning. The age limit was thirteen, which meant I was competing with people in the eighth grade.

I was now engaged in an enterprise that was more interesting to me than anything else in my entire life. I felt good again. When my mother was out of the house, I searched everywhere for a good picture of myself to enclose with the essay. I assumed they wanted a picture for two reasons—first, to help make sure you were the writer; second, so that if the essay was good they could look at the picture, and the artist who was doing the sculpture would tell them if you were handsome enough for his purposes. If two essays were equally good, they would choose the better-looking boy.

I found the gold Pickwick Chocolates tin where the family

snapshots were kept. The best, most good-looking picture was one taken before my operation, when I was leaner and with a firmer jawline. Donald had snapped it with my father's Kodak. It was not the newest of photos, it was from a few summers before, when my father had money and had taken us to the country for a vacation on a real working farm in Connecticut. But it had been shot fairly close up, so that you couldn't see how short I was then. I knew the picture had to go with the words and that the words would be good, so I couldn't send a picture that suggested that this boy, whoever he was, was too young to write so well. But this would do: it was a clear black-and-white photo, just the right size, and the sun lay across my face so that I squinted in a friendly attractive way. Behind me was an open field.

The evening I finally sat down to write my essay I propped my picture on the table in front of me. I thought of being in the country. My bold father liked the unusual, even in vacations, so together with our friends across the street, Dr. and Mrs. Perlman and their son Jay, we had all driven in the Perlman car to this farm. Connecticut was even farther out than Pelham Manor. At the time I thought of our going there as a foray into Christianity. Perhaps my mother did too. She was leery of the idea and would have preferred a place like White Lake, in the Catskills, at a real resort hotel with dancing in the evenings.

Instead of writing my essay, I fell to dreaming about our vacation. But it was really interesting. The farm was immense, with crops growing up everywhere in the sun. The farmer was a skinny buck-toothed man who laughed a lot and sat at the end of a long table as the boarders and the farmer's family and the farmhands in their overalls all had dinner together. Fresh corn grown right there, fresh milk from his own cows, eggs and chickens from his own coops. There were big soft tomatoes and sweet peas and chunks of hand-churned butter, and bread baked in the kitchen by the farmer's wife. She was a big woman who wore an apron all the time, her grey hair was bound behind her head in a bun, she had fat red hands that passed under my face as she put the bowls of food on the table. She had two daughters, who helped serve, and one of them who had hair the color of hay caused my father and Dr. Perlman to glance at each other when she came to their attention. My father was now inspired to recite the shortest poem in the English language. "It's called 'A Dissertation on the Antiquity of Microbes,' " he said, and cleared his throat. Everyone looked at him in alarm. " 'Adam had 'em,' " my father said. Everyone laughed.

Hanging corkscrews of flypaper turned slowly in the breeze coming in through the screen doors. Flies were stuck to the paper, clumps of them, some of the hanging swirls were all black. My mother could not look at them. There were two kinds of milk in pails on the table: milk the farmer's wife had boiled and raw milk straight from the cows. Of course my father wanted us all to try the raw milk. My mother gently suggested she would prefer the pasteurized for Donald and me.

"But these are certified cows," my father said. "Isn't that so?" he said to the farmer.

"Yes sir," the farmer said, smiling his buck-toothed smile. "Ain't nothing wrong with these cows," he said, but then, unfortunately, went into a coughing spell that turned his face red and shook his skinny chest. He cleared his throat and smiled.

"Well," my mother said as diplomatically as she could, "we're used to the pasteurized, if you don't mind."

My father continued to argue the point. He had no shame in discussing private feelings in public places; he did this too at restaurants, embarrassing everyone in the family by talking with the same directness as when we were home alone. "There probably isn't one TB bacillus left in New England," he said. My mother gave him a look, but it did no good. He seemed oblivious to the fact that the farmer and the two farmhands at the table were enjoying the discussion. My mother ladled the milk that had been boiled into our glasses. My father dramatically held his glass up to the light and poured the raw milk, lifting the ladle farther and farther away so that it made a rich froth in the glass and sounded delicious. He then drank off the milk in one draft, smacking his lips and putting the glass down on the table with a rap. He looked at us and spread his arms. "I'm still alive," he said. He was having a good time. Meanwhile, my mother quietly pushed from her place a soft-boiled egg in which she had discovered a blood spot.

One of the farmhands let us come haying with him. Donald and I rode the wooden wagon, you could feel the horse's exertion in the creak and lurch of the wagon over the rutted road. The wagon stopped and hay flew up in our faces and we laughed. Then I started sneezing and had to get down. The cows in the fields swished their tails about and flies rose from their flanks. Cow flop looking like disks of chocolate pudding was everywhere in the stony field. Down at the lake we rowed a boat about and found the water choked with weeds. My father and another guest found some chains, and from the rowboat we dragged these chains through the water and pulled up the weeds until we had made a clear place in the lake near the shore. Here we swam, or, rather, Donald and my father swam. I splashed about for a while and then left them swimming and went up the hill to play by myself. The sun shone, and what amazed me was the fact that no one paid attention to the animals and nevertheless they didn't run away. Pinky had always run away if you took her off the leash. The animals in the Farm in the Park had been in pens or corrals. Here the cows stood about in the open as far as you could see. Horses grazed in the field and they weren't hitched to anything. Chickens ran in the yard and a dog who didn't even have a collar lay asleep at the foot of the porch where the women guests sat. I had never seen animals left alone before. The sun and the sky seemed untethered too, I felt the freedom of things at this farm, and I could run everywhere I wanted and watch everything and still be on the farm. At night the air became cool, we wore sweaters after dinner and I went to bed under a soft eider quilt on starchy scratchy sheets. I became drowsy listening to the adults talking softly on the porch below my window. The crickets and the frogs of night grew louder in my ears, like my own pulse. I kept my face under the top sheet because of all the mosquitoes in the room. I might have complained and caused a disturbance except for what my father had said when I'd shown him my first mosquito bite on this day of our arrival. "Quick, Henry, the Flit" is what he said, smiling. That's what I said under the covers hearing the mosquito buzzing just above my ear, "Quick, Henry the Flit," although there was no Flit near, no spray can to put it in, and no Henry.

TWENTY-SEVEN

This is the essay I sent to the World's Fair on the theme of the Typical American Boy.

The typical American Boy is not fearful of Dangers. He should be able to go out into the country and drink raw milk. Likewise, he should traverse the hills and valleys of the city. If he is Jewish he should say so. If he is anything he should say what it is when challenged. He roots for his home team in football and baseball but also plays sports himself. He reads all the time. It's all right for him to like comic books so long as he knows they are junk. Also, radio programs and movies may be enjoyed but not at the expense of important things. For example he should always hate Hitler. In music he appreciates both swing and symphony. In women he appreciates them all. He does not waste time daydreaming when he is doing his homework. He is kind. He cooperates with his parents. He knows the value of a dollar. He looks death in the face.

Once I had done it, I copied it out in my best penmanship. I had to copy it twice because just as I got to the end the first time my pen leaked and I got a big blot in the margin. I mailed it according to all the rules, and then I stopped thinking about it.

I had given the American Boy contest everything I had, but now it was out of my hands and so I wanted it out of my mind as well. I knew these things took a very long time. Even when you sent away for something you had to allow six weeks for delivery. I had never understood why, but there it was.

Of course, since I had thought that the essay represented my last and only chance to get to the World's Fair, it was inevitable that an opportunity to go would arise immediately. It came by way of the shy soft voice of my friend Meg. "I go every Saturday," she told me. "Norma doesn't like to leave me alone all day, so she takes me with her. But I have to stay close by where she works and so it isn't much fun. If you came with me, we could take care of each other and Norma wouldn't worry. Edgar, we could see everything!"

Oh my dear friend—this was the longest statement she had ever made to me! She tucked her hair behind her ears and smiled her ambiguous smile. I could see her lovely slender neck. She had small hands and the largest, clearest grey eyes. We were sitting after school in the swings at Claremont Park. Our feet were on the ground and we were pushing ourselves back and forth in small arcs. I couldn't believe my good fortune, but I pretended to think about it very soberly. "It's a good idea," I said, finally. "Everyone would benefit."

As soon as I could, but without unseemly haste, I left Meg and ran home to talk to my mother. This would take some doing. A rill of disloyalty opened up in me. But Donald no longer lived at home and nothing could be further from the thoughts of my mother and father right now than the World's Fair. I had waited patiently and without making a pest of myself. So maybe it would be all right.

I marshaled my arguments over a glass of milk and two Oreo cookies. When my mother came home from shopping, I helped her put the groceries away and then I told her about the invitation. "Who invited you?" she said, sitting down with a cup of coffee. "Is it your friend's idea or the mother's?"

This was the tough question. Either answer was a calculated risk. The mother was not looked on favorably. But a child's invitation lacked substance. "It's the mother's," I said. "She asked Meg to ask me to ask you."

My mother gazed at me, not unkindly. "I suppose everyone has gone by now," she said. "How much would it cost?"

"That's the beauty part. We get in free, Meg's mother works at the Fair."

"Doing what, may I ask?"

"I don't know exactly," I said. "But it must be a good job because she has a discount pass for the rides. Most of the exhibits are free anyway. The souvenirs, I suppose, would cost something. But who needs souvenirs?" I said stoutly. "They're for children."

I saw the indecision in my mother's eyes. This was better than I had hoped for. "I'll talk to your father," she said. "Now go do your homework."

That evening it was time for bed, and my father had not yet come home. I turned off the light and decided to wait up in the dark. I watched the lights of the Concourse traffic on the ceiling. A light would hover in the corner of the room and then flare outward and disappear just as the sound of the engine became loudest. Then the sound would recede. I must have fallen asleep because I awoke to a conversation already under way.

"The phone bill," my mother was saying. "Consolidated Edison. Today I didn't even have the money to get your shirts out of the Chinese laundry."

"I have some money for you."

"You've been saying that for three days."

"I drew something against my commissions this morning. I don't like to do that, since it puts me in the hole."

"I'll tell you what puts you in the hole. Your card playing puts you in the hole."

"Does this go with dinner? What course is this?"

"Tell me of any other wife who waits to twelve o'clock to serve dinner? Where have you been? What have you been up to?"

"If you don't let me eat in peace, I'm going to walk right out of here."

"Walk. You don't frighten me. Do I ever have your company? Would I know the difference?"

But it was quiet for a while. I heard the sounds of silverware on a plate. The kitchen faucet ran.

"You want anything else?"

"No, thank you."

"I have another matter to discuss," my mother said. "Edgar has been invited to go with that little girl Meg to the World's Fair."

"Well?" my father said. "Why not?"

"Of course, you know whose child she is," my mother said.

"Whose?"

At this moment a bus pulled up to the curb under my window and the doors hissed and the engine idled loudly. The doors closed and the bus drew away, its gears grinding.

"I hate gossip," my father was saying. "In fact, that's worse than gossip, that's slander. How would you feel if people went around telling stories about you?"

"These are not stories, these are facts. Everyone knows. It's common knowledge in the neighborhood."

"Well, supposing it's true. That was years ago. The man is dead."

"How has she gotten by all these years?" my mother said. "Do people change that much?"

"I'm not interested," my father said. "She sounds like a nice enough woman to me. I've seen his little friend. She's a sweet girl. Let him go. He can take care of himself. I've been meaning for us to go to the World's Fair."

"One of your promises."

"Yes, one of my promises. And I will make good on it. In the meantime, if he has the chance he should go and enjoy himself. There's little enough for anyone to enjoy these days."

"You're telling me," my mother said.

When the day came, I was ready. I dressed in a shirt and tie and wore my school knickers and my new low shoes, of which I was very proud. I had until recently worn the old high lace-up kind. Folded in my pocket were two dollars that my father had given me with instructions that I didn't have to spend all of it if I didn't need to; but that if I needed to, then I had it to spend. I understood this instruction. It was a great morning of the spring. I raced down the hill from the Concourse, crossing Eastburn at 174th Street, and ran along past the schoolyard, crossed at 173rd, went right by my old house, turned left at Mt. Eden Avenue and ran through the Oval, and up the hill to Meg's house overlooking Claremont Park. My mother had wanted to walk me here so as to "thank" Norma, as she said, but I knew that wasn't a good idea and talked her out of it. She would have let Norma know what a great responsibility it was to take care of another woman's son for a whole day. I didn't think Norma needed to hear that. However subtle my mother believed herself to be, however delicately suggestive in her statements, she was in fact brutally direct. It was a characteristic I had come to rely on, knowing in no uncertain terms where I stood—that was her phrase, *no uncertain terms*—but it took getting used to. I didn't want Norma to hear from my mother in no uncertain terms.

I rang the bell and Meg opened the door. She stood there smiling. She wore a white dress and white shoes newly polished and a blue-ribbon bow in her hair. Behind her, Norma in a flowered dress was putting on her hat while looking at herself in the mirror. She stood tugging at it until she found the right angle. It was one of those hats with a wide brim that throw shade on the face. As I stepped in the door and Meg closed it behind me, their phone rang and Norma answered. "Oh, hello," she said, "this is she." Norma threw a glance in my direction, and I realized that my mother, not to be deterred, was on the other end of the line. "Oh, it's my pleasure," Norma said, and smiled at me. "We love having him, he's a joy to be with." She paused. "Well, fairly late, I should think. Yes. Right to the door. Of course." She listened some more. "No, I quite understand," she said, "I would make sure too. It does get a bit cool in the evening. I see he has his sweater with him. That should do him fine, I think."

My mother went on for a while and Norma sat down on the sofa and lit a cigarette as she held the phone cradled in her shoulder. She blew smoke and looked at me through the smoke. I was embarrassed about this but didn't know what to say. When Norma hung up she said, "Your mother likes you a lot, Edgar." I agreed. "But why would anyone like a monkey face like you?" Norma said, and we all laughed.

TWENTY-EIGHT

Even from the elevated station I could see the famous Trylon and Perisphere. They were enormous. They were white in the sun, white spire, white globe, they went together, they belonged together as some sort of partnership in my head. I didn't know what they stood for, it was all very vague in my mind, but to see them, after having seen pictures and posters and buttons of them for so long, made me incredibly happy. I felt like jumping up and down, I felt myself trembling with joy.

I thought of them as friends of mine.

We came down the stairs right into the fairgrounds. Banners flew from the pavilions. The wide streets were painted red, yellow and blue. They were absolutely clean. The buildings were mostly streamlined, with rounded edges, as I supposed buildings of the future should be. We walked on Rainbow Avenue. The day was fine. Thousands of people were here. They smiled and chatted and pointed things out and consulted their guidebooks. We walked along Constitution Mall. Brilliant tulip gardens were in bloom. The Fair had its own buses. It had its own tractor trains, and Norma decided we should have a ride. An orange-and-blue electric-powered tractor pulled a dozen rubber-wheeled cars behind it, and when the driver blew his horn it played the opening measures of "The Sidewalks of New York": "East side, west side, all around the town." Norma wanted us just to look around and get our bearings. We sat on the last car of the train, so that it whipped around a bit at the corners. Of course it was very tame, nothing like the roller coaster we could see in the distance in the amusement area; it had to go slow because it moved among great crowds of strolling people. Everywhere people walked in family groups and stopped to take their pictures in front of exhibit buildings. There were lady guides in grey uniform jackets and hats. The shuffle of feet was like a constant whispering in my ears, or what I imagined a herd of antelope would sound like going in great numbers slowly through high grass. We went around Commerce Circle and through the Plaza of Light and right around the Trylon and Perisphere, which, up close, seemed to fill the sky. The pictures of them hadn't suggested their enormity. They were the only white objects to be seen. They were dazzling. They seemed to be about to take off, they looked lighter than air. A ramp connected them, and I could see a line of people silhouetted against the blue sky. We passed the statue of George Washington. I had my map, which I consulted. But with Norma it wasn't really necessary. She knew everything. "Let's make our plans," she said. She had been so happy to have me with them that she'd arranged to join the fun. "I don't have to go to work yet, so I thought we'd start with a little education. I thought we'd look, for instance, at the interesting foreign pavilions like Iceland or Rumania." My heart sank. Meg said, "Norma, stop your kidding!" and I looked up and saw Norma laughing and realized she was funny for a mother, and she knew what children liked and what they hated. I laughed too.

We rode across the Bridge of Wheels and got out, of course, at the General Motors Building. That was everyone's first stop. We took our places on a long line that went up a ramp and turned a corner and up another, alongside this great stream-lined building of rounded corners and windowless walls. It reminded me of the kind of structure I would make by turning over a pail of wet sand at the beach and pounding the bottom of the pail and lifting it off the sand mold. The General Motors exhibit was the most popular in the whole Fair, and so I didn't mind the long wait we had, practically an hour. We inched along. Meg held my hand, and Norma just behind us smoked her cigarettes and fanned herself with her hat. We were quiet. In the momentousness everyone was quiet. It was the quiet World of Tomorrow, everyone all dressed up.

Finally we got inside. My stomach tightened and my heart beat as we prepared for the exhibit. We ran and took seats, each of us in a chair with high sides and loudspeakers built into them, they faced the same direction and were on a track. The lights went down. Music played and the chairs lurched and began to move sideways. In front of us a whole world lit up, as if we were flying over it, the most fantastic sight I had ever seen, an entire city of the future, with skyscrapers and fourteen-lane highways, real little cars moving on them at different speeds, the center lanes for the higher speeds, the lanes on the edge for the lower. Cars were regulated by radio control, the drivers didn't even do the driving! This miniature world demonstrated how everything was planned, people lived in these modern streamlined curvilinear buildings, each of them accommodating the population of a small town and holding all the things, schools, food stores, laundries, movies and so on, that they might need, and they wouldn't even have to go outside, just as if 174th Street and all the neighborhood around were packed into one giant building. And we passed bridges and streams, and electrified farms and airports that brought up airliners on elevators from underground hangars. And there were factories with lights and smoke, and lakes and forests and mountains, and it was all real, which is to say, built to scale, the forests had real tiny trees, and the water in the tiny lakes was real, and around it all we went, at different levels, seeing everything in more and more detail, thousands of tiny cars zipping right along on their tracks as if carrying their small beings about their business. And out in the countryside were these tiny houses with people sitting in them and reading the paper and listening to the radio. In the cities of the future, pedestrian bridges connected the buildings and highways were sunken on tracks below them. No one would get run over in this futuristic world. It all made sense, people didn't have to travel except to see the countryside; everything else, their schools, their jobs, were right where they lived. I was very impressed. No matter what I had heard about the Futurama, nothing compared with seeing it for myself: all the small moving parts, all the lights and shadows, the animation, as if I were looking at the largest most complicated toy ever made! In fact this is what I realized and that no one had mentioned to me. It was a toy that any child in the world would want to own. You could play with it forever. The little cars made me think of my toy cars when I was small, the ones I held between my thumb and forefinger, the little coupes and sedans of gunmetal whose wheels spun on axles no thicker than a needle as I drove them along the colored tracks of my plaid carriage blanket. The buildings were models, it was a model world. It was filled with appropriate music, and an announcer was describing all these wonderful things as they went by, these raindrop cars, these air-conditioned cities.

And then the amazing thing was that at the end you saw a particular model street intersection and the show was over, and with your I HAVE SEEN THE FUTURE button in your hand you came out into the sun and you were standing on precisely the corner you had just seen, the future was right where you were standing and what was small had become big, the scale had enlarged and you were no longer looking down at it, but standing in it, on this corner of the future, right here in the World's Fair!

That dazzled me. Perhaps it might only have been the sudden passage from darkness to daylight, but I actually wobbled on my feet. I had the feeling that I too had changed size, and it only lasted a moment but it was quite strange. It alerted me to the sizes of everything at the Fair. Norma took us to the Railroads Building. We sat in an auditorium facing a stage with a scenic diorama of O-gage trains and locomotives rolling through hills and valleys and over rivers and through cities. So we were big again. A model freight train would disappear around a bend just as a model passenger train came over a bridge. An announcer told us they had laid the tracks for this exhibit on seventy thousand tiny railway ties that were fastened with a quarter of a million tiny spikes. And then outside, in the daylight behind the exhibit hall, was a real railroad yard with ancient steam engines on display, "The General," the "Daniel Nason," and the newest most modern locomotive of all, a sleek and monumental monster of dark green whose wheels were taller than a man. So there it was again!

And then at the Consolidated Edison exhibit, again everything was shrunk—it was a diorama of the entire City of New York, showing the life in the city from morning till night. We could see the whole city and across the Hudson River to Jersey, the Statue of Liberty in the harbor. We could see up in Westchester and Connecticut. I looked for my house in the Bronx, but I couldn't see it. Norma thought she saw Claremont Park. But below us were the great stone skyscrapers, the cars and buses in the streets, the subways and elevated trains, all of the working metropolis, all of it sparkling with life, and when afternoon came there was even a thunderstorm, and all the lights of the buildings and streets came up to deal with the darkness.

Everywhere at the World's Fair the world was reduced to tiny size by the cunning and ingenuity of builders and engineers. And then things loomed up that were larger than they ought to have been. The Public Health Building had an exhibit showing the different parts of the body, each of them depicted many times their real size. An enormous ear, and nose, with their canals and valves and cellular bone marrow exposed—big pink plastic organs, bigger than I was. The eye was so big you walked into it! You walked into this eye, saw through its lens, which changed to make you nearsighted or farsighted. We all grew dizzy with that one. And then an enormous man made of Plexiglas, I suppose, with all his giant internal organs visible, but no visible penis, a mistake in representation about which I said nothing to Meg and Norma, thinking it was not polite.

And everywhere outside were stone statues of men and women in various poses, wrestling dogs, or bulls, swimming with dolphins, or standing on one foot, or carrying farm tools. They wore stone dresses or stone pants, or they were naked with stone breasts and backsides. You could see the muscles in their legs or arms, you could see their ribs and spinal columns of stone. They stood or lay about in pools or atop pylons or rose up from shrubbery. Some of them were pressed into the sides of buildings, so only the front halves of them showed, sculptures of concrete pressed in like sand molds. The same kinds of expressionless people were painted on the sides of buildings, enormous murals of them holding beakers of chemicals or blueprints in their hands. They looked like no one I knew, parts of them were immense, other parts were small. They intermingled, so you didn't know which arms belonged to which bodies. I was made light-headed by the looming and shrinking size of things.

We wanted to go everywhere, do everything. "Whoa, whoa, hold your horses," Norma said. We were getting wild. She took us to a dairy counter and we sat down and had egg salad sandwiches on white bread and malted milks, an excellent lunch. We sat at a little metal table under an umbrella and ate and drank while Norma leaned on an elbow and smoked a cigarette and watched us. She had bought a buttermilk for herself. When we had finished, she leaned forward and gently wiped with a paper napkin the malted milk around Meg's mouth, who lifted her chin and closed her eyes while this was done.

Then we were off again. It was late afternoon. We saw a rotating platform on which real cows were milked by electric pumps. The cows stared at us as they turned past. They were like the cows on that farm in Connecticut. That they had to be milked by machines while they were rotated I did not question. I thought this was a new discovery; perhaps it kept the cream from rising. We saw in the General Electric Building hall an artificial lightning generator. This was truly fearsome. Bolts of lightning shot thirty feet through the air. Meg screamed and people around us laughed. You could smell the air burn, the thunder was deafening. This was part of the exhibit showing General Electric Appliances for the home. There was so much to see and do. We watched Coca-Cola being bottled and Philadelphia Cream Cheeses wrapped and we saw France and Spain and Belgium. In the Radio Corporation of America Building, which was shaped like a radio vacuum tube, we saw a demonstration of wireless telegraphy saving a ship at sea, and a new invention, picture radio, or television, in which there were reflected on mirrors tilted over a receiver actual pictures of people talking into microphones at the very moment they were talking from somewhere else in the city, not the World's Fair.

We were tired now and stopped to rest on a bench, and to watch the people walk by. All you had to do was turn around and wherever you were you could see the Trylon and Perisphere.

"OK, kids," Norma said, "now I've got to go to work. I have it all planned out. If you're going to make it through this evening, you've got to rest awhile."

She took us on another tractor train to the section of the Fair where she worked. The Amusement Zone. This was very familiar to me. It looked like the boardwalk at Rockaway, with the same penny arcades and shooting galleries and scales to stand on while the concessionaire guessed your weight. But there were big rides too and showplaces like Gay New Orleans and Forbidden Tibet. Meg tugged my arm. "Look, Edgar!" We were going past what I had thought was only another building. But on the roof was a truly amazing sight, a gigantic red revolving National Cash Register, seven stories high. It showed the day's Fair attendance as if it were ringing up sales. Clouds floated peacefully behind it.

Norma's place of work was a wooden theater building with a platform and a barker's lectern in front. The doors were still closed. It was some sort of nautical show. An underwater scene with an octopus was painted on a curtain. Nothing was going on. Behind this building, in a little backyard with a broken-down fence, with towels and women's underwear hanging on a clothesline, was a canvas tent. The flaps were down. Norma found us deck chairs and told us to rest. When she raised the flaps and went into the tent, I saw women sitting at dressing tables.

The afternoon was turning dark now, a chill was in the air here in the shade behind the wooden building. I put on my sweater. Meg sat in her chair all asprawl with her legs hanging over the sides. She looked at me as her eyes glazed over. These chairs were old. The colored stripes were faded. Even two light children sank back into the old canvas—I saw the outline of Meg's back in her chair, the weight and roundness of her in the chair sling. It was very quiet here behind the World's Fair. I heard the murmur of voices but couldn't hear the actual words said. I heard a woman's laughter. I heard calliope music—a circus march that I recognized and that at any other time would have made my heart pound with excitement. I closed my eyes.

TWENTY-NINE

Norma's job was to wrestle with Oscar the Amorous Octopus in a tank of water. First she stood outside with five or six other women on the platform stage in front of the building. The women wore bathing suits and high-heeled shoes and stood up there while a barker, in a straw hat and holding a cane, told the people who had gathered what they would see inside. Norma looked down and smiled at us. Her bathing cap was turned up on the back of her head. Her one-piece woolen bathing suit was dark blue.

When the doors were opened we pushed inside and got right in front of the glass tank; it was like a small swimming pool made of glass. People pushed behind us. Inside the tank, on the floor, was an octopus. I could tell immediately it was not real. First of all, I had read that octopuses were smaller than people generally believed, their heads were not much bigger than grapefruits; their tentacles were seldom more than a few feet long. This was a rubber model, with a head the size of a sack of potatoes; the tentacles rippled along the floor of the tank in a kind of mechanical way. The eyes ogled us, and the creature moved to the glass and pressed against it as if it wanted to get at us. The audience laughed. He had eight tentacles, and they swished around in more or less independent searching patterns. Occasionally one of the tentacles curled back and touched his mouth, as if he had found something to eat and was eating it, the way an elephant will bring its trunk to its mouth. But it was always the same one. I didn't believe the octopus was real. The little suckers at the end of each tentacle looked molded. The whole thing was the amber color of a rubber nipple.

We could see the women now. They were kneeling at the back edge of the tank on a kind of deck or standing with their hands on their knees and peering in. They were in shadow. The light was in the water where Oscar was. He lifted that one tentacle and curled it back toward himself, like someone saying "Come here" with his index finger. The crowd appreciated this. Then music began, an electric organ playing "The Blue Danube Waltz," and Oscar began to sway in time to the music. One of the women dove in smartly and rose up past the tank window and looped over herself neatly and touched Oscar on the top of his head and then hoisted herself out of the tank. Another dropped in and Oscar grabbed for her, but she eluded him and swam past us, smiling with her eyes open, even though she was underwater, kicking her legs right past us, and she too climbed out of the tank just before the octopus almost grabbed her foot. They were all playing a game with him. Norma dove into the tank now, she dove well. She did the bravest thing of all, she actually allowed Oscar to put his tentacles in her hands and they did an underwater dance together, swaying in time with the music, an underwater ballet, although Oscar looked out at us while he danced and one tentacle came up behind Norma and attached itself to her backside while he ogled at the audience, rolling his eyes, and his mouth curled back in a kind of leer. The audience laughed.

But Norma got away, up the ladder, and now two by two the women jumped in and flirted with Oscar and touched him and swam away before he could get his tentacles on them, although sometimes he did. And soon they were all in the tank with him, and their white legs flashed by, or their arched backs, or they came up from the bottom along the glass front with their hands over their heads, their palms pressed together and their bathing suits stretched taut over their bodies. I couldn't tell anymore which was Norma.

All this time underwater lights were playing through the water, turning it different colors, light blue and green and dark green and red that at first looked black. Now the music had changed, and it was hard to see what was going on, it was dark and foreboding music, like the music of *Inner Sanctum,* a horror-story radio program, very dark music. A white body pressed up to the glass and was tugged back into the murk. And then I felt Meg's hand in mine. She pulled me through the crowd to the door. I understood why. We let the crowd flow around us. It was mostly men, a few women, we were the only children that I could see.

Norma had told us we could wander as we wished around the Amusement Zone, she had even given us money so that we could do what we liked. The only condition was that we had to check back with her every half hour or so during the time when she was offstage. Meg had pulled me back from the tank because we were losing valuable time watching her mother when we could be seeing the Fair.

Yet as we ran along not knowing what to do first, it became clear that we would have to be organized. There were lines everywhere at the big important rides. If we had to show up back at Norma's tent every half hour or forty minutes, it was clear we would have only one thing each time around; we should plan what that was beforehand.

"What is your absolutely essential ride?" I said.

"Parachute," Meg said after a few moments of thought.

I dreaded going up in the parachute, but couldn't let on. "Me too," I said. "Now, what is the absolutely most important exhibit as far as you're concerned?"

"The babies in the incubators," she said. That was a keen disappointment.

"I thought you saw that already."

"I know," Meg said. "So what?"

"I'd rather see Frank Buck's Jungleland," I said. Nevertheless we were getting somewhere. Neither of us was interested in Little Old New York or the Winter Wonderland, despite its contingent of penguins brought back from Antarctica by Admiral Byrd. And we both could do without Merrie England. And we agreed that if we had time, we would like to visit the Odditorium, which was supposed to have amazing freaks of all kinds, according to my friend Arnold.

So with our agenda set, we ran into the night. In front of the Infant Incubator building was a giant thousand-pound sculptured stone baby on its back with its arms and legs waving in the air. But inside, behind glass partitions, attended by nurses in white, these real ugly little scrawny ratlike babies jerked their hands around or slept. How they could sleep in bright light I didn't know, although I understood that babies this age are still blind. Before the invention of the incubator, babies born too early would not have lived. Meg pressed her face against the glass. A nurse saw her and wheeled over an incubator so that she could see it more clearly. The little kid inside was all hooked up to things. It had the face of a wrinkled nut or peach pit. But Meg thought it was cute.

We ran back to Norma. She stood in front of her tent behind the Octopus building. She wore a terrycloth robe and her hair was combed back, all her makeup was gone and her face looked very white, and her eyes red, from swimming in the tank. She smiled when she saw us, she had been awaiting us anxiously. We hugged her. I put my arm around her lower back. I could feel the swell of her hips under my forearm. She wore pink mules on her feet.

Almost immediately we were off again, running down the Midway to Frank Buck's Jungleland. At last! It was a zoo technically, he had lots of different animals, but the railings were wood and the cages were portable, so it was more makeshift

than a zoo, more in the nature of a camp. There were three
different kinds of elephant, including a pygmy, and there was a
black rhinoceros standing very still, as still as a structure, and
who obviously understood nothing about where he was or
why; there were a few sleeping tigers, none of them advertised
as a man-eater; and tapirs, an okapi, and two sleek black pan-
thers. You could ride on a camel's back, which we didn't do.
On a miniature mountain, there lived, and screamed and
swung and leaped and hung hundreds of rhesus monkeys. We
watched them a long time. I explained Frank Buck to Meg. He
went into the wilds of Malaya, usually, but also Africa, and
trapped animals and brought them back here to zoos and circuses and sold them. I told her that was more humane to do
than merely hunt them. In truth, I had worshiped Frank Buck,
he lived the life I dreamed for myself, adventurous yet with
ethical controls, he did not kill. But I had to confess to myself,
though not to Meg, that I had now read his book twice and
realized things about him I hadn't understood the first time.
He complained a lot about the personalities of his animals. He
got into scraps with them. Once an elephant picked him up
and tossed him away. An orangutan bit him, and he nearly fell
into a pit with a certified man-eating tiger. He called his animals devils, wretches, pitiful creatures, poor beasts and specimens. When one of them died on the ship to America, he felt
sorry for it, but he seemed sorrier to lose the money the speci-
men would have brought. He called the Malays who worked
for him in his camp "boys." Yet I could see now in the Malay
village in Jungleland that these were men, in their loincloths
and turbans, and they handled the animals in their care quite
well. Frank Buck himself couldn't have been more impressive.
They laughed among themselves and moved in and out of
their bamboo shacks with no self-consciousness, barely attending to the patrons of Jungleland. I looked around for Frank
Buck, knowing full well he wouldn't be here. I understood his
legendary existence depended on his not being here, but I
looked anyway. The truth was, I thought now, Frank Buck was
a generally grumpy fellow, always cursing out his "boys" or

jealously guarding his "specimens" or boasting how many he had sold where and for how much. He acted superior to the people who worked for him. He didn't get along with the authorities in the game preserves, nor with the ships' captains who took him on their freighters with his crated live cargo, nor with the animals themselves. I saw all that now, but I still wanted to be like him, and walk around with a pith helmet and a khaki shirt and a whip for keeping the poor devils in line. The Jungleland souvenir was a gold badge, with red and yellow printing. I pinned Meg's to her dress and mine to my shirt.

We wandered up and down. We bought jelly apples, the good kind with the hard clear red casing. There was a strolling jazz band and we followed it along the Midway. As the evening wore on I forgot everything but the World's Fair. I forgot everything that wasn't the Fair as if the Fair were all there was, as if going on rides and seeing the sights, with crowds of people around you and music in your head, were natural life. I didn't think of my mother or my father or my brother, or of school or the Bronx or even of keeping my wits about me and watching my step. After each of our forays we returned to Norma in her robe and damp hair. We were in the rhythm of the thing. She received us sitting in one of those striped canvas beach chairs with her knees up and her arms around her knees, or with her legs crossed and a dreamy thoughtful look as she smoked one of her cigarettes.

We went to the Odditorium, where the freaks were shown, terrible-looking poor beasts, some of them looking worse for wear than the animals in Jungleland: a half-bearded man/lady wearing half of a bathing suit on one flank and half of a dress suit on the other; something that had fur all over its body; male Siamese twins joined at the hip; a man with enormous webbed feet; a man who claimed to be made of rubber and proved it by suspending heavy weights from rings in his chest—when he stood up, his skin came out toward the weights like bat wings; a woman in a basket who had no arms or legs, just little flippers at the shoulders and hips, which were covered with woolen pink gloves and pink booties; and so on.

Meg didn't like any of this, which I could understand. She perked up in Little Miracle Town, the community of midgets. The midgets were grown-ups, they acted with all the assurance and confidence of grown-ups—they really ran things all by themselves—except that they were tiny, with tiny voices as if they talked through telephones. They had little pug faces, like Mickey Rooney. They looked up in your face and patronized you. They had their own cars and railroad line, their own theaters and stores and toy and doll factory. They sang and showed you around, there were many of them, they showed you their city hall and let you peer in the windows, and some of them were even dressed as soldiers and they stood guard at their bivouac of tiny tents.

Typically of the Fair, almost next door to the midgets was a genuine human giant who sold rings from his finger for fifty cents. He had an English name, Albert something. He was real, all right, every few minutes he stood up to prove it, though most of the time he was seated because in actuality to be that large puts a great strain on the heart. He didn't speak. A card said he was eight feet tall and came from the English Midlands. He had heavy eyebrows, large facial features, his teeth were not good, but he seemed a kind man, if bored by what he was doing. Of course if he got too bored he might become angry. His hair was black and nicely combed. His hands were enormous. He wore a baggy suit. The ring was cheap stuff, I could tell. Each time he sold a ring he got another one from a cardboard box and put it on his finger for the next customer. The price was steep. Nevertheless, I decided Meg should have a ring.

She didn't want one. She was shy. I pulled her by the hand till we were right in front of him. I held out one of my dollars. The large hand gently took it from me. I was surprised at the humanity of this commerce. The giant hand deposited a half dollar in my palm. Some sort of sound, like distant thunder, issued from him, and then found tone. He was chuckling. Meg's eyes went wide and she held her breath. The giant removed a ring from his enormous finger and lifted her arm and slipped the ring over her hand and onto her wrist. We ran off.

All night Meg had been waiting for the Parachute Jump. I'd held off as long as I could. I saw no way out of it. We took our place on line. The Jump was sponsored by the Life Savers candy company. I looked up. Big Life Savers of every color were affixed to the metal lacework of the parachute tower. That was consoling. The line moved quickly. People were pulled up into the black night under the large circular frame that was like a mushroom cap at the top of the tower. Then they floated down, their parachutes billowing. As we were buckled in I noticed that rigid guy wires kept us from swaying and would keep the parachute from actually falling. This was not a true parachute jump, but more like the feeling a fireman would have sliding down a brass pole. That was fine with me. There was a lurch, and we began our rise. My heart beat furiously. I went rigid and held my breath. Up we rose, higher and higher, I could see the whole Fair dropping away under us, the shining white Trylon and Perisphere were bathed now in pale blue light. I saw the Lagoon of Nations, its fountains lit in many colors. I saw the Aquacade. I heard music from a dozen directions, and then, as we rose the breeze added itself to the music like a string section, but in a mocking way of fluctuating sound, as if we would never stop rising from the earth and were bound now for another realm of fierce winds and darkness, a sky life, and we would be blown about in it forever.

Meg was holding my arm so tightly it hurt. "Edgar," she shouted. She held on to my arm with both hands. Her eyes were wide with panic. "I'm scared! Let me down, tell them to let me down!"

"Close your eyes!" I shouted. "Close them!" I was terrified she would squirm so, she would slip right through the harness and fall to her death. "Don't move! Hold on to me! We'll be back down in a few seconds!"

"I'm scared!" she wailed and buried her face in my neck.

"This was your idea!" I shouted as the wind blew about our heads. It was not a gracious thing to say but I couldn't help myself. I saw out over the world now, over the Fair. I saw Manhattan, I saw clouds over the city lit from below by electric light. I grew dizzy. I closed my own eyes and held on to Meg as tightly as she held me. I swore that if I came out of this alive, never again would I go up in such a contraption.

Then we jerked to a stop. And for one moment hung there like pendants from the neck of the night. That is what I thought, that is what went through my head. That we were jewels on the breast of an enormous giantess. My eyes were closed but the bright bulbs of the parachute tower lit my lids, and gave me the illusion of a shelf of white flesh behind me. Then we were falling, gliding, and shouting in our terror; but it was thrilling too. I looked up and opened my eyes, and over our heads a beautiful red parachute streamed up like an immense flower and gathered the wind into itself and flooped out to its fullness. I laughed. We were floating to the earth, I heard the calliope again, I heard the insouciant horns of "The Sidewalks of New York." I was shouting and laughing. Meg had pressed her face against me and I was telling her to look up, but she wouldn't. I had one more scare as I saw the ground rising toward us at an alarming speed, but then we were braked, gently, and dropped the last few feet in a mechanical way, as an elevator comes to a stop; and a few moments later we were on the ground again.

Now Meg permitted herself to look up at where she had been. She was very pale. Her hand in mine was moist. "It was fun, wasn't it," she said as we walked quickly back down the Midway to Norma. "I liked it." And I nodded and didn't say anything. I was too pleased with my own courage, and quietly surprised by it, to tease her or make her feel bad.

I think by now we were beyond exhaustion. Our eyes shone unnaturally. Norma put her hands on our cheeks and insisted that we not do anything else but sit and wait for her while she finished the last show. A man was with her. He wore a leather jacket, and trousers that were like pipes on his legs. He wore a soft cap with the peak pulled down at an angle. He jiggled the change in his pocket as he looked at us. He had broad shoulders and a friendly face but he needed a shave. Pinned to his cap just over the peak was a button with a number printed on it. He smiled as Norma introduced us, Joe was his name, but I could tell watching him watch her as she tucked her hair up under her bathing cap and then folded back the earflaps that he was her boyfriend.

Norma said to us that she had to go to work. Joe said to us, "And my job is to watch from out front." Norma smiled, removed her robe, and put her arm in his as they went through the alley to the Midway.

I wanted very badly to see those women in the water with the octopus. It seemed to me important. Meg was slumped in a deck chair. She had wrapped Norma's robe around her legs. She examined her collection of badges and pins from the different things we had done. I felt she knew what I wanted and by studiously ignoring me was telling me she had no objection. I ran down the alley to the side door and got into the crowd just as it was filing into the theater. Taking advantage of my size, I squeezed between people and crawled under their legs till I was in the first row, by the rail.

There was Oscar. I thought I could make a pretty good guess now which of the two tentacles had a man's real arms inside them and which two had his legs. The legs were easier. As the women swam by or drifted past him he seemed to rear himself off the floor of the tank, and after the place in the act when the water grew dark and the music mysterious, he seemed more loomingly agile than he had before, a kind of suspended potato sack with ogling eyes that caught what small light there was and shone eerily through the ink. His tentacles waved sinuously. Now when the lights brightened again, Oscar the Amorous Octopus had caught one of the swimmers and had pulled her to him under the water, and as she struggled he pulled her bathing-suit straps off her shoulders and down her back. She got away finally, shooting upwards, but for a moment her breasts were visible, as Fay Wray's had been when after she took the steep dive off the cliff while Kong was occupied with the pterodactyl she came up in the water right past the camera. It was this way now. The audience was not laughing anymore as Oscar seemed to be able to catch the women who swam with him and turn them upside down and pull at their suits. Some of them flailed their arms and legs, some were quite still, as if playing dead, but the music got faster, and Oscar's tentacles more efficient, and soon he was chasing all the women at the same time. They did not climb out of the tank now, but swam about, you could see their legs underwater. One after another they were caught by the monster and dragged under and exhibited. He turned them around and over and upside down, and feigning a clumsy curiosity, he pulled off their bathing suits. Light began to suffuse the water, until it was a pale green. The women were all naked now and came up to the glass of the tank and drifted upwards like dancers, lifting their arms and scissor-kicking their legs right in front of us. They all did this holding hands now, swimming down to the bottom of the tank, coming forward and floating up past us. I needed to know which was Norma, and I found her, her face was blurred by being underwater, but she was the only blond lady, and that became clearer as the light became white. She was the most beautiful. She floated up past me, breasts and thighs, and kicked her legs open and did a somersault. After that the women left the tank one by one until only Norma was left. Oscar went after her. He had been lying exhausted on the bottom of the tank, with his tongue hanging out, as if octopuses had tongues, but now he seemed revived by the sight of her. He chased her and caught her. Now he was doing something she really seemed not to want him to do, one of his tentacles went between her legs and up her back, she had to push him off and dismount the tentacle, rolling around with him in the process, all bent double and rolling around up past the glass and the eyes of all of us. I couldn't breathe. I felt a thrumming kind of heat between my legs but I felt sick too, as if I were going to faint, my ears rang and I was hot and my mouth had gone dry; but my stomach felt cold as if it were filling with the cold water in that tank after the lights had faded and it turned to ink. There was a scattering of applause.

A while later we were on our way home in Joe's taxi. He was a cabdriver, like my uncle Phil. Because he was Norma's friend, Joe had not put down the flag on the meter.

Meg and I had the back to ourselves. We had lots of room to sprawl in. I leaned against a corner and she lay across the seat with her head in my lap. Joe drove with his arm around Norma and she sat huddled against him. Her hair was still damp. I could see it shining in the light of the World's Fair.

We made our way slowly past the fairgrounds. "Look!" Norma said, and we sat up. The big fireworks show had begun over Fountain Lake. We watched it on our knees in the backseat, first through the side window, then through the rear. Great cascades of booming color, showers of red and green and white, pops and swirls and parachutes of color firing the sky and exploding in our ears. It was a most terrible racket. The World's Fair stood in separate instances of daylight. The cab seemed to shake and shudder under the concussive explosions, sparks whirled in circles over our heads, as if we were under attack. We turned a corner, now hearing more than we saw, only the highest rocket showers visible through the window.

Meg sank down on the seat and I joined her. We lay again as

we had been. Soon everything was quiet once more.

Meg had said nothing to me about her mother nor acted as if anything unusual had happened under water this evening. She was used to this. I tried to put the images of Norma out of my mind. I knew no one like her. She acted free. I did not think of her as a bad woman but as someone who probably took a different view of things. Otherwise she would not be this way. I could not talk to her about this, of course, but I wondered what she would say. I thought about the casual recklessness of her life. There she was sitting in the front seat of the cab with her boyfriend's arm around her and they were like some new mother and father still in love. I again saw her body in its underwater ballet. I didn't want to think about it. I felt queasy thinking about it, the picture of it produced the faintest illness from somewhere under my stomach, something between nausea and an ache; I knew, though it was there for everyone at the World's Fair to see, I shouldn't have seen it. Norma's freedom made life more thrilling and more dangerous. I felt the danger now. Meg had been born to the thrilling freedom that I only now suspected was possible. The burden of it made her quiet and beautiful. I loved her. The weight of her small body against me now I took as some natural condition of my life, as if we were joined and we shared the same blood, like those Siamese twins, although the twins had been men. Or perhaps we were like swimmers under water, undulating and drifting over each other, rolling about around each other's limbs. I was very sleepy now, and could not distinguish the hum of the taxi on the streets from the resonance of my own thoughts. The fireworks echoed in my mind as a kind of congratulations to me for what I knew. I saw once again Norma's body, the tremors of the muscles of her inner thigh as she swam through the water, the extension and contraction of musculature under the quivers of flesh of her buttocks and belly. And the other women too, that revolving underwater dance of them in their exertions with Oscar. I found now if I held myself the nauseating ache was bearable. Then I pressed Meg's head against myself. I knew everything now, the crucial secret, so carelessly vouchsafed. After all, I had not intended this, it had come to me without my bidding, without any planning or calculation on my part, presented, in fact, as an accident of the adventure. It was not my fault. I had worried before, all the time in this enormous effort to catch up to life, to find it, to feel it, comprehend it; but all I had to do was be in it and it would instruct me and give me everything I needed. As I fell asleep the fireworks went off over and over again like me pounding my own chest and sending my voice to the heavens that I was here.

THIRTY

A few weeks later I found out that Norma and Meg were moving to Brooklyn as soon as the school term was over. Norma was going to marry Joe the hackie, as she called him, and they were going to live in a private house in the Bensonhurst section, wherever that was. "Oh, Edgar," Norma said to me one day, "the only bad thing is how we're going to miss you!" I affected nonchalance. Meg, too, seemed undisturbed by the prospect, we both left it to Norma to express the regrets of the matter.

But then we had the last week of school, with its half days, and then a class party, and then school was out and Meg was gone. I went to the park across the street from their house and I looked up at the windows. The shades were up. I could see sunlight on the walls, it was obviously a vacant apartment. My mother asked me after a day or two if I missed my friend, by which she meant to show sympathy, I suppose, but which sounded to me like a tactless annotation of my pain. I denied that I did. "Well, that was nice of them anyway to take you that day to the World's Fair. What did you say the mother's job is?"

"She's one of the guides," I said. "They have these guides in uniform and she is one."

Norma had said that as soon as they got settled they would get in touch and invite me to their new home. This was not a promise I took seriously, Brooklyn being so far from everyone's experience as to be a foreign country. I knew it had the baseball Dodgers but I was not fond of the Dodgers. People liked their pugnacity, as if they were a street gang. Sports cartoons showed them pitching and batting with black stubble on their faces, and cigar butts in their mouths. The whole borough offered itself in that characterization—raucous, rowdy, proud of its lack of manners, like the Dead End Kids. That was all right, except that they meant to claim for themselves the essential New York spirit. I was a Yankee fan myself. I liked the quiet brilliance of Joe Di-Maggio, the derring-do of Tommy Henrich. Bill Dickey was a solid professional, strong and fair-minded. All the Yanks were like that—Red Ruffing, Joe Gordon. They were good players who concentrated on what they were doing, who were modest about their tremendous skills and never argued with umpires or played to the crowd. When things were going badly for them, they did not complain but bore down harder. They were civilized and had a naturally assured way about them. That was the true New York quality of spirit. Not bumhood.

Meg did write a letter and then another, but I couldn't bring myself to answer. I kept promising myself that I would write but I didn't. Baseball was a new passion of mine and I didn't think she would be interested. I liked to listen to the games on the radio. Even when the Yankees were out of town, the game circumstances were telegraphed to the studio in New York and the announcer described the game from the telegraph wire, but as if he were on the scene. That interested me more than the game itself. Crowd background noise, the bat hitting the ball, crowd cheering noise. You could hear the telegraph clicking, but the announcer could make you picture the field all the same. "Joe McCarthy's going out to the mound now with that duck's waddle of his. The manager takes the ball from Lefty and waves to the bullpen. So that's all for Lefty Gomez. He walks slowly to the dugout. The Boston fans give him a good hand. He tips his cap."

I played my own baseball games with cards or dice. Aces were home runs, kings triples, queens doubles, jacks and tens were singles, there being more of these in a game. I kept scoreboards and made up player names and kept the batting averages. Before my friend Arnold went away to camp, we played strikeouts in the schoolyard. This was a hard game for us but we changed some of the rules to make things easier. We brought the pitcher's mound closer to the schoolyard wall. One out per team per inning, otherwise first man up would bat all day. Hitting was much easier than fielding. We played for hours in the sun inside the chain link fence on the great concrete expanse of the schoolyard.

I didn't know anybody who lived on the Concourse, and by July, when I went down the hill to my old street, there was rarely anyone there. Most families had gone for the summer. My father struggled to make good in his job—he could not afford to give us a vacation. My mother was glad we had moved away so that none of the neighbors would be aware of this. We went to the movies a lot, sometimes the three of us, but most often just my mother and I. I was bored by the movies she liked, which were usually about love, except if they were funny. She didn't have favorite movie actors, she thought most of the leading men were dopes. But she liked and admired actresses. She liked elegance, and wit. She liked women who spoke well and stood up for themselves. She made a point of seeing a movie if Loretta Young or Margaret Sullavan or Irene Dunne or Rosalind Russell was in it. My favorite actresses were Fay Wray and a beautiful woman I had seen only once or twice, but whom I loved, named Frances Farmer. In one picture Frances Farmer played both a mother and her daughter. That reminded me of Norma.

My father when he came with us couldn't sit still for a whole double feature. The newsreel always interested him. He told me that sometimes when he had a free hour during the workday he would go to one of the Trans-Lux newsreel theaters and watch the news and maybe a travelogue. He always wanted to know what was going on, keeping up with the world was what mattered to him more than stories.

Donald came home once or twice on the weekend and he took me to the beach or the movies. He was very relaxed and happy and was a sport with his money. He bought me lunch in a

Chinese restaurant. He showed me his bug, an intricate-looking technical device in a black box. He removed it and gave me a demonstration. It was like a tuning fork laid on its side. You didn't tap down, as with an old-fashioned telegraph key, but rattled the key between your thumb and forefinger, thus doubling the rate of clicks. I gave him a sentence from a book and he clicked it out almost as fast as I read it. He explained that every operator developed a sending style that was as recognizable over the air as his signature on paper. That interested me. I resolved to learn the Morse code. You could write it out in dots and dashes. A dot followed by a dash was an *a.* Maybe I would send Donald a letter all in Morse code.

In the heat I lay around a lot and read. My mother wanted me to go out, but I had no place to go. I was very lazy. I thought about the World's Fair. I came upon the Little Blue Book no. 1278, *Ventriloquism Self-Taught,* that I had ordered through the mail long before but had never read. I had always been attracted to ventriloquism. It was a powerful magic, throwing your voice and fooling people, although the author warned that the expression "throwing the voice" was misleading: "A large part of the otherwise intelligent public still labor under the delusion that the ventriloquist is endowed by nature with the power of throwing his voice . . . but what the ventriloquist really does is to imitate as exactly as possible a sound as it is heard by the ears after it has travelled some distance. . . ." I got past this nitpicking and into the training. The most difficult consonants to say without moving your lips were *b* and *p.* But in the context of a sentence you could get away with "vhee" for the *b* and "fee" for the *p.* Thus, a big piano would be a vhig fiano. But before I could even work on the letters, I had to master the *ventriloquial drone.* "To acquire this," the manual said, "take a long deep breath and, holding it, make a sound at the back of your throat as though you were trying to be ill. . . ." This I did, over and over. I was aiming for the resonant drone tone that the author assured me I would recognize as soon as I found it vibrating in my vocal organs. But what kept coming out was a very liquid gurgle that attenuated, as my breath ran out, to the sound of someone choking to death. "Edgar," my mother said, "what is the *matter* with you!" She fervently wished for the end of the summer when, by law, I would have to return to school.

And to my delight as well as her gratitude, September did arrive and I reported for the fifth grade in my first pair of long pants.

I had always loved the beginning of the school year. All the children looked older and more serious. There was a shyness among us for the leaps in height we had made over the summer. Growth required us to become reacquainted. We were older and wiser, and had put childhood behind. Even the louts and fools appeared at their best for the first few days of the term. Everyone arrived with combed hair, clean shirts or middies, and new pencils and erasers. Some of the girls wore stockings instead of socks. We listened to our teacher outline the planned course of work and realized we were respected for the responsible scholars we had become. It was all very engrossing.

Best of all was the equipment our advanced studies required. New notebooks with more lines per page, compasses, protractors. Thicker textbooks than any we had known. And new subjects, such as Civics. I was always eager to do my assignments at the beginning of the school year. I liked having a fresh Composition notebook, whose binding of pressed cardboard layers had not begun to separate at the corners and whose black-and-white marbled design was still shiny with varnish. I had not drawn on the inside of the covers yet, no airplane dogfights, no masked and booted avengers, no block letters that made my name appear hewn in stone. That would all come later, with boredom.

One evening as I was doing my homework on the living room floor I looked up and found my father peering at me over the edge of his newspaper. His eyes blinked. He kept staring at me and so I was not able to avert my gaze. I might have thought something was wrong, except that his eyes had no concern or anger in them. When he lowered the page to reveal his face, his mouth was set in the faintest of startled smiles.

"How many boys with your name, do you suppose, live at 1796 Grand Concourse, The Bronx?"

"Just me," I said. In fact there were no other boys of any name in this house that I had ever seen.

He consulted his paper for a moment. "Well then, this must be you," he said.

I got to my feet. "What must be me?"

"It must be you who won honorable mention in the World's Fair essay contest for boys."

"What now?" my mother said, standing in the door and wiping her hands on her apron.

"Our son entered a contest and won," my father said.

I was peering over his shoulder at the news story. I was one of six honorable mentions. The winner was an eighth grader from P.S. 53.

"Not exactly," I said. I was trying to appear casual about the whole thing, but there was my name in black and white in the newspaper. My mother had sat down on the couch. "When did this happen?" she said. "I knew nothing about a contest."

"My name is in the newspaper!" I shouted. "I'm famous! I'm in the newspaper!"

Then we were all laughing. I hugged my father. I ran across the room and hugged my mother. "You're full of surprises, aren't you?" she said.

My father read the entire news story aloud. Included in the account was an excerpt from the winning essay. " 'The typical American boy should possess the same qualities as those of the early American pioneers. He should be handy, dependable, courageous, and loyal to his beliefs. He should be clean, cheerful and friendly, willing to help and be kind to others. He is an all around boy interested in sports, hobbies, and the world around him. . . . The typical American boy takes good care of public property he uses. He enjoys the comics, the movies, outdoor games, pets, and radio programs. He is usually busy at some handicraft or hobby and is always thinking up something new to do or make. That is why America still has a future.' "

I folded my arms across my chest. "It's not that good," I said. "It sounds like the Boy Scout pledge. A Scout should be courteous, friendly, clean and all that drivel."

"Now, Edgar," my mother said.

I was upset. I had had sports in mine too, and kindness. He had pioneers. Why hadn't I thought of that? And he had brought in the future of America. He was right—the typical American boy mentions America.

"Shouldn't they inform the winners directly?" my mother said. "Supposing we didn't happen to read the *New York Times*?"

"Has anyone checked the mail recently?" my father said.

"I'll go," I said. "Where's the key?"

"Before you do," he said, "bring me your essay, I'd like to read it if I may."

I brought out my first copy, the one I couldn't send because I had gotten an inkblot in the margin, and gave it to my father. Then I went out and ran down the stairs to the bank of mailboxes in the front hall at the bottom of the stairs.

Inside the box was a long white envelope addressed to me with the word "Master" in front of my name. A small blue-and-orange Trylon and Perisphere were stamped on the back flap. The letter was from Grover Whalen, chairman of the Fair Corporation. I knew him from the newsreels, he had a moustache and liked to cut ribbons and congratulate people. Now he was congratulating me. He said that by merely presenting this letter at the gates I and my family would be entitled to a free day at the Fair with privileged access to all exhibits and events and free admission to all shows and rides. He said that I was a fine boy, and a good citizen. And he congratulated me again. I wouldn't have known who he was if he hadn't typed his name, that's how badly written his signature was.

"We can go to the Fair!" I shouted as I came into the apartment. "The whole family! It's free!"

But my father held up his hand. My father was reading my essay aloud to my mother.

" 'He should be able to go out into the country and drink raw milk. Likewise, he should traverse the hills and valleys of the city. If he is Jewish he should say so. . . .' "

It sounded good in my father's voice. He read it with feeling. He read it better than I could have. I was thrilled that he thought it worth reading aloud in his own voice. As he reached the end he spoke almost in a whisper.

" 'He knows the value of a dollar. He looks death in the face.' "

Neither of them said anything. They were staring at each other. I realized my mother was crying. "What's the matter?" I said. "Ah, Ma," I said and felt that old despicable thing in me in which tears came to my eyes at the least provocation. She shook her head and lifted the hem of her apron to her eyes.

"Nothing's the matter," my father said. "She's very proud of you, that's all. Come here."

I went to him and he opened his arms and pulled me to him and he held me. It was awkward for me but I did not protest. When he released me, he stood up and fished around in his pocket for a handkerchief and blew his nose.

I still didn't like it that my mother was crying. "Come on, Ma," I said. "We have free tickets!" She laughed through her tears.

My father said, "Don't be disappointed that you didn't get first prize, Edgar. You are not a typical American boy and that's all there is to it." He cleared his throat. "Let's celebrate! What do you say? Let's go out for the evening!"

"Won't that get him to bed very late?" my mother said.

"We'll go to Krum's," my father said.

"He has school tomorrow," she said.

"Rose," my father said, "this boy has done something wonderful. Come along, don't dally, get dressed. The night is young."

She gave in readily enough, it was what she wanted too. And so a few minutes later we were on our walk up the Concourse, my mother and my father and I. He was in the middle. My mother's arm was in his and on the other side I held his hand. They looked very nice. She wore her flowered sundress with a matching jacket and a smart hat with the brim pulled over on one side, and he wore his double-breasted grey suit and his straw boater tilted at a rakish angle. I had put on a clean shirt and tie and had washed my face. "Don't we look swanky!" I said. We were all very happy. Krum's was up near Fordham Road. At their fountain were devised the best ice cream sodas in the Bronx. Perhaps in the world. The evening was balmy, the sun had set but the sky was still blue. The Concourse was alive with cars and people strolling in the early evening. The trees on the road dividers were in full leaf. The streetlamps had come on, and some of the cars drove with their parking lights, but the underside of the passing clouds in the sky were sunlit. My father strode along as he did when he felt good, his shoulders moving from side to side, it was almost a dance. His head bobbed. "Shoulder back," he said to me, "chin up, eyes straight ahead. That's it. Look the world in the eye."

"We should call Philadelphia and tell Donald the good news," my mother said. "We'll do that when we get home," she said after a moment. "He's probably out for the evening anyway. And where did you *get* that stuff," she said to me, leaning forward across my father to catch my eye. "Appreciating all women, indeed. You're a chip off the old block, all right," she said, and when we laughed she laughed with us.

I thought to myself that I was, too, in another way. Perhaps what so pleased my father—beyond my essay, beyond my enterprise—was that I had gotten us into something, in the least likely way I had come up with the tickets.

THIRTY-ONE

The following Friday night Donald came home, and the next day we all went to the Fair. Donald enjoyed very much the way it had happened that the family was finally going. He claimed not to be able to believe it. He hit his forehead with the heel of his hand.

The minute we entered the fairgrounds I felt at home. Everything was there just as I had left it. It was even more amazing to see the second time. We were admitted just as the letter promised, each of us was given a special pass to pin like a badge to our clothes. I was proud, I enjoyed it when people looked at us and then looked again.

We stood in the shadow of the Trylon and Perisphere, and I felt these familiar forms, huge and white, granted some sort of beneficence to my shoulders. It was hard to articulate, but it was as if I were in some invisible field of their guardianship.

I was eager to show my family what I knew. The first thing I wanted them to see was the General Motors Futurama. They all pored over the guidebook. Donald planned the itinerary. Futurama would be on it, of course, yet it made more sense first to see Democracity, the diorama inside the Perisphere. So that is what we did. We rode an escalator up inside the Trylon and walked across a pedestrian bridge into the Perisphere. It was a strange globelike room. We stood on a moving belt that went

360 degrees around the inside of the shell. We were looking down at a totally planned planetary city of the future. Everything had been designed to eliminate all problems and difficulties. A recorded narration told us about it. "In this brave new world," said H. V. Kaltenborn, my father's not terribly favorite radio news commentator, "brain and brawn, faith and courage, are linked in high endeavor, as men march on toward unity and peace."

"M'God," said my father, "he's here too."

The music of an orchestra and choir directed by André Kostelanetz rose from the background. Everyone stared intently at the display, but I was not terribly impressed because nothing moved except us. It was not quite as exciting as a merry-go-round, which is itself fairly dull. My mother was made slightly dizzy moving sideways in this manner. My father pointed out that he knew the music, the score was by a Negro composer named William Grant Still. It was available on records, and he had sold quite a few copies when he had his store.

We left via the Helicline, a ramp leading from the Perisphere to the ground. From this close both structures could be seen in their texture, the sunlight illuminating the gypsum board of their siding. The rough siding made dimples of shadow on the Perisphere. At one point the whiteness turned silver and I could imagine it as the flank of a great airship. Then I could see where the paint was peeling, which was discouraging. But then as we neared the ground the two structures loomed in their geometry, gradually becoming more and more monumental and revealing more of their familiar form, until everything was all right again.

Even though it was Saturday, the Fair was not as crowded as it had been on my first trip, and with fewer people filling the avenues it wasn't as pretty a place. With fewer people in their dress-up clothes the Fair wasn't as clean-looking or as shiny, I could see everywhere signs of decay. Perhaps this was just in my mind; I knew that in only a month the World's Fair would close forever. But the officials who ran the exhibits seemed less attentive to the visitors, their uniforms not quite crisp. Many empty

stroller chairs stood about in banks, their operators in their pith
helmets talking to one another and smoking cigarettes. Now the
tractor-train horn playing "The Sidewalks of New York" seemed
plaintive because so few people were aboard. I hoped my family
didn't notice any of this. I felt responsible for the Fair. However,
it all seemed interesting enough to them, they were intent on the
main things.

At the Westinghouse building, before we entered the Hall of
Science, where Electro the Robot was the star, we stopped at the
Time Capsule—or rather the site of its burial. I had seen it
before it was put in the ground, because one Saturday afternoon
at the Surrey Theater it was shown in the Movietone newsreel,
a polished steel cylinder suspended from a crane, twice as tall
as a man and pointed at both ends, like a double-headed bullet.
The president of the Westinghouse Company spoke into microphones from all the radio stations that were set up there, and
then they sank the Time Capsule into this hole they had dug that
was just a bit wider than the capsule itself, and into which a
slightly larger casing had been sunk so that the capsule would
not be eroded by water in the soil and so on. And down it went
into its Immortal Well, as the hole was called, and the audience
applauded and then workmen screwed a cap over the whole
thing and then they built a sort of concrete observation platform
around it and that's where we were now, peering down at the cap
and reading the descriptive material they had posted.

The Time Capsule had been devised to show people in the
year 6939 what we had accomplished and what about our lives
we thought meaningful. So they had put articles of common use
in there, like a windup alarm clock, a can opener, and a tooth-
brush and a can of tooth powder and a Mickey Mouse plastic
cup, and a hat by Lilly Daché; and they had put in material like
asbestos and coal, and messages from scientists, and a U.S.
silver dollar and the alphabet in hand-set type, and an electric
wall switch; and they had put in the Lord's Prayer in three
hundred languages, and a dictionary and photographs of factories and assembly lines, and assorted comic strips and *Gone with
the Wind,* by Margaret Mitchell, which I had not yet read; and

finally newsreels of President Roosevelt giving a speech, and scenes of the United States Navy on maneuvers and the Japanese bombing of Canton in the war with China, and a fashion show in Miami, Florida.

My father wondered aloud what the people five thousand years from now would derive from these things collected in the Time Capsule. "They will think we were good engineers for a primitive people," he said, "and had in our religion only one prayer, which we spoke in a babble of tongues, and that we wore odd hats and murdered each other and read abominable books."

"Not so loud, Dave," my mother said. Other people were standing there and listening. One man laughed but my mother didn't want my father to offend anyone. Of course her reaction only provoked him into even more embarrassing comments. He asked my brother and me why we thought there was nothing in the capsule about the great immigrations that had brought Jewish and Italian and Irish people to America or nothing to represent the point of view of the workingman. "There is no hint from the stuff they included that America has a serious intellectual life, or Indians on reservations or Negroes who suffer from race prejudice. Why is that?" he said as finally we edged him away from the Immortal Well and into the Hall of Science.

It wasn't as if my father couldn't have a good time. On the contrary, he was enjoying himself tremendously. He could be critical of something and admire it at the same time. He just liked to use his mind. By contrast, my mother lacked any capacity for irreverence. She could be bitter, but never disrespectful. When we went through the Town of Tomorrow, a sample community of modern detached houses, each in its own new yard, she became incensed. "What's the point of showing such houses," she said, "when they cost over ten thousand dollars and no one in the world has the money to buy them?"

I was happy when it was time to eat. We sat in the sun and ate waffles with different kinds of topping, which we shared, and not a voice was raised in criticism.

I thought when I got them all to the Futurama, even they would be impressed. And as we rode sideways in our speaker chairs, the whole splendid panoply of highways and horizons before us, all lit up and alive with motion, an intricate marvel of miniaturization, they oohed and aahed as anyone else would. I felt better. It was exhausting to use your mind all the time, education was exhausting, particularly when it was administered by one's parents.

My father understood that I had a proprietary interest in the occasion. So afterwards, outside, he was very gentle and said many things to show his appreciation and his delight. "It is a wonderful vision, all those highways and all those radio-driven cars. Of course, highways are built with public money," he said after a moment. "When the time comes, General Motors isn't going to build the highways, the federal government is. With money from us taxpayers." He smiled. "So General Motors is telling us what they expect from us: we must build them the highways so they can sell us the cars."

Even I had to laugh at that. Everyone did, we were having a good time.

"That may be so," my mother said a moment later to me as my father and brother walked on ahead. "But it would be very nice to own a car."

I can't recall much more of that final day at the Fair. My parents, growing tired, decided to concentrate their energies on the foreign pavilions. My mother wanted earnestly to see the Jewish Palestine pavilion. She was proud that Jews had a place among other countries. She had contributed a bit of money to the building of it. "They show how the Jewish farmers have made Palestine fertile again, with irrigation and forestry programs," she said. "They show that Jews can be like everyone else."

My father was interested in the Czechoslovak pavilion because of what had happened in that country. "Chamberlain betrayed them to Hitler," he said. "I want to go there and pay my respects. Also the Netherlands, now also lost. They have a carillon —those bells we heard a while ago? That's the Netherlands."

Donald and I had no particular interest in these things. We agreed to split in two groups and arranged when and where to meet. My parents rode off in a hand-pushed chair, like children in a stroller. "I'm sorry they tore down the Soviet pavilion," my father said to no one in particular. "I'd like to have seen it." He turned and waved to us the hand that held the cigar.

Donald and I took the bus down Rainbow Avenue, across the bridge and into the amusement section. Here it was more crowded. I didn't let on I knew about the amazing Oscar, but secretly I hoped to see my friend Meg. I imagined her sitting in the back, in a faded deck chair. I strolled along with Donald and just happened to bring him to the place. But there was no more Oscar the Amorous Octopus, the building was occupied by jugglers and fire-eaters. So we rode a Dodgem electric car with rubber bumpers, in a great mad crackling horde of similarly equipped drivers, all murderously intent. We bumped them and they bumped us, and we laughed hysterically. Donald let me drive, his arm over my shoulders, as we spun about crashing and banging into people and being bashed in return, everyone's head threatening to fly off. Donald yelled over the din: *"This* is the Futurama!" Then we went to a fun house and watched ourselves bend and flatten and elongate in the mirrors, our recognizable selves disappearing into nothing, and looming over us a moment later. We ended up at the Savoy, a place where swing was played and people danced to a band on the bandstand. Donald was entranced, the Jimmy Lunceford band was on the stage and we stayed for two whole shows while Donald shook his head in time to the music and closed his eyes and rapped his fingers on the tables like drumsticks. The dancers jitterbugged and did the Big Apple. It was good music.

Later it rained, and I remember seeing the fireworks go up in the black night and lighting the rain as if some battle were being fought between the earth and the sky.

M y winning honorable mention in the essay contest brought
me a degree of celebrity for a few days at P.S. 70. The detestable
Diane Blumberg, whom I had yet to beat in a spelling bee,
looked at me with a new respect, I thought. The principal, Mr.
Teitelbaum, saw me in the hall and stopped to shake my hand.
"That's the kind of student we turn out at Seventy," he assured
me in case I had thought the credit should be mine. Perhaps my
sense of accomplishment is what kept the World's Fair in my
mind, a kind of dwelling in secret amazement at the boy I was
for having boldly done the job; or perhaps it was the recollection
of those clean and painted streets, red and yellow and blue, and
the flower gardens and the whiteness of the future as it ex-
panded in my mind perispherically and thrust its needle into the
sky. One day in October I decided to make up my own time
capsule. I think the idea came to me when I found a cardboard
mailing tube my father had brought home. I lined the tube
inside and out with tinfoil I methodically collected from the
insides of cigarette packs and gum wrappers. My friend Arnold
found out what I was up to and joined in. And one day after
school he accompanied me to Claremont Park, the place I had
chosen as the burial site.

I led us fairly deep in the park where there was a little clump
of bushes. Here the ground was soft, and also one could dig
something and be circumspect about it. Meg and I had played
close by here. Arnold helped dig the hole. We measured it with
the tube itself until finally it could be slipped down and not
show.

Ceremoniously I showed Arnold the items I had chosen to
represent to the future my life as I had lived it: my Tom Mix
Decoder badge with the spinner shaped like a pistol. My hand-
written four-page biography of the life of Franklin Delano
Roosevelt, for which I had gotten a grade of 100. This had to

be rolled like a cigar. My M. Hohner Marine Band harmonica in its original box that was Donald's but which he had given me when he got the larger model. Two Tootsy Toy lead rocket ships, from which all the paint had been worn, to show I had foreseen the future. My Little Blue Book, *Ventriloquism Self-Taught,* not because I had succeeded but because I had tried. And finally something I was embarrassed to let Arnold see, a torn silk stocking of my mother's, badly run, and which she had thrown away and I had recovered, as an example of the kind of textiles we used—although it was true I had heard that women no longer wore silk stockings in protest against the Japanese, but now wore cotton or that new nylon stuff made of chemicals.

Arnold had brought something too and he asked if he could drop it in the tube. "It's my old prescription pair of eyeglasses," he said. "The frame is cracked but they might understand something about our technology when they look through the lenses." I said OK. Once, long ago, Arnold had showed me he could start a fire in dry brush with those glasses. He dropped them in and I screwed the cover on the tube and slipped it into the ground.

Then I pulled the tube back up and unscrewed the cap and removed the ventriloquism manual. It seemed to me a waste of a book to bury it like that.

I dropped the tube back down in the hole. Looking around to make sure that we hadn't been seen, we filled in the hole with dirt, and stood up and stamped the ground to make it as hard as it was everywhere else. I think we both felt the importance of what we were doing. We brushed some leaves and crumbs of dirt over everything for camouflage.

I remember the weather that day, blustery, cold, the clouds moving fast. The dead leaves flew in the gusts, and the great trees creaked in Claremont Park. My way home headed me into the wind. I put my hands in my pockets and hunched my shoulders and went on. I practiced the ventriloquial drone. I listened for it as I walked through the park, the wind stinging my cheeks and bringing a film of water to my eyes.

ABOUT THE AUTHOR

E. L. DOCTOROW's first novel, *Welcome to Hard Times*, was published in 1960, followed by *Big as Life* (1966), *The Book of Daniel* (1971), *Ragtime* (1975), *Loon Lake* (1980), and *Lives of the Poets* (1984). A play, *Drinks before Dinner*, was produced at the New York Shakespeare Festival Theater in 1978 and has since seen productions in regional and university theaters all over the United States as well as England and Scotland. Mr. Doctorow's work is published in over twenty languages. He is a member of the American Academy and Institute of Arts and Letters, and makes his home in New York.